Administration

NVQ Level 2

Second edition

Lynda Bourne and
Pamela Scott

FINANCIAL TIMES
PITMAN PUBLISHING

LONDON · HONG KONG · JOHANNESBURG
MELBOURNE · SINGAPORE · WASHINGTON DC

This book is dedicated to the memory of
Clifford Protheroe

FINANCIAL TIMES MANAGEMENT
128 Long Acre, London WC2E 9AN
Tel: +44 (0)171 447 2000
Fax: +44 (0)171 240 5771
Website: www.ftmanagement.com

A Division of Financial Times Professional Limited

© Longman Group Limited 1994

First published in Great Britain 1993
Second edition published 1994

British Library Cataloguing in Publication Data
A CIP catalogue record for this book is available
on request from the British Library.

ISBN 0-273-60619-0

10 9 8 7

Typeset by 🅰 Tek-Art, Croydon, Surrey
Printed in Great Britain by Bell and Bain Ltd, Glasgow

*The Publishers' policy is to use paper manufactured
from sustainable forests.*

CONTENTS

Contents

Unit 6   Maintain data in a computer system   145

Unit 7   Prepare documents   177

Unit 8   Receive and transmit information   200

Plus one unit from the following option units:

Unit 9   Maintain and issue stock items   251

Unit 10   Process documents relating to goods and services   274

Unit 11   Organise travel and accommodation arrangements   307

Unit 12   Contribute to the arrangement of events   328

INTRODUCTION

This book has been developed to provide trainers and trainees with a fully comprehensive, easy to understand and logically sequenced text for NVQ 2 Administration. Each unit has been written in accordance with the performance criteria, range statements and knowledge/ understanding required by awarding bodies such as RSA and LCCI.

Do-it-yourself tasks are included throughout each unit and can be selected to assess a particular skill or provide evidence of understanding for APL (accreditation of prior learning). Units can be selected and used as discrete, stand-alone modules, or as part of a complete text as a guide towards a full NVQ award. The authors have used, wherever possible, DIY tasks that are different to those used in the previous NVQ 2 edition.

Completion of DIYs will build a comprehensive work folder, to support evidence of practical assessment carried out in the workplace. It is important to remember that NVQ assessment is based upon a trainee's demonstration of practical ability over a period of time and cannot therefore be proven by written work alone. However, evidence must be provided that supports the trainee's practical ability and proves underpinning knowledge.

Unit and element numbers follow those in the NVQ assessment folder or book provided by the awarding body. DIY tasks have been given a reference number to help trainers and trainees record progress. Questions that may be asked by assessors and verifiers have been included throughout each unit. Each element concludes with information on the evidence required for completion and how to claim competence. Sample competence record statements are also provided but should be used only as a guide by trainees and not copied word for word.

GUIDELINES FOR SIMULATED ACTIVITY

The term 'workplace' refers to an area where naturally-occurring administrative activities are carried out. This should include the normal day-to-day constraints, pressures, deadlines, working relationships and activities experienced in a working office environment. Work being assessed can take the form of 'real' work or 'structured activities' carried out for the purpose of assessment.

If competence is to be assessed outside the workplace, eg in a model office, training office or training centre, the structured activity must be carried out in realistic working conditions which reflect those found in the workplace. This must include facilities, equipment and materials appropriate for the activities being assessed. The activities must include the relationships, constraints and pressures met in the workplace.

Simulation should be treated as a second choice mode of assessment. Only high quality simulations which reflect the reality of a workplace are acceptable. When using this mode of assessment the following guidelines should be observed:

a Simulation must allow the candidate to carry out activities to the required standard.
b Activities must reflect those that would be carried out in the workplace.
c The activity must take place in a complete working situation.
d Simulation must include constraints, time and work pressures, contingencies, work patterns, demands on personal responsibility and accountability in the job role.
e Paper-based projects, assignments, case studies, etc, may contribute towards evidence of competence but should not form the main evidence.

ACKNOWLEDGEMENTS

During the writing of this book we have had the support of company representatives, colleagues and friends. In particular we would like to mention Mr R D Dyer, Environmental Health Department, Poole Borough Council, and Martin Bedford, Customer Services Centre, Royal Mail Letters, Bournemouth.

We would also like to thank Dennis Scott and Sara Lippett for their endless proofreading, Sharon and Jayne for typing and printing, and Jerry, Pete, Kris, Carly, Natalie, Leila and Perri for their patience.

We should like to thank the following for permission to reproduce forms and documents:

Acco-Rexel Group Service plc
ATEP UK Ltd
British Telecom plc
Canon (UK) Ltd
The Controller of Her Majesty's Stationery Office
Ferranti GTE
M Flanagan
GBC (United Kingdom) Ltd
Hewlett-Packard Ltd
IBM (United Kingdom) Ltd
R B Jackson
London Electricity plc
Pitney Bowes plc
The Post Office
The Royal Society for the Prevention of Accidents (RoSPA)
WordPerfect Corporation

UNIT 1
Develop self to improve performance

■ **Element 1.1**
IDENTIFY AND AGREE OWN DEVELOPMENT NEEDS

Performance criteria

- Sufficient relevant information on own prior and current achievements is collected, to enable a valid assessment of development needs, to be made by self and relevant others
- Opportunities for developing self are identified through matching own achievements against organisational needs
- Identified needs for development relate to current work activities and potential career advancement
- A formal statement of development needs is agreed with appropriate persons

This unit is about helping you to recognise and plan your personal development. To make the most out of yourself and your working life you must learn how to manage your own personal development; you must identify what you want to achieve and how to achieve it if you are to be successful. It is of no use waiting for others to help you achieve your personal and professional goals if you are unable to identify your own needs as a starting point.

You must plan, monitor and control your career path by constantly assessing, reviewing and recording your development. Remember that development is a life-long process that is important not only in work but also in life itself. If you become competent at managing your work, this will help you to identify and achieve what you want from life.

It is important for you to understand that you can learn something every day, and it is only through such learning that individuals and

1

organisations prosper. Success depends on having the right people with the right skills doing the job most suited to them. This is why there must be a commitment by you, the people that manage your progress and the government itself to ensure that training and development is a continuous process that is available throughout your working life.

Your career is based on how well you do a particular job and your ability to identify and prepare for future roles. In order to do this, you must continually review your development needs in the light of new opportunities and personal goals.

Your goals will be related to your personal and professional life and can be measured in the form of short, medium and long term. Short-term goals are those that you wish to have accomplished within the next few weeks. Medium-term goals relate to things that you wish to have completed within the next year and long-term goals cover a period of 1–5 years. Nothing in life stands still – you must constantly assess your achievements against the goals you have set yourself in order to decide upon your next set of goals.

Your personal development needs are governed by 3 factors, as shown in Fig. 1.1.

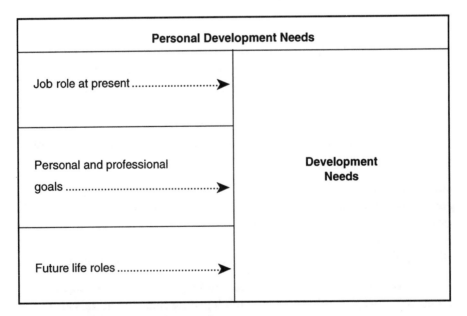

Fig 1.1 Personal development needs

■ DIY 1.1.1

Copy the development needs self-assessment sheet in Fig. 1.2 and, in your own words, complete the empty boxes. You may wish to discuss each part with your supervisor or a colleague. Try to insert as much information as possible as this will help you to complete the last section.

In order to have completed the above DIY you would have had to take into account your prior and/or current achievements. Think about how you did this. Did you use your Record of Achievement, a Curriculum Vitae or did you rely on memory? In order to identify your development needs you must have readily at hand all the relevant information. If you rely solely on remembering your achievements you will, without doubt, forget some of them. You should be building upon your life experiences and achievements and can only do this if you have recorded your progress in a logical and clear way.

Your prior and current achievements will reflect how you have responded to the need for change in both your personal and professional life. It is likely that you have set yourself goals, the success or failure of which has ultimately affected the next stage in your personal and career development. Once you have achieved a goal it is very easy to under-value or forget the process that you have been through in order to achieve the goal. This is why it is so very important to record your achievements in a logically sequenced, concise but descriptive manner. Using a Record of Achievement or Curriculum Vitae such as that shown in Fig. 1.3 is a sure way of doing this.

■ DIY 1.1.2

Prepare a curriculum vitae for yourself that lists:

Personal details
- Education/Training
- Qualifications
- Work Experience
- Personal Statement (this should be a positive statement about yourself that details your personal qualities, aptitudes and goals in life)
- References.

Development needs self-assessment sheet		
My job/training role at present is:	My personal goals are:	My professional goals are:
	Short-term	Short-term
	Medium-term	Medium-term
	Long-term	Long-term
My future life goals are:		
My development needs at present are:		

Fig 1.2 Development needs self-assessment sheet

Curriculum Vitae

Name   Susanne Elizabeth Tarrant
Address   88 Western Avenue, Dartford, Kent DA1 4JJ
Telephone   0033 446657
Date of Birth   5 January 1968 **Age** 25 years

School   Ashurst High, Bromley Road, Sidcup
Qualifications   GCSE – Typewriting, Biology, Home Economics
                       French, Mathematics, English – Grades D–E
                       RSA – Typewriting Stage 1, Shorthand 60 wpm
College   Henley College, Sidcup (day release)
Qualifications   RSA – Typewriting Stage 2, Shorthand 80 wpm

Work Experience
Carlton Cars, Blackheath (1983–1987)
Office Clerk dealing with sales and related documentation. Duties included bookkeeping and banking responsibilities.

De Verney Hotel, Lewisham (1988–1994)
Secretary to General Manager, later promoted to Personnel Officer. Dealing with staff training and recruitment.

Hobbies
Playing netball in local league. Fully qualified netball umpire. Walking, reading and cinema. Secretary of Drama Club.

Personal Statement
I am a fit and healthy person who enjoys working with the public. I have an outgoing personality and relate well to others. I have gained secretarial qualifications at college and I am currently attending shorthand evening classes. I am ambitious, hard-working and dependable. I would like to broaden my career by taking on a more challenging position where I can put my organisational and communication skills to greater use.

References
Mr J B Peasbody, Carlton Cars, Manor Road, Blackheath
Telephone: 081-778 8576

Mrs Bushard, De Vernay Hotel, Trafford Way, Lewisham
Telephone: 081-477 7380

Fig 1.3 Example of Curriculum Vitae

You may have already prepared a CV. If so, check that it contains all the details listed above. Use your CV to carry out the following task:

Exchange your own CV with that of a colleague or your supervisor. Ask them to read through the information to ensure that it is easy to understand and presented in a logical sequence. Take notice of any comments they make and amend your CV accordingly. Remember that your CV should be concise but descriptive. Think about whether this DIY has made you change your mind about your development needs detailed in DIY 1.1.1.

▶ *What is assessment?*

In order for you to identify your development needs you must be able to evaluate your achievements. You will use assessment to make judgements about your own performance. Assessment of your performance can be undertaken using written, oral and competence-based assessment. Written and oral testing proves your academic ability, while competence-based assessment proves that you are able 'to do' a particular task or job. A good CV or Record of Achievement will show a combination of both academic and practical ability.

The NVQ assessment system checks that you are able to meet the standards required by the Awarding Body and the National Council. To do this you will be required to present evidence based upon assessment carried out in the workplace or training centre. The assessment by your supervisor or training co-ordinator will verify that you are able to do a task in accordance with the performance criteria and range statements detailed in your NVQ folder or book. You must prove that you have met all criteria and covered the full range before you may be judged as competent.

NVQ assessment is based on what you know, what you do and how you do it. You must provide evidence that you have the underpinning knowledge and understanding required prior to attempting the task. The task itself must then be assessed, to a national standard, to prove that you can put into practice what you have learned. The assessor must judge your ability to perform whole work roles rather than one-off tasks and this in turn leads to continuous assessment of achievement and progress towards a national qualification.

6

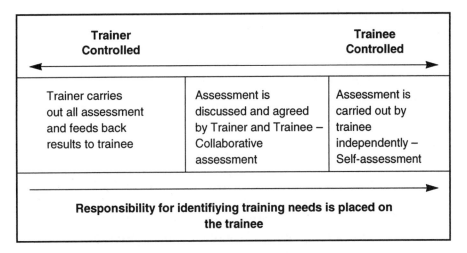

Fig 1.4 Responsibility for identifying training needs

Assessment can be carried out in a number of different ways. Fig. 1.4 shows how your autonomy is affected by the different methods that can be used. The word 'autonomy' relates to your own independence, in your training environment it means that you take some, or all, of the responsibility for identifying your training needs. Self-assessment is therefore often used as a method to involve the trainee in identifying their own training needs. Collaborative assessment should then be carried out so that an opportunity exists for the trainee to discuss the needs they have identified with their supervisor, trainer or training co-ordinator.

It would be foolish to expect a trainee to progress through their NVQ without help and guidance. But it is important to remember that the trainee must be encouraged to take responsibility for their training. Self-assessment allows you, the trainee, to set your own goals, monitor your progress and judge the final outcome. It encourages a more active interest and helps you to understand reasons for your own training performance.

■ DIY 1.1.3

Self-assessment is often discussed as an aspect of Records of Achievement or 'profiling'. It should be used to help you reflect and evaluate your performance, provide information to let others know your feelings and points of view about your training, and as a result of this enhance your motivation and support your self-development.

This is quite a tall order. But for the purpose of this DIY have a go at writing a statement about your training needs that gives details of the elements/units completed to date and how you feel you should progress in order to complete your final award. There is no set format provided for this, but try to fill a sheet of A4 paper with your statement.

You will use your self-assessment skills to plan your development needs. The outcome of your self-assessment will indicate positive areas of your work or life together with the less positive areas for which you may need to seek advice, guidance and/or support. Areas of need, once identified, must be discussed with your supervisor or training co-ordinator so that a training plan can be negotiated between you.

A Personal Action Plan is a useful way of documenting decisions concerning your personal development. Look at the example in Fig. 1.5. If you have already identified your own development needs the negotiating procedure will be a 2-way process with your supervisor or training co-ordinator that takes into account your own personal feelings, achievements and aspirations. Remember that we have already said that it is of no use waiting for others to help you achieve your personal and professional goals if you are unable to identify your own needs as a starting point.

The organisation that you work for may have an appraisal system in operation that allows you to carry out your own self-assessment prior to an appraisal interview with your line manager. A similar system may also be in operation within your training centre, where you are given the opportunity to identify your own training needs prior to discussion with your supervisor or training co-ordinator. This is often referred to as 'profiling' and should form an integral part of your training programme. In either situation you must realise that this procedure has been set up to give you an opportunity to have an influence on your own work role and future – make sure you use it!

In order for your organisation to support your training and development needs, it is important for them and you to identify that your own needs match those of the organisation. Remember that training and development costs money and it is unlikely that an

Personal Action Plan

Name .... *Sally Simmons* .... Work Role ... *Clerk Typist* ....

Period of training ... *Nov 93–Jan 94* ....

Part A – Self-Assessment

NVQ Elements/Units	Name of Unit	Completion Date
NVQ 2 - Units 1 *2* *3* *4*	*Develop self* *H & S* *Workflow effect* *Working Rels*	

Other goals I wish to achieve	
Finish CLAIT and take exam. *Can I do WP level 1 exam?*	*Selected unit:* *Unit 15 Shorthand*

Part B – Action required

By me	By my trainer	By the organisation
Arrange assessments *for units. Need assg.* *for Units 2 & 3.* *Discuss Unit 1*	*Help me with Unit 1* *Arrange assessment* *with supervisor for* *for Unit 2 & 3.*	*Arrange time for* *me & supervisor* *to complete Unit* *4.*

Part C – Agreement made

Help with Unit 1 - but should be ongoing until end of programme.
Arrange assessment with supervisor -Unit 4 but not yet ready for
Unit 3. Assignments for Unit 2 have been provided.

Trainer's signature ... *A Trainer* .... Date ... *1/11/93* ....

Trainee's signature ... *S Simmons* .... Date ... *1/11/93* ....

Date and place of next review ... *5/1/94* ....

Part D – Review

Trainee's review of progress *I have completed Units 5, 6 & 7 as I do this*
type of work every day. I will leave Unit 8 until last because this
should be easy to complete. I'm now doing Units 1, 2, 3 & 4.

Trainer's review of progress *Sally has started to review her progress in a*
logical way by working through the units in order. I have explained that this
is acceptable but that she should always be collecting evidence and
completing logs/diaries ready for other units. We intend to complete Units 4
and 2 by end of period but Unit 1 should be ongoing. Unit 3 will be reviewed
in February.

Trainer's signature ... *A Trainer* .... Date ... *5/1/94* ....

Fig 1.5 A completed Personal Action Plan

organisation will support your development plan if you have identified areas that do not complement your work role. You must look for relevant methods of development that will enhance your own work role and will also make you a more valuable asset to the organisation.

The Personal Action Plan specifies the training, development and assessment that your organisation has agreed you follow as part of your work or training role. The plan must detail the programme of activities, training, work experience, projects, assignments and simulations necessary for you to fulfil the performance standards set by the organisation.

Your Personal Action Plan is used to detail 4 major areas:

1 Your development needs based on your own self-assessment and the outcome of your previous plan.
2 Comments made by your supervisor, trainer or training co-ordinator based on a 2-way discussion.
3 The agreement you have reached regarding your future development needs and how these will be implemented.
4 Self-assessment and review at a set future date, discussed with supervisor, trainer or training co-ordinator, resulting in an agreed review of progress and assessment of performance.

Your NVQ is broken down into elements and units that cover a discrete part of your work activities and it is your responsibility to identify the elements and units that can be carried out in the workplace. Use your Personal Action Plan to detail the element and/or unit numbers for which you wish to prove competence during the period of time covered by the plan. You should also include details of other goals you wish to achieve. This information can then be used as a base upon which a formal interview can be carried out and your development needs discussed and agreed with a person in authority.

■ DIY 1.1.4

Copy the outline of a Personal Action Plan shown in Fig. 1.6. Use the following guidelines to help you fill in your own example of a Personal Action Plan. Ask your supervisor or training co-ordinator if they will complete the bottom section of the plan.

Personal Action Plan

Name ....Work Role..

Period of training...

Part A – Self-Assessment

NVQ Elements/Units	Name of Unit	Completion Date

Other goals I wish to achieve

Part B – Action required

By me	By my trainer	By the organisation

Part C – Agreement made

Trainer's signature .... Date......................................

Trainee's signature .... Date......................................

Date and place of next review..

Part D – Review

Trainee's review of progress

Trainer's review of progress

Trainer's signature .... Date......................................

Fig 1.6 A blank Personal Action Plan for DIY 1.1.4

Part A – Self-assessment

- Insert your name, work role and period of training to which your plan relates.
- Insert the element/unit numbers you wish to achieve during this period of time. Also include other details of goals you wish to achieve during this time.
- Leave the date column blank as this will be completed when each area of development has been achieved.

Part B – Action required

- List the actions that you, your trainer and your organisation will have to take to ensure your action plan is achieved. This may include work activities, projects, assignments, training, discussions, self-study, simulations, etc, as well as named personnel, dates, resources and equipment needed.

Part C – Agreement made

- You must now discuss your entries with your trainer and he/she must complete the next section of your plan. This will provide an opportunity for you to discuss your needs and agree a plan of action that is acceptable to you and the organisation.
- You must both sign the plan to confirm that it has been agreed and that both you and your trainer will work towards your success.
- You should also agree a date and place for your next review and put details of this on the plan. However, intermittent reviews should be arranged to check progress and identify any problems.

Part D – Review

- The last part of the plan is left to the end of the training period when you can self-assess your progress. Complete this section before attending your review. Discuss your progress with your supervisor or training co-ordinator, who will in turn write an account of your progress to date. This information will form the basis of your next personal action plan.

Completing Element 1.1

To complete this element on identifying and agreeing own development needs you will need to put all the DIY tasks in your folder and carry out a final assessment. This must show that you are aware of self-assessment methods and relevant methods of development. You must prove that you are able to collate and analyse information and provide information about your prior and current achievements in oral and written form. Opportunities for development must be matched against your organisation's needs and relate to your current work role and potential career advancement. A formal statement of development needs must be agreed with appropriate persons.

Claiming credit

Once you have completed your final assessment, you will need to write in your record book or folder how, when, where and what you have done to prove that you are competent.

The following is an example of how one trainee completed this claim:

As part of my training programme at Coopers & Co I have attended monthly reviews with my supervisor. Prior to my review I complete a self-assessment plan where I detail all of my achievements compared against the information on my last review. When I first started the programme I had to complete a CV and update my Record of Achievement from college. These documents provided me with the information I needed to start my first personal action plan and enabled me and my supervisor to make a valid assessment of my development needs. We matched my needs against those of the organisation and a plan was completed which related to my current work activities. We both signed the plan to show that it was agreed with both parties.

■ Element 1.2
PREPARE AND AGREE A PLAN OF ACTION TO DEVELOP SELF

Performance criteria

- Opportunities for meeting own development needs are identified and agreed with appropriate persons
- Specific objectives for development of self are agreed with appropriate persons
- Specific actions to facilitate development objectives are agreed with appropriate persons
- Planned actions are documented in accordance with organisational procedures

You must now be aware that there is no one with more interest in your career than you. If you wish to succeed, you must treat the learning process as your own responsibility and seek out the opportunities and people who can help you. Your supervisor, tutor, trainer and/or training co-ordinator are all people who are employed to assist you with your role as worker, trainee or both.

It is also important that you recognise your preferred style of learning, that you understand the process and methods for learning being used and that you identify the competences you need to complete in order to gain a full award.

We are all different and therefore it is obvious that different people will prefer different learning styles. The 4 main styles are:

- **Experimental** – learning by experimenting, sampling and actually putting things into practice.
- **Reflective** – learning by listening and observing what is going on; thinking about what has been observed before making a decision.
- **Experiential** – learning as part of a group involved in a group exercise, where discussion and feedback from other members forms part of the learning.
- **Theoretical** – learning through principles, models and theories using a scientific approach that analyses concepts.

The learning process must be supported by reviewing the outcome of the experience, learning from it and then applying it to new situations. The process has 4 important aspects, as shown in Fig. 1.7.

The learning process is about:

- **experiencing** a situation by being involved
- **thinking** about the experience and evaluating what has been learned
- **analysing** how the experience could be of use in other situations
- **testing** the learning in new situations and under various circumstances.

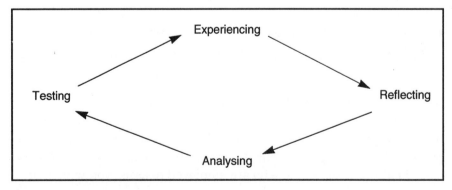

Fig 1.7 The process of learning

14

Try to understand the way in which you learn best and then seek out opportunities by discussing your needs with appropriate persons. This may be your line manager, supervisor, trainer or your own colleagues. Seek out advice and information on the training and development offered by your own organisation or training centre. There should be many different methods of learning available to suit your own style:

- Discussion
- Self-study
- Work experience
- Projects
- Simulations
- Open learning packs

- Audio/video programmes
- Attending training courses
- Reading
- Observation
- Lectures
- Practical activities

Finding the right learning style depends on individual preference, but it is important for you to identify as quickly as possible the learning style that best suits your needs. With this in mind you can start to be more selective about different training opportunities so as to choose the one in which you are most likely to succeed because it matches both your needs and the way in which you prefer to learn.

The learning process also takes into account assessment, review and evaluation. In terms of the NVQ award, the assessment is carried out to check your competence. Competence is your ability to perform a task to the standards required. The standards are those required by a real working environment and include all the related pressures. By proving competence you have shown that you have the underpinning skills, knowledge, understanding and skill to apply yourself in a real work situation.

▶ What type of training may be available to you?

Before starting work it is likely that you will have carried out training, either at school or at a training centre or college. This training is called 'off the job' as it is carried out away from any job of work. The type of training you receive is usually to teach you the basic skills required for a job. This may include typewriting, word processing, databases and spreadsheets, filing, answering the telephone, dealing with the post etc. When you have a part-time or full-time job you will need training on how to use your skills within the organisation you are working for. For example, you may be capable of creating a database, but you may not be familiar with the structure of the database used in the organisation or you may not be familiar with the packages they use on the computers. The training you receive whilst working in the company is called 'on-the-job' training. It makes sure that you are totally familiar with the organisations rules, regulations and procedures.

▶ *What are the advantages and disadvantages of on-the-job training?*

The procedures and skills are learnt whilst carrying out the job. A supervisor will usually spend time with you demonstrating how the job is done and then watch while you have a go. If you make mistakes the supervisor will correct you and, if necessary, demonstrate again. Once you are able to carry out the task without supervision you will be able to do the job. You are in the company of the people you work with and will be able to see how your part of the job fits into the section or department you are working for. You will be able to see the problems – and deal with them – that occur in everyday work, ie the interruptions, the telephone calls and visitors.

However, the supervisors are not usually qualified trainers. They know how to do a job but do not necessarily have all the knowledge and understanding that surrounds the task. The information that they pass on may be relevant to the organisation worked in but may not be useful when changing jobs to another company. The interruptions, such as the telephone, visitors, urgent work and the demands of other staff, may cause the training to stop and start. Quite often you need a quiet period of time to get to learn a new skill or procedure. In addition people expect you to get all your work finished as well as carry out the training. The duties carried out in one job are unlikely to cover all the areas you wish to develop. For instance, if you wished to acquire your Administration qualification, there may be some units that are not dealt with by the section in which you work.

▶*What are the advantages and disadvantages of off-the-job training?*

Most training centres have qualified specialist staff to train and assess you in the skills and knowledge covered. The equipment available is selected for training purposes and you will have uninterrupted time to learn the new skills and procedures. The training staff will also negotiate action plans with you and help you to develop a programme to suit you and enable you to acquire your qualifications. If you have special needs then these are usually provided for with special equipment or specially trained staff. Textbooks will be available and special training manuals; in addition resource centres containing books, computers, videos, tapes and other facilities will be available. You will be able to mix with others that are learning the same procedures and skills. In addition the skills you gain are general and can be adapted to suit any organisation or company.

However, although the staff are qualified trainers they may not have experience of working in an organisation and carrying out the procedures and skills that they are teaching. The equipment at the centre may become dated and faulty through over-use and by careless handling by inexperienced trainees. Individual attention may not be available in large groups of trainees. Some of the procedures and skills may be difficult to learn in a training room, such as greeting and assisting visitors. It is difficult to learn how to become part of a team and learn how to deal with unexpected interruptions such as telephone calls and visitors.

As you can see there are many advantages/disadvantages of on- and off-the-job training and you can probably think of more. Some large companies have the advantage of having their own training section, where staff can be released from their normal place of work to attend on a day or half-day basis. The staff within these training centres may be fully qualified trainers but may also have worked within the company on everyday duties.

■ DIY 1.2.1

List down the advantages and disadvantages of the training that you are currently carrying out. If this includes on- and off-the-job training, make 2 separate lists.

17

▶ *So what is the best type of training?*

Ideally a trainee can arrange to link both types of training. As we have seen some things are better learnt in a specialist training centre, others in the workplace. Quite often you will be the only person that sees both places and will be in the best position to decide which things you learn in the training centre and which you learn at work. This will become an important part of your action planning.

This means that if you have the opportunity of going to work, even if it is only for a few weeks, you must take full advantage of the facilities that will be available to you. Make sure that you list everything that you want to know and cover whilst on work placement and talk to your supervisor about it. Do not be too disappointed if you cannot do everything. If you do not have a definite action plan you may be disappointed with the work that is given to you.

In the same way, if you have the opportunity of going to a training centre one day a week or during the evening, make sure you have an action plan. Only you will know what opportunities you have at work and what you need to be included in your off-the-job training. You should complete a Personal Action Plan and discuss it with your centre trainer to make sure that the training programme you are entering will fulfil your requirements.

■ DIY 1.2.2

Make a list of the elements that you must cover to complete your Administration award. Next to each element indicate where you think it would be best to cover the performance criteria required. You will need to indicate either 'on-the-job' or 'off-the-job' next to each of the performance criteria.

▶ *How does a record of achievement fit into this?*

Part of your training at school or college will probably be recording your achievement. You will usually have a Record of Achievement issued by your tutor in which you write all the qualifications and experience you have gained whilst training. This should be the start of your record of self-development which should be added to when you achieve further qualifications or carry out more training.

One of the first things to do will be to update your Record of Achievement. If you have gained a new qualification then the certificate, or a copy, should be placed in your record and your Curriculum Vitae updated. If you have attended a training course or learnt a new skill a statement from you, signed by your trainer or supervisor, would be a suitable document to put in your record. Always include the dates of training on your record – this will ensure it is accurate and up to date. Later it may be difficult to remember exactly when and what you did.

Your Record of Achievement should not contain any spelling errors as you may wish to use it at future interviews. The way in which you organise your records will reflect the type of person you are. A Record with documents and certificates falling out and dirty and torn statements will not impress a future employer. Your Record should be something you are proud to show anyone.

▶ *Why would a company ask you to use an action plan?*

Many companies are taking training more seriously than in the past and are introducing action plans to their staff. Action planning and training has the advantage of ensuring that the employees cover everything they need and want to know. They are taught how to carry out tasks properly, and this usually means more efficiently, therefore saving time. Action planning has become widely used as a method of planning what you and your company need to do to ensure you receive the right kind of training.

▶ *What period of time does an action plan cover?*

An action plan may be short, medium or long term, or include all 3. A short-term plan may cover the areas of training needed in the next few weeks or months, medium term up to 1 year and long term 1–5 years. When written, however, the action plan may need to alter to take into account changes in your circumstances. When writing your short-term action plan you will need to think about:

- what you want to achieve in the next few weeks and months
- what you need to know and be able to do to achieve your aim

19

- who you need to contact and what equipment and materials you will need
- what time you will have to commit to your plan and what arrangements need to be made

Once you have a skeleton plan you can start to break it down into sections. For instance, you may look through the units of the qualification and identify which ones you can carry out quite quickly, with only a little training because you are already doing those particular jobs at work. You will also be able to identify those elements and units which are best covered either on- or off-the-job. (DIY 1.2.2 will have already helped you to do this.)

■ DIY 1.2.3

Complete a short-term action plan for one of the units or elements in Administration that you have not yet completed. List down what you need to know, the equipment you need to use and who can help you achieve this. Photocopy the action plan in Fig. 1.6 or use one that you already have.

Most action plans will need changing on a regular basis because you and your circumstances change. You may change your job at work, move from the area, have an upset at home – literally anything may affect your action plan. When these changes occur you should update your action plan to take account of the changes. Discuss any problems with your supervisor and/or trainer and make sure they are aware of your new action plan – especially if you are expecting them to help.

▶ *Who is there to help you?*

Most organisations can see the benefit of training and action planning, but not all will offer it to their staff. If you wish to carry out personal development without the assistance of your company you may need to attend training sessions in the evening or at weekends. You will still need to complete an action plan and identify who and what you need to access to achieve your aims. There are several places that you can go for information. First start with your supervisor or personnel department, if you have one. They will advise you as to whether the company will support you in what you wish to do. Sometimes a company will pay for the training course, but only after the employee has been successful. If the company will not support you, then you will be able to find out further information from your local Careers Guidance Office, local training centres and colleges, council libraries, job centres and local Training Enterprise Councils (TECs). Many of these contacts now have a computer-based information system that lists all the training and support (including grants) available within the county. There are usually projects run by the government to support individuals wishing to attend training and development programmes. Some of these are supported financially – which means the cost to you will be kept to a minimum.

■ DIY 1.2.4

Find out your local sources of information on training. Write down the names and addresses of the organisations that may prove useful. Keep these on file, or as part of your action plan documentation. Your tutor, supervisor or personnel department should be able to help you. If not, contact the local TEC or Careers Guidance Office, both of which are listed in the telephone directory.

▶ *What else can you get from your organisation?*

Some companies and organisations have appraisal or review systems in place. This is a regular review (usually once a year) of your progress that helps you and the organisation to identify where your future development may be. It is at this time that you will have an opportunity to identify any opportunities or training that you wish to follow. Do not be afraid to discuss your ambitions at an appraisal interview. It is also an opportunity to identify any training and development needs that you feel are required to help you in your work. The company will be unlikely to be able to help everyone do everything but there is usually a system to ensure that the assistance given by the organisation is fairly distributed around the staff.

■ DIY 1.2.5

Draw up a medium-term (up to one year) action plan for yourself. Identify what achievements you would like to make, who and what you need to assist you to meet these achievements. Keep your action plans on file and review them in 6 months (make a note in your bring forward file or diary). Photocopy the Personal Action Plan given in Fig. 1.6 or use one that you already have.

Completing Element 1.2

To complete this element on preparing and agreeing a plan of action to develop self you will need to put all the DIY tasks in your folder and carry out a final assessment. This must prove that you have identified your own development needs, specific objectives for development and the specific actions needed to facilitate your development. These details must be recorded and planned actions agreed with an appropriate person (this may be colleagues, line managers, supervisors, tutors). You must record all conversations, whether formal or informal, and details of your actions in terms of training, discussions and self-study of relevant material. You must follow your organisation's training and development policy and their procedure for recording development.

Claiming credit

Once you have completed your final assessment, you will need to write in your record book or folder how, when, where and what you have done to prove that you are competent.

The following is an example of how one trainee completed this claim:

During my 2-year course at Sealands Ltd I have discussed with my supervisor and training co-ordinator my development needs. Discussions have been formal and informal. The formal discussions are written down on my action plan (see evidence folder). We have identified objectives to be achieved and the actions necessary for this. I have attended training sessions, discussions and have used self-study using open learning packs. I have gained advice regarding my training from my supervisor and training co-ordinator who have helped me to link my training to the company's training and development policies and procedures.

■ Element 1.3
IMPLEMENT AND REVIEW A PERSONAL DEVELOPMENT PLAN

Performance criteria

- Actions are undertaken in accordance with agreed plan
- Where planned actions cannot be met, alternative methods of achieving objectives are agreed with appropriate persons
- Agreed objectives are reviewed with appropriate persons to determine achievement
- An up-to-date record of progress against plan is maintained
- A personal portfolio of achievements is established and maintained

Taking control of your career is about action planning what you wish to achieve, organising resources and others around you in order to achieve your plan, taking action and then monitoring your progress. If things do not go exactly to plan – and it is unlikely that they will – your next job will be to decide upon the corrective action to take in order to achieve the goals you have negotiated and agreed with your supervisor or trainer. There will be a number of unforeseen circumstances that will affect your action plan, although these things should not be seen as a setback – remember that many things in life do not go exactly as planned.

Your success will be based upon your ability to continually assess your progress, identify and resolve problem areas and make corrections that will get you back on course. This is why it is so important to work according to a negotiated action plan that is reviewed at regular intervals to assess your progress. Regular reviews provide an opportunity for you to discuss your plans with somebody who is interested in your progress. Your supervisor or trainer is there to help you work through any obstacles you have encountered and identify possible solutions. Likewise, remember that other people such as your family, friends, work colleagues and other trainees can play a part in helping you to plan ahead for your future.

▶ *How can you review your progress?*

The first step in the cycle is to complete an action plan that sets down

23

the progress and achievement you wish to accomplish within a set period of time. The plan is not rigid. It is as flexible as you and your supervisor wish it to be – you are the people doing the negotiations and agreeing on the plan.

If you are being over-ambitious others are there to slow you down, and if you are being lazy they are there to help you quicken up. The action plan must be signed by both of you to prove that it has been discussed and agreed by both parties.

It is normal practice for one formal review to be carried out each month, although this may vary from place to place. Your aims and objectives will be discussed and your progress compared against your long-term aim – in other words, the qualification(s) you wish to achieve at the end of your training period. The outcome of each review will form the basis of your next action plan and will be written in terms of elements and units that have been completed. The grid shown in Fig. 1.8 can be used to map your progress as you work through your Level 2 Administration award.

The grid can be placed at the front of your evidence portfolio and can be used to record your progress. The form is completed by you and signed when you have checked through your evidence and confirms that you wish to claim that you are competent in all the units that you have ticked. This will be checked by your trainer or supervisor and signed to confirm that they are in agreement with you. Finally, the evidence must be checked by a person in the organisation acting as an Internal Verifier, and then signed. Your completed evidence portfolio is then checked by the awarding body's External Verifier who is likely to ask you a number of questions to confirm your knowledge and understanding of certain units.

■ DIY 1.3.1

Take a photocopy of the progress chart in Fig. 1.8 and put a cross under each of the elements your have already completed. Also include the date of completion. If you already have a form to complete to show your progress, insert this into your folder and make sure it is up to date.

NVQ 2 – ADMINISTRATION
Progress Chart

Name _____

(X + date in box = completion)

Unit 1			Unit 2		Unit 3			Unit 4	
1.1	1.2	1.3	2.1	2.2	3.1	3.2	3.3	4.1	4.2

Unit 5		Unit 6			Unit 7		Unit 8	
5.1	5.2	6.1	6.2	6.3	7.1	7.2	8.1	8.2

Extra Units

.1	.2	.3

Additional Unit

1.1	1.2	1.3	.1	.2	.3

Completion date _____

Trainee's signature _____

Trainer's signature _____

Internal verifier's signature _____

Fig 1.8 Progress chart

25

▶ *How should the evidence portfolio be presented?*

As you progress through your qualification you will see that you can help your assessor by presenting clear, organised, documented evidence. Your portfolio should be organised in element and unit order (dividers are good for this) with the use of clear, descriptive statements that explain what you have done and which put the work into its proper context. Cross-referencing can also be used if you have evidence in one element or unit that is relevant to another, but make sure this is logically sequenced so as not to cause confusion.

Your competence records must be completed with your own account of what you have done to prove that you are competent – there is one record for each element of the award. These records must be completed by you with a personal statement detailing what you have done; this must be supported by relevant evidence that can be cross-referenced. At relevant points in your statement indicate where you have provided evidence in your portfolio. You may have noticed that there are sample competence record statements at the end of each element in this book – use these as a guide but do not copy them word for word.

You should also include in your portfolio an up-to-date Curriculum Vitae that summarises your personal background – this is particularly useful to the External Verifier who knows nothing about you. You should also ensure that your portfolio contains sections that describe your organisation and responsibilities. Remember to include past certificates that are relevant to the award and for which you may have claimed APL (Accreditation of Prior Learning – this will be explained later).

Perhaps the most important thing to remember is that you have produced your portfolio in order to gain a Level 2 award in Administration. This qualification is made up of units that test your ability to organise files, plan and organise work, use a computer system, prepare documents and so on, therefore your ability to do all of these things must be reflected by the quality of your evidence portfolio. Above all, your ability to present well written, error-free evidence will be at a premium.

■ DIY 1.3.2

This DIY provides you with an opportunity to make sure that your evidence portfolio is presented correctly. Insert dividers that detail each element and use plastic wallets in which to store your evidence. This keeps your work clean and tidy. At the front of your portfolio you should have an up-to-date CV.

Use the grid shown in Fig. 1.9 at the front of each element as a check that all performance criteria and range statements have been covered by your evidence. The completed form will help you to write a descriptive account of what you have done to prove that you are competent.

■ DIY 1.3.3

Photocopy the Element/Unit Completion Sheet shown in Fig. 1.9 and place one copy behind each element divider. When you have completed the unit enter the details required for the form, check your work and make sure you have all the evidence required. When you have done this pass your work and the form to your supervisor or trainer for them to check it and sign it.

▶ *What type of evidence can be used to prove competence?*

Your evidence can come directly from your own work performance or indirectly from other people who have observed your performance.

Direct evidence is the best as it is evidence of what you have done and helps assessors to judge your outcomes against performance criteria – it demonstrates that a certain level of performance has been achieved. Performance evidence can be achieved through direct observation by an assessor. Although this assessor must be trained and hold a D32 Assessors Award, the assessor should work to an assessment plan that allows them to 'tick off' the actions that match performance criteria and range statements. The assessment plan is essential as the performance evidence must be documented if it is to be placed in your portfolio. Supplementary evidence such as questioning and testing off the job may also be used to support observation of work.

NVQ 2 – ADMINISTRATION

Unit/Element completion sheet

Name _____

Unit No _____ Element No _____

Name of element

_____

Performance criteria

_____

_____

_____

_____

Range statements

_____

_____

Evidence provided in personal portfolio

_____

_____ Date

_____ _____

_____

_____ Date

_____ _____

_____

_____ Date

_____ _____

_____

_____ Date

_____ _____

Trainee's signature_____

Trainer's signature _____

Date completed _____

Fig 1.9 Unit/Element Completion Sheet

Work examples such as letters, memos, log books, computer/financial data, reports, documents, etc, can be used to clearly demonstrate results from your actions. However, direct observation of a piece of work or general observation over a period of time can also be used but must be supported by a testimonial from the observer stating that you have achieved the standard of performance required.

Simulation can be used to fill in the gaps. This means that you must use actual work evidence whenever possible, but as it will not always be possible to provide on-the-job evidence, it is acceptable to carry out a simulation that shows you can perform to the required standard. Work such as assignments, case studies, projects, exercises, DIY tasks and skills tests can be used for this. (Further guidelines on using simulation can be found on page xi.) But always remember that on-the-job evidence is classed as a primary source and should be used wherever possible.

▶ *What is Accreditation of Prior Learning?*

APL allows you to use your past experience to show that you are competent. Things that you have done in the past can be used as evidence against a particular element to show that you have met a competence standard. However, you must still prove that your competence is 'current' and that you are able to repeat today a competence demonstrated months or years ago. Your APL assessor will discuss with you the means by which you are to prove that you are still competent. This may involve a one-off assessment, question and answer session and/or a written testimonial from you and/or employers, customers, suppliers and other people in authority who will testify to your level of competence.

APL recognises that you have learnt through previous experience and does not expect you to be part of a formal training programme in order to prove competence. The APL process accepts that people learn through experience in the same way as acquiring ability through a traditional learning programme. You are able to use APL for individual elements and units of your award or as a means to a full award providing you have the required experience and can provide relevant evidence such as that already detailed above. In order to gain credit using the APL process you must still complete personal action plans and an evidence portfolio. You must also complete the competence records for each of the elements for which you are claiming credit.

■ DIY 1.3.4

In Element 1.2, DIY 1.2.2, you completed a list of performance criteria and next to each indicated whether you could be assessed on-the-job or off-the-job. Go back to the list and make a note against criteria that you feel you could cover using the APL process. This will be based upon your past experience and any certificates that are relevant to the award.

▶ *What are Lead Bodies?*

NVQ awards are based on the requirements of industry. There are various Lead Bodies that have been set up for different sectors of employment and it is these bodies who decide upon the content of NVQ Awards. The Qualifications and Standards Branch of the Employment Department keeps a list of all Lead Bodies together with a contact name. The list can be obtained by writing to:

> Mr D Wright, Qualifications and Standards Branch, Room W736, Moorfoot, Sheffield, S1 4PQ. Telephone: 0742 594888.

The Administration Lead Body, which covers administration and secretarial awards, can be contacted through:

> Ms Imogen Hobbs, Secretary, Administration Lead Body, The Institute of Chartered Secretaries and Administrators, 16 Park Crescent, London, W1N 4AH. Telephone: 071-580 4741

Local government, office skills and post office counters also come under this body.

The Lead Bodies design national standards relevant to the requirements of industry. These national standards are produced as elements and units which are supported by the performance criteria and range statements that are found in your NVQ folder or book. The actual qualification is designed by the Awarding Body and checked by the National Council for Vocational Qualifications before it is given its NCVQ stamp of approval.

▶ *What is an Awarding Body?*

The Awarding Body for each vocational area has the job of taking the standards laid down by the Lead Body and making them into a qualification. The Awarding Body will then advertise and co-ordinate each award making sure that quality standards are followed. A document called the 'Common Accord' sets out the way that all Awarding Bodies should operate in terms of quality control, terminology and so on, to make sure that standardisation is maintained.

The Awarding Bodies that you are most likely to be interested in are:

- BTEC (Business and Technology Education Council), Central House, Upper Woburn Place, London, WC1H 0HH. Telephone: 071-413 8400.
- City and Guilds of London Institute, 46 Britannia Street, London, WC1X 9RG. Telephone: 071-278 2468.
- London Chamber of Commerce and Industry Examinations Board, Marlow House, Station Road, Sidcup, DA15 7BJ. Telephone: 081-302 0261.
- Pitman Examinations Institute, Catteshall Manor, Godalming, Surrey, GU7 1UU. Telephone: 0483 425321.
- Royal Society of Arts Examinations Board, Progress House, Westwood Way, Coventry, CV4 8HS. Telephone: 0203 470033.

The Awarding Bodies design schemes of training and assessment according to the national standards laid down by the Lead Bodies. These schemes are accredited by the NCVQ or SCOTVEC who keep an up-to-date database of all awarding bodies and the awards they offer. The following addresses may be of interest to you:

- National Council for Vocational Qualifications, 222 Euston Road, London, NW1 2BZ. Telephone: 071-387 9898.
- Education and NVQ Unit, Training and Enterprise Agency, Clarendon House, 9–21 Adelaide Street, Belfast, BT2 8DJ. Telephone: 0232 895668.
- Scottish Vocational Education Council, Hanover House, 24 Douglas Street, Glasgow, G2 7NQ. Telephone: 041-248 7900.

■ DIY 1.3.5

As you have worked through this unit you have completed a number of different forms and records that will help you to record progress and provide you with a Personal Action Plan. If you have not already done so, you should now complete a Personal Action Plan that will cover your next period of training. This must be discussed and agreed with your tutor or training co-ordinator and a review date agreed. The completion of this unit depends upon you showing evidence of the use of action planning and the completion of an indexed personal portfolio of achievements.

Completing Element 1.3

To complete this element on implementing and reviewing a personal development plan you will need to put all the DIY tasks in your folder and carry out a final assessment. This must provide evidence of the use of personal action planning which has been discussed and agreed with appropriate persons. If planned action cannot be met, alternative methods must be discussed and agreed during the review. An up-to-date progress record must be maintained and an evidence portfolio established and maintained.

Claiming credit

Once you have completed your final assessment, you will need to write in your record book or folder how, when, where and what you have done to prove that you are competent.

The following is an example of how one trainee completed this claim:

During my 2-year training programme at Seahalls Ltd I have completed a number of Personal Action Plans (see evidence folder). These plans were checked each month with my supervisor and we discussed my progress and agreed on the next action plan. I kept an up-to-date record of my progress that helped me to see outstanding elements or units that needed to be completed (see folder). I was able to discuss my progress, aims and objectives with other trainees and my supervisor who were all interested in how I was progressing and any problems that I have encountered. I have completed a personal evidence portfolio which is divided into elements. Each element has a separate divider which has the element number and the name of the element typed on it. I have used plastic wallets to keep my work neat and tidy. Before I handed my completed portfolio to my supervisor I checked it myself and made sure each element contained relevant evidence and a completed competence record.

UNIT 2
Monitor and maintain a healthy, safe and secure workplace

■ **Element 2.1**
MONITOR AND MAINTAIN HEALTH AND SAFETY WITHIN THE WORKPLACE

Performance criteria

- Existing or potential hazards are put right if authorised
- Hazards outside own authority to put right are promptly and accurately reported to the appropriate person
- Actions taken in dealing with emergencies conform to organisational requirements
- Emergencies are reported and recorded accurately, completely and legibly in accordance with established procedures
- Work practices are in accordance with organisational requirements
- Working conditions which do not conform to organisational requirements are promptly and accurately reported to the appropriate person
- Organising of work area minimises risk to self and others

Employers have a duty to protect their employees and keep them informed about health and safety, in the same way as the employees have a responsibility to look after themselves and others. If you identify a problem this should be discussed with the employer or safety representative if there is one. It is possible for you to contact the Health and Safety Executive, your local authority or perhaps the local fire brigade direct if you feel your employer is putting people's health or lives at risk.

▶ *What are all employees expected to know about their workplace?*

All employers, employees and trainees in the workplace or training centre should know:

1 how to contact 'first-aiders'
2 where to locate the first-aid box
3 what to do in the event of a fire
4 where to locate fire equipment
5 how to select/operate fire equipment
6 where to locate the accident book
7 who to report hazards to
8 how to lift/handle materials correctly
9 when/where to use protective clothing

This information should be covered in the safety policy, rules and emergency procedures of the organisation during induction training. If you do not know the answers to the 9 points above, now is a good time to ask your supervisor for advice.

Fig 2.1 Some safety hazards in the office

▶ What are the possible hazards?

There is a wide range of possible hazards in an office and it is the responsibility of everyone to ensure that potential accidents are prevented before they happen. Examples are: drawers left open; cabinets placed in front of fire extinguishers; open scissors or sharp objects left on desk tops; chairs left in gangways; and overloaded electric sockets. Are you guilty of throwing items such as sticky tape or correction fluid across the room to a colleague? Many people do this and it is only after an accident has occurred that they think twice before doing it again!

It is imperative that you appreciate the dangers that can occur from hazards such as:

- slippery or poorly maintained floors
- lifting heavy items without bending properly
- staircases and fire exits used as storage facilities
- poorly maintained or frayed carpets
- standing on chairs to reach high shelving
- removing safety guards on machines
- trailing electric or telephone leads
- obstacles in gangways
- using faulty electrical equipment
- faulty storage/stacking of business items
- improper treatment of hazardous substances
- unsuitable positioning and use of furniture

The above list is by no means exhaustive as the potential hazards are many and changeable. All you need to do at any one time is to look around your own working area and spot any potential hazards – pay particular attention to the list above but always be on the lookout for other, less obvious, hazards. It is very important that we all understand and try to reduce risks by ensuring that we are fully aware of safe working practices.

■ DIY 2.1.1

Use the list shown in Fig. 2.2 to carry out a safety check in your workplace or training centre. The checklist should not only cover equipment, fixtures and fittings within your own working area, but all areas within the organisation. Look

35

SAFE AND TIDY CHECKLIST			
Question?	**Answer**		**Comments**
	Yes	**No**	
Filing cabinets 1 Are drawers left open? 2 Can more than one drawer be opened at once? 3 Are drawers overcrowded?			
Telephones 1 Are they easy to reach? 2 Are wires kept out of the way? 3 Are mouthpiece/earpiece kept clean?			
Computers 1 Is brightness correct? 2 Are screens and keyboards positioned correctly? 3 Is there enough light without glare?			
Desks 1 Are they tidy? 2 Are any desks an obstruction? 3 Are desks the right height? 4 Is all equipment stored safely?			
Chairs 1 Are they comfortable? 2 Do they support your back? 3 Are chairs left in gangways?			
Electrical equipment 1 Are there trailing wires? 2 Do you know how to treat faulty equipment? 3 Do you know how to check the mains supply? 4 Do you know how to recognise faulty equipment?			
Hazards 1 Do you know to whom you would report a hazard? 2 Do you know how you would report a hazard? 3 Do you know how to deal with the following emergencies? (a) illness (b) accident (c) fire (d) evacuation			

Fig 2.2 Safe and tidy checklist

around your office or training area and then answer the questions on the checklist.

Figure 2.2 lists a number of possible hazards in an office environment. Make a list of the common forms of accident and/or health emergency that you may have to deal with.

▶ *What health and safety laws should you be aware of?*

There are legal minimum health and safety requirements that have to be followed in both the office and other working areas. Health and safety legislation covers lighting, heating, space, cleanliness, ventilation, and so on to ensure people are offered a safe and comfortable place in which to work. It is in the company's interests that standards and procedures are followed in order to reduce absenteeism through poor working conditions, illness or accident.

Legal action against an employer failing to provide a healthy and safe place of work include fines, closure of premises and even imprisonment for persistent offenders. However, health and safety at work is such an important aspect of the welfare of employees that most employers do not need the threat of legal punishment to provide good working conditions.

There are about 30 Acts of Parliament governing the working environment; some of the more important aspects are discussed below.

Health and Safety at Work Act 1974 (HASAWA)

This is an enabling Act, which means that it is designed to bring together all the previous legislation and make sense out of it. However, at the moment many of these earlier Acts exist side by side with the HASAWA. The basic idea of the Act is that there should be a joint effort by employers and employees to provide a safe and healthy working environment.

The employer has to provide safe:

- equipment and systems of work
- working conditions and adequate arrangements and facilities for welfare

- use, storage, transport and handling of substances and articles
- means of access to and from work.

If an accident should occur the employer must investigate this fully and all staff should be fully informed, supervised and trained in accordance with their work role.

Employees are responsible for:

- taking care of their own safety
- the safety of other people affected by their actions
- co-operating with employers and any other persons involved in carrying out duties under this law.

The HASAWA includes the Electricity at Work Regulations 1989 and The Reporting of Injuries, Diseases and Dangerous Occurrences Regulations 1985 (RIDDOR).

Fig 2.3 Employees are responsible for taking care of their own safety . . .

Electricity at Work Regulations 1989

The Electricity at Work Regulations 1989 have been made under the Health and Safety at Work Act of 1974 and cover establishments such as colleges, hospitals and commercial premises. The purpose of these regulations is to require precautions to be taken against the risk of death or injury from electricity at work. Injury or death caused by electric shock, electric burn, fires of electrical origin, electric arcing or explosions initiated or caused by electricity are covered by these regulations.

There are maintenance guidelines for all electrical equipment – even the office kettle, word processor and electric fan have to be inspected and maintained on a regular basis. Employers are required to label their electrical equipment with details of when it was last checked and the date of the next inspection, as shown in Fig. 2.4. Green labels are used for equipment that has passed its test and red labels used for equipment that is not satisfactory. If a piece of equipment is found to be dangerous it must be removed.

Reporting of Injuries, Diseases and Dangerous Occurrences Regulations 1985 (RIDDOR)

The Reporting of Injuries, Diseases and Dangerous Occurrences Regulations 1985 (RIDDOR) state that an accident book must be kept by anyone who employs workers. In the event of an accident the employer must maintain a written account of what happened, which must be made available for inspection by the relevant authority. If an employee is off work, due to an accident, for more than 3 days the employer must inform the local authority's Environmental Health Department or an inspector from the Health and Safety Executive depending on who has legal responsibility for that particular premises.

Fig 2.4 An example of a completed green label

The relevant authority must be informed verbally within 24 hours of the accident occurring, and in writing using form F2508 within 7 days. This information is used to identify accident trends and unsafe working practices.

The type of accident report is not stated by RIDDOR, it is left to the responsible person to use a form or record that best suits the purpose. A photocopy of form F2508 kept in a file would be acceptable.

Statements of health and safety policy

Section 2(3) of the Health and Safety at Work Act 1974 states that if 5 or more people are employed then, by law, the company has to have a written statement detailing its health and safety policy. The statement should be specific to the company and set out the general policy for protecting the health and safety of employees at work and the arrangements for putting that policy into practice. This statement must be brought to the attention of all employees and others who may be affected by the employer's business and it should be updated when working conditions change.

▶ *How should accidents be reported?*

If an accident has occurred it is important this is reported. An accident report form can be used to give details of the accident. It is vital that this form is completed after an accident, so that if the same accident occurs again and again the trend will be identified and can be put right. If, for example, a number of staff had all injured themselves falling over a broken drawer in the filing cabinet then it would be the employer's responsibility to have the drawer repaired before another accident occurred. An example of an accident report form is shown in Fig. 2.5.

All accidents at work should be reported to your supervisor and recorded in writing using an accident report form. The reasons for this are:

- the information can be used to investigate the cause of the accident and help to reduce hazards in the future
- a written record of the accident may be required by law
- the injury, no matter how small, should be given attention. It may happen that what seems to be a small injury may give rise to serious problems later

Accident Report Form (To be completed by Line Manager)	
Accident Details:	Location:
	Department:
	Date: Time:
	Name & Address:
	Sex: Age:
Details of Injuries:	Occupation:
Signature _____ (Line Manager)	Witnesses:

Distribution: Copy 1 to Human Resources
Copy 2 to Facilities Manager
Copy 3 to Health & Safety Representative
Copy 4 to Facilities Manager Central Services

Notification of Unsafe/Unhealthy Conditions form completed.   YES/NO*
(Only complete where necessary)   *Delete as applicable

Fig 2.5 Accident report form

■ DIY 2.1.2

1 Photocopy a page from your accident report book or photocopy the example in Fig. 2.5. Insert the following information.

At 11.00 am today the Personnel Secretary, Danielle Harvey, who was celebrating her 25th birthday, tripped over a filing cabinet drawer in the secretarial section of the Personnel Department. The drawer had been left open after a file was removed. Ben Roberts was with her at the time and was able to administer first aid to Danielle's cut and bruised ankle. Danielle was taken home to 25 Morton Drive, Ernesford Grange, Coventry, and is expected to have the next 4–5 days off work.

2 Write a memo to the Health and Safety Officer explaining how this accident occurred and what action you think should be taken to ensure that the same accident does not happen again.

41

The Offices, Shops and Railway Premises Act 1963

This Act is much more specific than the HASAWA which has a general approach to health and safety in the workplace. The Offices, Shops and Railway Premises Act stipulates working requirements and informs employees of their rights.

This Act states specific requirements, such as:

- adequate floor space for each employee
- temperature above 16°C and a thermometer displayed
- adequate ventilation without draught
- adequate, separate toilets
- washing facilities with hot and cold water
- soap and clean drying facilities
- fresh drinking water
- facilities to hang and dry clothes
- isolation of noisy machinery
- safe and clear floors and stairways
- machinery or correct procedures to lift heavy weights
- chairs provided for employees who stand to do their work
- availability of trained first-aid staff
- adequately stocked first-aid boxes
- machine guards where necessary
- clear gangways and fire exits
- fire drills/assembly points brought to notice of all staff
- adequate fire extinguishers in working order

Under this Act the **Information for Employees Regulations 1989** provide employers with a large poster that has to be displayed clearly in all offices. The poster informs employees of their rights and gives local information detailing the employees' local enforcing authority and the address of the local employment medical service.

There are other Acts in operation including:

- The Fire Precautions Act 1971
- The Employers' Liability (Compulsory Insurance) Act 1969
- The Employers' Liability (Defective Equipment) Act 1969
- The Occupiers' Liability Act 1957

■ DIY 2.1.3

In order to revise your knowledge of the most important health and safety laws, complete the following sentences with the missing words. It is advisable to write out the whole sentence so that it can be used as evidence of understanding. Try to fill in the missing words without referring to the previous text, work through each question and pencil in your answers before checking them.

1 The Health and Safety at Work Act 1974 (_ _ _ _ _ _) is designed to bring together all the previous legislation and make _ _ _ _ _ out of it.

2 The basic idea of the Act is that there should be a joint effort by _ _ _ _ _ _ _ _ _ and _ _ _ _ _ _ _ _ _ to provide a safe and healthy _ _ _ _ _ _ _ environment.

3 The employer has to provide safe:
   a _ _ _ _ _ _ _ _ _ and _ _ _ _ _ _ _ of work
   b working conditions and _ _ _ _ _ _ _ _ arrangements and facilities for welfare
   c use, _ _ _ _ _ _ _ _, transport and _ _ _ _ _ _ _ _ of substances and articles
   d means of access _ _ and _ _ _ _ work.

4 Employees are responsible for:
   a taking care of their _ _ _ safety
   b safety of other _ _ _ _ _ _ affected by their actions
   c co-operating with _ _ _ _ _ _ _ _ _ and any other persons involved in carrying out _ _ _ _ _ _ under this law.

5 The HASAWA includes the _ _ _ _ _ _ _ _ _ _ _ at Work Regulations 1989 and the Reporting of Injuries, Diseases and _ _ _ _ _ _ _ _ _ Occurrences Regulations 1985 (RIDDOR).

6 The _ _ _ _ _ _ _ _, Shops and Railway Premises Act stipulates working requirements and informs employees of their _ _ _ _ _ _.

7 This Act states specific requirements, such as:
   a adequate floor _ _ _ _ _ for each employee
   b temperature _ _ _ _ _ 16°C and a thermometer displayed
   c adequate _ _ _ _ _ _ _ _ _ _ _ _ without draught
   d adequate, separate _ _ _ _ _ _ _ _
   e washing facilities with _ _ _ and cold _ _ _ _ _
   f soap and clean _ _ _ _ _ _ facilities
   g fresh _ _ _ _ _ _ _ _ water

h facilities to _ _ _ _ and _ _ _ clothes
i isolation of _ _ _ _ _ machinery
j safe and _ _ _ _ _ floors and _ _ _ _ _ _ _ _ _
k machinery or correct procedures to _ _ _ _ heavy weights
l chairs provided for _ _ _ _ _ _ _ _ _ who _ _ _ _ _ to do their work
m availability of _ _ _ _ _ _ _ first-aid staff
n adequately stocked _ _ _ _ _ - _ _ _ boxes
o machine _ _ _ _ _ _ where necessary
p clear _ _ _ _ _ _ _ _ _ and fire _ _ _ _ _
q fire drills/assembly _ _ _ _ _ _ brought to notice
   of all _ _ _ _ _
r adequate fire _ _ _ _ _ _ _ _ _ _ _ _ _ in working order.

8 Under this Act the Information for _ _ _ _ _ _ _ _ _ Regulations 1989
provide employers with a _ _ _ _ _ _ that has to be displayed
_ _ _ _ _ _ _ in all offices.

9 The poster informs employees of their _ _ _ _ _ _ and gives information
detailing the employees' _ _ _ _ _ enforcing authority and the address of the
local employment _ _ _ _ _ _ _ service.

Control of Substances Hazardous to Health (COSHH)

A wide range of substances, from chemicals used in industrial
processes to cleaning preparations or even natural substances like
fungus are capable of damaging health. In all types of business –
factories, farms, leisure activities, offices, shops, to name but a few –
workers' health can be at risk from the hazardous substances staff
encounter from day to day if the right precautions are not taken. There
are essential requirements for controlling exposure to hazardous
substances and employers are responsible for protecting people who
might be affected by these substances.

The basic principles of occupational hygiene are listed below.
Employers must:

1 Assess both the risk to health arising from workplace exposure to
   hazardous substances and decide upon what precautions are
   needed.
2 Introduce appropriate, effective measures to prevent, or adequately
   control, the exposure.

3 Ensure that control measures are used, that equipment is properly maintained and procedures observed.

4 In some cases monitor workers' exposure and carry out appropriate health checks.

5 Inform, instruct and train employees about the risks and precautions to be taken.

Substances that are hazardous to health include substances labelled as dangerous, for example very toxic, toxic, harmful, irritant or corrosive substances. Agricultural pesticides and other chemicals used on farms and substances with occupational exposure limits are also classified as hazardous to health. These substances may also include harmful micro-organisms and substantial quantities of dust, indeed any material, mixture or compound used at work, or arising from work activities, which can harm people's health.

Figure 2.6 shows some signs you may have already seen indicating a warning about hazardous substances.

Fig 2.6 Hazardous substance signs

Employers have to ensure that the exposure of employees to hazardous substances is prevented or adequately controlled. The employer has to decide which control measures are required for the employees' workplace in order to deal effectively with any hazardous substances that may be present. This may mean preventing exposure by:

- removing the hazardous substance, by changing the process
- substituting with a safe or safer substance, or using it in a safer form

Where this is not possible then they must control exposure by, for example:

- totally enclosing the process
- using partial enclosure and extraction equipment
- general ventilation
- using safe systems of work and handling procedures

It is the employer's responsibility to choose the method of controlling exposure. The use of personal protective equipment, for example respirators, dust masks and protective clothing, can be used as a means of protection in those situations only when other measures cannot control exposure.

The employer has an obligation to ensure that all control measures are kept in efficient working order and good repair. Controls should be examined and tested regularly and respirators and breathing apparatus also have to be examined frequently. The employer should monitor the exposure of workers in certain cases, for example:

- where there could be serious risks to health if control measures were to fail or deteriorate
- if they cannot be sure that exposure limits are not being exceeded
- where they cannot be sure that particular control measures are working properly

It may be the case that medical examinations have to be carried out. The services of a doctor, trained nurse or trained supervisor could be used to check employees for effects such as severe dermatitis, or to ask questions about breathing difficulties, if the work involves substances known to cause asthma. A simple record must be kept of any examinations carried out.

It is the employer's responsibility to keep their employees informed about:

- the risks arising from their work
- the precautions to be taken

and, if carried out:

- the results of monitoring
- the results of health surveillance

■ DIY 2.1.4

Make a list of any hazardous substances you use whilst at work. Write a brief report on the procedures you must follow to ensure safe handling and storage. Take a photocopy of Fig. 2.7 below showing types of protective clothing. On a separate sheet of paper write out why each of these items may be required and the type of hazard for which they are used as protection.

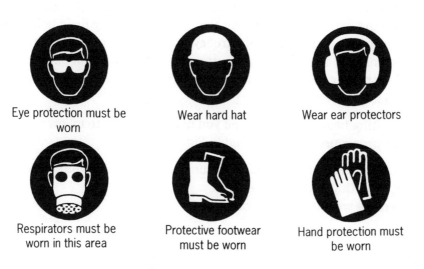

Eye protection must be worn

Wear hard hat

Wear ear protectors

Respirators must be worn in this area

Protective footwear must be worn

Hand protection must be worn

Fig 2.7 Requirements for safety clothing

▶ *What type of protective clothing might be used?*

Depending upon the type of materials you, or other members of staff, deal with it may be a requirement to wear protective clothing (see Fig. 2.7). This may be a simple apron or overall to prevent you from getting dirty or it may be a hard helmet, protective footwear or perhaps goggles to prevent injury if an accident occurred. It is important that you know where protective clothing is kept and how to use it properly. The clothing must be maintained and cleaned according to instructions and always replaced in the correct location.

It may be the case that it is your job to give out protective clothing to members of staff or people visiting your company. This may be carried out on a booking in and out basis or the clothing may be available for them to help themselves. However, it is important that this clothing is worn at all times and that visitors are informed of the rules and regulations regarding protective clothing operated by your employer for the visitors' safety.

▶ *How should you lift and handle materials?*

Lifting and handling everyday working materials will cause no concern and can be dealt with on an everyday basis. However, it is important when dealing with materials that are heavy or awkward to move that you use the correct procedure for this. Firstly, you may need help, and this may come in the shape of a trolley or another person. If an item is far too heavy to lift then it may be the case that arrangements can be made with the caretakers to move the item for you. A written request for this may have to be made.

When lifting heavy items yourself you must take care to follow the correct procedures, as illustrated in Fig. 2.8.

1 Bend your knees and take the strain on your legs not your back.
2 Lift smoothly and do not jerk.
3 Keep the weight close to your body.

Fig 2.8 Correct method for lifting heavy items

4 Stand upright and do not lean sideways.

5 Keep your spine straight.

6 Use trolleys and other aids if available

7 If in doubt, **get help**, or use mechanical aid.

8 Realise your limitations and do not risk your health.

The majority of back injuries are caused by people lifting heavy items incorrectly. Follow these procedures and you will use the strength of your legs to lift the item and not the weakness of your back.

▶ *What is correct handling?*

The type of handling and storage will depend upon the kind of stock and the size of the business or training centre. Large organisations will have a stockroom with specialist staff employed purely to take charge of the stock. A small organisation may only have a stock cupboard with one person in charge of the key.

Every item of stock must be stored neatly and be easily accessible when required. Shelves should be labelled so that it is easy to find what is needed, and the stockroom or cupboard should always be locked. It is important that the storage area is kept dry at all times to prevent paper-based items from becoming damp and going mouldy. Large or heavy items should be kept low so that lifting is not required and when new stock arrives it should be placed at the back or at the bottom so that the older stock is used first.

It is important that you treat hazardous stock with care. Any liquids that are toxic, inflammable or give off fumes, for example thinners, glue or duplicating fluid, must be kept in a separate area and you must never smoke in this area or in the stockroom itself. It is also very important that you are aware of the action to take to prevent accidents and to be able to carry out remedial action if an accident does occur. If you identify any hazards, or problems arise with storing certain stock items this should be reported to your supervisor or the health and safety representative immediately. Likewise, if damage occurs to any stock while it is being stored this should be reported – it may still be under guarantee and the supplier could arrange for exchange or repair, or alternatively the business may be able to make an insurance claim.

■ DIY 2.1.5

Health and safety procedures are there for a reason. Answer the following questions in full to prove that you understand how these procedures operate in your training centre or workplace.

1 What type of hazards would you be authorised to put right?
2 If the hazard is beyond your authority, how would you report this to your supervisor.
3 What are your organisation's procedures for dealing with emergencies?
4 How do your work practices operate in accordance with organisational requirements? (This should include your own work station.)
5 What instructions are provided by the organisation to ensure you comply with legal requirements and codes of practice?

▶ *What are the most common forms of accident?*

Common forms of accident or health emergency include fire, flood, risk of explosion, toxic fumes and accidents. In any of these events it is important that you know the correct procedure to follow to minimise the emergency and act efficiently. The procedures you may need to follow in any of these incidents include evacuation, activating alarms, detaching equipment from mains supplies and reporting accidents correctly. It is vital that you understand your own limitations when dealing with emergencies and that you know when and how to contact help if necessary.

▶ *What are the relevant procedures to follow in an emergency?*

A busy organisation is likely to be crowded with staff, visitors and customers and it is important that in order to protect these people and the organisation's property that much thought is given to fire and accident procedures. If the organisation stores inflammable, toxic or perhaps corrosive materials then even more attention should be paid to emergency procedures and every member of staff should know exactly what to do in the event of an emergency. Staff will be expected to escort visitors or customers who are unfamiliar with the evacuation procedure from the building.

When you join an organisation as a new member of staff you should undergo induction training which will show you what to do in the event of an emergency, how to recognise or sound the alarm and how to follow the evacuation procedure. It is important for you to know how to raise the alarm, who to contact in the event of an emergency and how to evacuate yourself and possibly others from the building as quickly and safely as possible. You must know the quickest route to follow out of the building and at which point outside you should assemble for a name call.

■ DIY 2.1.6

On a piece of A3 paper draw a plan of the area in which you work. This may be a large office, training room, library or one floor of a small organisation. On your plan show the following:

doors	water buckets
windows	fire escapes
stairs	sprinklers
fire extinguishers	fire alarms
fire blankets	smoke detectors
furniture	emergency notices
sand buckets	fire exit location signs.

Also note on your plan where you would find:

1 accident report book/form
2 organisation's 'Information for Employees Regulations poster'
3 nearest, trained first-aid person
4 nearest first-aid box

▶ *Fire precautions*

Fire precautions must always be strictly followed. There must be an effective means of giving a fire warning, for example a loud ringing bell or hooter that all staff recognise as being a fire alarm. Fire-fighting equipment must also be available and must be maintained properly so it is always ready for use. Familiarise yourself with the type of fire-fighting equipment available, in particular the different coloured fire extinguishers that can be used for different types of fire.

All fire exits and fire doors must be marked. A fire door must never be left open as the purpose of this door is to hold the fire back to give you more time to escape – it will be of little use if it is left open. Fire exits must be clearly marked as members of staff, visitors and customers will need to find them in order to get out of the building in an emergency. Fire exits must never be locked and must be kept clear at all times; they should never be blocked by items such as boxes or office equipment that is not in use.

All fire procedures should be displayed on a noticeboard and brought to the attention of all members of staff regularly. Most organisations have details of fire procedures in each separate room giving details of the assembly point and the quickest route out of the building from that particular room. Remember that you should never smoke in a non-smoking area and you should never put lighted cigarette ends in to a waste-paper basket. If you work in a non-smoking area it means just that. Do not be tempted to smoke in toilets or quiet areas as this is likely to offend other members of staff and could be dangerous.

▶ *What types of fire extinguishers are there?*

It is important that you understand the use of each of these fire extinguishers and the fires for which they are designed. There are six commonly used fire extinguishers, as illustrated in Fig. 2.9.

Green fire extinguishers contain CFC gases, which affect the ozone layer, and as part of the Montreal Agreement it has been agreed that the use of these extinguishers will be phased out. However, they will still be in existence for a while yet as it is important to remember that however much they affect the ozone layer, the fire itself is more harmful. When green fire extinguishers are no longer in existence, black or blue extinguishers can be used in their place.

There are other types of fire-fighting equipment that may be available for use in an emergency. Equipment such as fire blankets, sand buckets, sprinklers, smoke detectors, hosepipes and fire alarms are there to protect you in the event of a fire and to give you an opportunity to prevent a large fire breaking out. However, never under any circumstances risk your own life by trying to tackle a fire without giving the alarm signal first.

FIRE EXTINGUISHERS		
Colour	**Contents**	**Use for fires**
GREEN	Halon, BCF	Paper, wood, fabric, liquids, fat, paint, spirits, oils, gases (such as oxygen, butane and propane), and electrical fires.
CHROME	Gas	As above.
CREAM	Foam	As above, but not electrical fires.
BLACK	CO_2	Liquids, fat, paint, spirits, oil, gases and electrical fires.
BLUE	Powder	Metals, such as magnesium, on fire.
RED	Water	Paper, wood and fabric fires.

Fig 2.9 Types of fire extinguisher

■ DIY 2.1.7

You have already drawn a plan of the area where you work. Check that you have included all the fire-fighting equipment, including sand buckets and so on. On your plan colour in each extinguisher according to its colour. Add an information sheet to your plan explaining each of the different coloured fire extinguishers and their uses. Describe what each extinguisher contains and for which fires it can be used.

You will also note that each extinguisher carries details on how to operate it in an emergency. Add these details to your A4 sheet including diagrams to clarify the information.

▶ *Why have an evacuation procedure?*

Remember that an organisation may have to be evacuated not only in case of fire. It may be that there has been an explosion, accident, flood, bomb alert or perhaps a suspicious package has been found.

Fire, police or ambulance services may have to be called, but do not do this yourself unless you are the person who is responsible – it is likely to be your supervisor's or switchboard operator's responsibility to call the emergency services.

In the event of an evacuation customers and visitors and possibly other members of staff will need help evacuating the building as quickly and safely as possible. It is important for you to act quickly, but to keep calm and never panic. There will be a set procedure to follow in order to evacuate each office, department, floor and so on, and this will include making sure that no one is left behind.

Every person in the work area should be encouraged to leave the building quickly but not to panic and run. In the event of a fire never use the lift when evacuating as heat, smoke and fire is likely to be sucked upwards through the lift shaft; also the lift may break down and leave you stranded. It will be your supervisor's responsibility to ensure that all members of staff have left the building and it is likely that they will do this by carrying out a name call. In order to help your supervisor make sure that you report to them as soon as you have left the building so that they know you are out of the building and safe. Never re-enter the building until you have been told it is safe to do so and be on the lookout for other members of staff who have not reported in.

It is very important for you to understand that fire exits, fire doors and fire-fighting equipment are there to help you in the event of fire. They must never be hidden or obstructed in any way and if access is blocked this should be reported to your supervisor immediately. It is too late once someone has been injured or possibly killed.

In the event of a fire it is useful for you to know how to use the fire-fighting equipment, but if it is a real emergency never risk your own life by trying to tackle the fire. It is more important that you sound the alarm and evacuate the building along with other members of staff and leave the fire-fighting to the experts.

■ DIY 2.1.8

You may think that an office is not the most dangerous of places. However, accidents still happen! Look at Fig. 2.3 on page 38 and make a list of all the hazards you can identify.

▶ *What is 'first aid'?*

In the event of a customer, visitor or another member of staff being injured or taken ill it is important to have access to a first-aid box like that shown in Fig. 2.10 so that treatment may be given, perhaps whilst

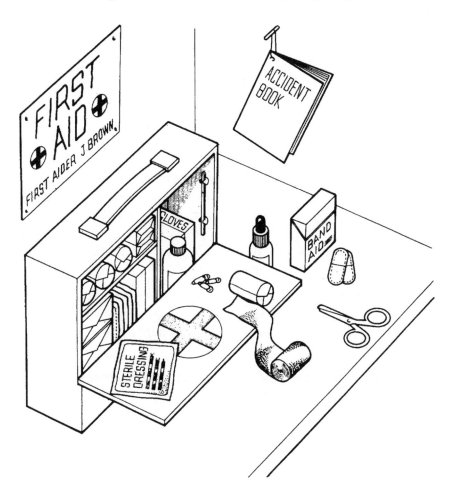

Fig 2.10 A first-aid box

waiting for an ambulance to arrive. If a first-aid box is not required it is still important to know how to make the person comfortable and safe whilst awaiting help.

There should be qualified first-aid staff available who will be able to use the contents of an adequately stocked first-aid box. In a large organisation it is likely that first-aid staff will carry pagers so that they may be contacted quickly and given details of the incident.

The first-aid box should contain:

1 Individually wrapped sterile dressings of assorted sizes.
2 Sterile eye pads with attachment.
3 Individually wrapped triangular bandages.
4 Safety pins.
5 Medium/large/extra large size, sterile, individually-wrapped, unmedicated wound dressings.
6 Cleaning tissues, cotton wool, antiseptic, disposable gloves.
7 Disposable wipes.
8 Guidance notes on the use of the first-aid box.
9 Reorder forms.
10 List of contents.

The first-aid box should only contain items that a qualified first-aid person has been trained to use. They should not contain medication, for example aspirin, of any kind as the first-aider is not a trained doctor. The first-aid box should be kept in a central place for all staff to use and it is reasonable to expect that at least one member of staff in your organisation will have first-aid training.

As an employee it is important that you follow safe working practices. If you see a potential hazard report it to your supervisor immediately before somebody has an accident and make sure that you are aware of the following:

1 Who has had first-aid training in your office or training centre.
2 Where the first-aid box is kept.
3 Who to contact in the event of an emergency.
4 How to record/report accidents.

Unless you have been trained to use the first-aid box yourself do not try to treat an injured person. Summon someone who is trained as quickly as possible. If the accident has been caused as a result of a broken fixture or fitting, or something which has been spilled on the floor, make sure that you clean up or clear up so that the accident spot is removed as soon as possible.

It is important that you do not panic. You must remain calm and clear headed. This will reassure anyone who has been injured and give them confidence that help is on hand and you know what you are doing.

▶ *What should you do if someone has an electric shock?*

To help a person suffering from electric shock:

1 Shout for help.
2 Switch off the power.
3 If the power cannot be switched off immediately, pull or push the casualty clear with a broom or wooden chair.
4 Unless wearing thick, rubber-soled boots, stand on lino, rubber or wood.
5 Do not touch the casualty with bare hands unless the power is switched off.
6 If the casualty is breathing place them in the recovery position.
7 If the casualty is not breathing apply rescue breathing, check pulse, and if absent, apply heart compression.

▶ *What is 'rescue breathing', 'heart compression', and the 'recovery position'?*

Immediate and proper examination and treatment of injuries may save life – and is essential to reduce pain and help injured people make a quick recovery. All organisations must have an appropriate level of first-aid treatment available by law. An appointed person should take charge in an emergency, call the ambulance and look after the first-aid equipment. The first-aid box should contain guidance on the treatment of injured people, in particular how to keep someone alive by artificial respiration (rescue breathing), how to control bleeding and how to deal with an unconscious person.

There are government guidelines that cover 4 main areas of resuscitation:

RECOGNISE A LACK OF OXYGEN **ACT AT ONCE**

Arising from

ELECTRIC SHOCK
DROWNING
POISONING
HEAD INJURY
GASSING etc

May be causing

UNCONSCIOUSNESS
NOISY OR
NO BREATHING
ABNORMAL COLOUR

SWITCH OFF ELECTRICITY, GAS, etc.,
REMOVE CASUALTY FROM DANGER
SEND SOMEBODY FOR HELP

GET A CLEAR AIRWAY ...
REMOVE ANY OBSTRUCTION ... then

BREATHING MAY RESTART ... IF NOT ...

3 **APPLY RESCUE BREATHING** **4** **IF NONE, COMBINE RESCUE BREATHING & HEART COMPRESSION**

START WITH FOUR
QUICK DEEP BREATHS

SEAL NOSE AND
BLOW INTO MOUTH

  or

SEAL MOUTH AND
BLOW INTO NOSE

KEEP FINGERS ON JAW
BUT CLEAR OF THROAT

MAINTAIN HEAD
POSITION

PLACE CASUALTY
ON A FIRM SURFACE

COMMENCE
HEART COMPRESSION

HEEL OF HAND ONLY
ON LOWER HALF OF
BREASTBONE
OTHER HAND ON TOP,
FINGERS OFF CHEST

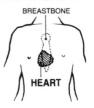

AFTER BLOWING INTO
MOUTH or NOSE,
WATCH CASUALTY'S
CHEST FALL AS
YOU BREATHE IN

REPEAT EVERY 5 SECS

KEEP ARMS STRAIGHT
AND ROCK FORWARD
TO DEPRESS CHEST
1½ INCHES (4 cm)

APPLY 15 COMPRESSIONS
ONE PER SECOND ... then
GIVE TWO BREATHS

**AFTER FIRST FOUR
BREATHS TEST FOR
RECOVERY SIGNS**

1. PULSE PRESENT?
2. PUPILS LESS LARGE?
3. COLOUR IMPROVED?

PULSE POINTS

RE-CHECK PULSE ...
IF STILL ABSENT
CONTINUE WITH
15 COMPRESSIONS
TO TWO BREATHS

IF PULSE RETURNS
CEASE COMPRESSIONS
BUT CONTINUE
RESCUE BREATHING

Fig 2.11 RoSPA poster 'Emergency Aid'. Reproduced courtesy of RoSPA

1 **Recognise a lack of oxygen**. This may arise from electric shock, drowning, poisoning, head injury, gassing, etc, and can cause unconsciousness, noisy or heavy breathing or abnormal skin colour.

2 **Act at once**. Switch off electricity, gas, etc, remove casualty from danger and send someone for help. Get a clear airway and remove any obstruction. Tilt the casualty's head back and lift their jaw. Breathing may now restart.

3 **Apply rescue breathing**. Start with four quick, deep breaths, seal nose and blow in to mouth. Keep fingers on jaw but clear of throat. Maintain head position. After blowing in to mouth or nose watch casualty's chest fall as you breathe in. Repeat every 5 seconds. After first four breaths test for recovery signs such as: pulse present, pupils less large, colour improved. The pulse points can be checked by feeling the wrist or neck.

4 **If none, combine rescue breathing and heart compression**. Place casualty on a firm surface and place heel of hand only on lower half of breastbone with other hand on top, keeping fingers off the chest. Keep arms straight and rock forward to depress chest 4 cm. Apply 15 compressions, one per second, then give two breaths. Re-check pulse and if still absent continue with 15 compressions to two breaths. If pulse returns cease compressions but continue rescue breathing.

A member of staff who has had training in first aid will know how to carry out rescue breathing and heart compression if this is necessary. However, such action will only be required in extreme cases such as those listed above. In the case of fainting, unconsciousness, epileptic fit and so on, where the casualty requires time to come round, the recovery position should be used so that they may recover in a comfortable position where they cannot cause harm to themselves (see Fig. 2.12).

Fig 2.12 The recovery position

If the casualty is lying on their back:

1 Place their right arm slightly under their body, lean over them and pull them towards you so that they roll on to their front.
2 Move the casualty's head so it is on its side facing you and bend their left arm upwards so that the hand is placed flat on the floor by their face.
3 Bend the casualty's nearest leg upward at the knee so that the body is turned slightly and is supported by the leg.
4 Cover the casualty with a blanket if in a cold position and stay with them until they recover or further help arrives.

▶ *How could you prevent machine accidents?*

There are special rules for some machines used in offices. Some are classed as dangerous machines which people can use only after full instruction and sufficient training under close supervision. Examples include packaging equipment, guillotines and other cutting equipment.

Before you use such a machine make sure:

1 You know how to switch it off before you switch it on.
2 All guards are fitted and working.
3 All materials are clear of working parts of the machine.
4 Area around machine is clean, tidy and free from obstruction.
5 Your supervisor is told at once if you think a machine is faulty.
6 You are wearing appropriate protective clothing.

Never:

1 Use a machine unless you are authorised and trained to do so.
2 Try to clean a machine when it is still plugged in or switched on.
3 Use a machine with a danger sign or tag attached.
4 Wear dangling chains, loose clothing, gloves, rings or long hair that could get caught in moving parts.
5 Distract people who are using machines.

▶ *How should you use visual display units safely?*

The Health and Safety (Display Screen Equipment) Regulations 1992 affect workers who habitually use VDUs for a significant part of their normal work. Although this description does not apply to workers who use VDUs occasionally, the employers still have general obligations to protect them under health and safety legislation. The Regulations do not contain detailed technical information, but instead set more general objectives.

Employers have to:

- analyse work stations of employees covered by the Regulations and assess and reduce risks
- ensure work stations meet minimum requirements
- plan work so there are breaks or changes of activity
- on request arrange eye and eyesight tests, and provide spectacles if special ones are needed
- provide health and safety training
- provide information.

In order to reduce any possible negative effects on health through the use of VDU-based equipment for lengthy periods of time, the Health and Safety Executive has recommended a series of guidelines for ensuring that the office environment is compatible with the introduction of new technology. Leaflet IND(G) 36(L) *Working with VDUs* is published by the Health and Safety Executive and provides useful information regarding the use of VDUs in an office environment.

The guidelines recommend that in the operation of VDUs adjustable brightness and contrast controls should be used to improve the displayed image, which together with screen filters will reduce eye strain. VDU keyboards should be detached from the screen so that the distance between the screen and operator can be adjusted according to personal preference, and the keys themselves should have a matt surround to minimise glare and have concave tops with adjustable slope to maximise operator comfort.

VDUs generate heat and this will have to be taken into account when heating an office environment to an acceptable temperature; adequate ventilation and humidity also needs to be maintained. Lighting has to be adequate enough for the operator to read documents but not too bright or directed so that it glares on the screen and makes it difficult to read. Undue noise is also disruptive and therefore printers and other noisy office machinery should be sited away from operators or provided with acoustic covers.

Time spent at a VDU will depend upon the nature of the work being performed. Lengthy periods of keying in text may require rapid keyboarding but will not involve extensive concentration on the screen itself. However, if the work involves composition of text, work with spreadsheets, databases or desktop publishing this may require shorter work periods as far greater concentration on the screen is necessary.

■ DIY 2.1.9

If you are not already in possession of the leaflet *Working with VDUs* contact: HSE Information Centre, Broad Lane, Sheffield S3 7HQ, or contact their free leaflet line on (Tel) 0742 892346, (Fax) 0742 892333, and ask for a copy. Use this leaflet to produce information sheets that can be distributed to VDU operators in your work place or training centre. Your information sheet should cover at least one side of A4 paper.

Completing Element 2.1

To complete this element on monitoring and maintaining health and safety within the workplace you will need to put all the DIY tasks in your folder and carry out a final assessment. Competence must be proven in dealing with existing or potential hazards and taking actions that conform to organisational requirements. Hazards and working conditions outside your own authority must be promptly and accurately reported to an appropriate person. Actions and reporting of emergencies must conform with established procedures and work practices must be carried out in accordance with organisational requirements. Competence must be proven in dealing with all equipment, fixtures and fittings within your own area of responsibility and all areas within the organisation. Emergencies must cover illness, accident, fire and evacuation. All legal requirements and codes of practice must be followed.

Claiming credit

Once you have completed your final assessment, you will need to write in your record book or folder how, when, where and what you have done to prove that you are competent.

The following is an example of how one trainee completed this claim:

While employed at Coopers & Co I was able to report hazards such as trailing leads and eating and drinking around computing equipment. I reported these hazards in a memo (see evidence). During induction training I was shown what to do in an emergency and how to evacuate the building (see induction training pack evidence). The office supervisor was responsible for completing accident report forms but I have completed 2 forms from given information (see evidence). I am not a trained first-aider; however, I know that in the event of an accident I must make the casualty comfortable in the recovery position and contact a first-aider immediately. I would do this by dialling 222 (the internal emergency number) or by sending a runner. I organised my own work station so that there were no hazards, such as trailing leads and overloaded electric sockets. My VDU was placed away from the light so that there was no glare on the screen. I also made sure my chair was set at the right height with the back support in the correct position. I used the HE leaflet called Working with VDUs *for advice. I kept the telephone, and equipment I used regularly, close by so that I could be efficient and safe.*

■ Element 2.2
MONITOR AND MAINTAIN THE SECURITY OF THE WORKPLACE

Performance criteria

- Organisational security procedures are carried out correctly
- Security risks are correctly identified
- Identified security risks are put right or reported promptly to the appropriate person
- Identified breaches of security are dealt with in accordance with organisational procedures

Whether you work for a large or small organisation, the way in which you deal with visitors is very important. A visitor is anyone that comes to see you or your colleagues and does not work in your department or organisation on an everyday basis.

This could be someone from:

- another department or section
- another branch

- another company or other organisation
- a customer or client
- people attending a meeting
- people delivering or collecting items
- people attending an interview or asking about vacancies

Some of these visitors will be expected and others will be unexpected. The way in which these visitors are greeted and your attitude towards them is very important. However, whilst creating the correct company image you must be constantly aware of security and ensure that information is not given out to the wrong person in the name of politeness. Security relating to people, equipment and information should always be treated as a priority.

▶ *In terms of security, how should visitors be treated?*

When receiving visitors you should always try to be:

- polite
- courteous
- positive
- friendly
- helpful
- patient

However, to protect the security of your organisation you must also be prepared to be:

- tactful
- diplomatic
- firm
- direct
- assertive

Above all, you should always be on the lookout for anything suspicious or out of place, and be prepared to act on your suspicions by reporting to an appropriate authority, such as your supervisor, as quickly as possible.

Unless a caller is authorised, no confidential information should be given (verbal or written) to them. Confidential information includes personal details of staff, their exact whereabouts and appointments schedule, financial details about the organisation and its customers, details of future projects or contracts, etc. If you are unsure whether information may be passed on or not, always check with your supervisor.

■ DIY 2.2.1

How do you ensure that your organisational security procedures are carried out correctly? Give full details of the action you should take if you become suspicious – what are the reporting procedures for this?

Many companies now have strict rules about the security of the building. Callers and visitors may not be allowed to walk round the offices without a member of staff accompanying them. Usually a member of staff will collect the visitor from reception and accompany them to the meeting office. A receptionist should not leave reception unattended in case another visitor arrives and is left to wander round the building unsupervised.

In the majority of organisations visitors are still allowed to find their own way to the office they require, but care must be taken to ensure the visitor is given clear directions so that they do not get lost. When the business is complete and the visitor wishes to leave, the member of staff with them should make sure that they know how to get out of the building. There may be a quicker route from the building than the one by which they entered or the visitor may be required to leave the building through reception so that their name can be logged out of the visitors' register. (Fig. 2.13).

Some organisations rely solely on the visitors' register as a means to record visitors' details and the nature of their business. In some cases, such as government offices or high-risk areas, the visitor may need to have their bag, briefcase or belongings searched before being allowed to enter the building. The visitor may even be required to leave items at reception, and these should be labelled with the visitor's name and kept in a safe and secure place until their return. In some extreme cases a body search may be carried out. Any company carrying out such procedures is likely to employ specialist staff such as security guards to attend to these duties.

VISITORS' REGISTER						
DATE						
Identity Badge No.	Time in	Time out	Name	Company	Appointment with	Action Taken

Fig 2.13 Visitors' register

Some organisations issue visitors with a badge or pass at reception to show that they have been authorised to visit the building (Fig. 2.14). The badge or pass should be returned when the visitor leaves the building. Plastic badges bearing the name of the organisation and the word 'visitor' are often used, or badges with a blank space for the visitor's name to be inserted are popular and provide a more personal touch. Special reception registers can also be used that allow the visitor to enter details of their business alongside their name, a copy of the name portion of the register can be torn from the register and inserted in to a small plastic holder which can be attached to the visitor's lapel as identification. In this way the visitor's entry and exit to and from the building is fully monitored.

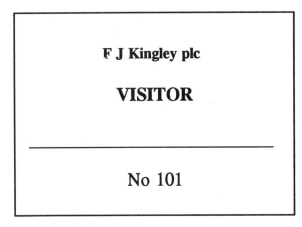

F J Kingley plc

VISITOR

No 101

Fig 2.14 Visitors' lapel badge

■ DIY 2.2.2

How does your workplace or training centre register the entry and exit of visitors? Is the visitor asked to show personal identification before being issued with a visitor's badge?

1 If your organisation already has a security procedure in action, write a report explaining how it operates. Also include copies of the visitors' register, badges and any other form of security measures.
2 If your organisation has no security procedures, now is a good time to produce some. Write a memo to your supervisor explaining the advantages of such a system and suggest the measures that could be taken in your own workplace or training centre to improve security.

▶ *How can equipment be made secure?*

A busy office is likely to be filled with expensive equipment such as computers, word processors, printers, photocopiers, fax machines, telephones, and so on. It is unlikely that a thief would try to steal large equipment such as photocopiers or main frame computers. However, smaller equipment such as word processors, that can be dismantled into a number of smaller, separate parts, may be the target for a thief.

It is usual practice to lock an office that is to be left unattended, not only to secure equipment but perhaps personal items such as coats and handbags.

67

Equipment should be labelled with an indelible ink pen stating the name or initials of the organisation together with the postcode – if the equipment is stolen but later found by the police it can be easily traced back to its rightful owner using this information. Small, valuable equipment such as a desk-top franking machine or a lap-top computer must always be locked away in a secure place unless it is being used. Most office equipment will carry a serial number and this should be noted when the equipment is first installed, by doing this the equipment can be identified if it is stolen.

▶ *How can information be made secure?*

All company files could be classed as confidential. Personal information, company reports, financial accounts or minutes from a business meeting should never be discussed with people outside the company. It is important to recognise that information dealt with on a daily, routine basis may be of interest to a rival company. A member of staff may be interested in a colleague's salary or perhaps their home address and telephone number. Therefore, it is important that you do not leave paperwork lying round the office, however innocent you may think it is.

To secure paper-based information make sure all files are kept in one place under lock and key. Folders containing sensitive information should be marked 'CONFIDENTIAL' and must not be left on a desk or lent out to unauthorised personnel, however nice and friendly they may seem. Dead files should never be put in a bin or skip, they should be shredded or incinerated so they are unreadable.

Confidential information held in a computer must also be protected. Use passwords or keywords to restrict access and protect information; only authorised staff should know the password or keyword which should be changed regularly and never written down. Printouts should be kept in a folder marked confidential and disks should be kept locked away in a cupboard, not just locked in their disk box. Information stored on a computer database will be covered by the Data Protection Act (see page 161 for more information).

■ DIY 2.2.3

How is the equipment in your workplace or training centre made secure? Is there a procedure in operation that labels and records all equipment?

1 Find out if this is so and write a report explaining how this procedure is carried out and how the equipment is logged.
2 If there is no such labelling and logging in progress, you should write to your supervisor explaining why and how this should be done.

▶ *How would you deal with a breach in security?*

Situations such as a member of staff being threatened, equipment being stolen or information about the company being leaked would all be treated as a breach in security. In any of these cases it is important that you know the correct procedure to follow. You may need to get assistance quickly if you have an aggressive, suspicious or unauthorised visitor. In this case you may need to contact your supervisor quickly, dial an internal emergency number to summons a security guard, or contact the police.

If you are suspicious of a person, or even another member of staff, who you think is or has been stealing from the organisation you must report this to your supervisor immediately. It is only by your quick action that further theft can be prevented. Also, remember that if you identify a potential security risk you must report this immediately so that something can be done about it. Make sure that you follow all security procedures properly and that potential security risks outside your own authority are reported to the appropriate person. Never under any circumstances risk injury to yourself and recognise your own scope for dealing with security risks.

■ DIY 2.2.4

You are the receptionist at Coopers & Co Chartered Surveyors and you are just about to close the reception area at 5 pm. A member of staff, Mr Collins, runs back into the building and explains that he has left something in the office. He asks you if you can hang on for 5 minutes while he goes and gets it. All the other members of staff have gone home and it is your supervisor's afternoon off. You agree, but 20 minutes later you are still waiting to go home. You decide to go to the office to see if the member of staff has found what he is looking for. When you open the office door you see him coming out of the Managing Director's office with a computer disk in his hand. He looks surprised to see you and explains that he had just popped into the office to close a window. It is now 5.30 pm and you finally see the member of staff out of the building and go home yourself. Some weeks later your supervisor tells you that there have been problems with security and that details regarding the financial planning of the company have been leaked to a rival. Apparently they were copied from the Managing Director's database.

1 Write a memo to your supervisor explaining the events of the evening when Mr Collins returned to the office. (Do you think this memo should be confidential?)
2 If you were to remain silent about this incident what might happen?

Completing Element 2.2

To complete this element on monitoring and maintaining the security of the workplace you will need to put all the DIY tasks in your folder, and carry out a final assessment. This must prove that you are able to identify security risks and follow your organisation's security procedure. You must also show that you are able to put right security risks or, where relevant, report these to your supervisor – this must be in accordance with organisational procedures. You must prove an understanding of the security systems for checking personal identification, entry and exit of visitors and the security of equipment.

Claiming credit

Once you have completed your final assessment, you will need to write in your record book or folder how, when, where and what you have done to prove that you are competent.

The following is an example of how one trainee completed this claim:

When I completed 3 weeks' work experience at Coopers & Co reception I was told to issue all callers to the company with a visitor's badge. The visitor's badge had a number on it and this was entered in the visitors' register (see copy in evidence folder) alongside the name, company name and type of business. The visitor had to book out of the company and return the badge before leaving. All visitors had to report to reception and no one was allowed into the building unless they had an appointment; if they did not I would contact the relevant person and ask if they could see the visitor, or I would offer to make them an appointment. If an unauthorised person tried to enter the building I would call security on Extension 123 and tell them. I recognise that I could request a person not to enter the building but under no circumstances should I try to stop someone physically myself. I did not identify any potential security risks at Coopers and Co but if I had I would have reported these verbally to my supervisor. I have carried out a task where I identified risks and wrote a report to my supervisor with details of how these could be put right (see work folder) as well as a report explaining how equipment is made secure (see evidence folder). I have also written a report to my supervisor explaining that identity badges should be worn by visitors so that they can be identified and their presence verified.

UNIT 3

Contribute to the effectiveness of the work flow

■ Element 3.1
PLAN AND ORGANISE OWN WORK SCHEDULE

Performance critiera

- Routine and unexpected tasks are identified and prioritised according to organisational procedures
- Appropriate planning aids are used to schedule work
- Where priorities change, work schedules are adapted accordingly
- Anticipated difficulties in meeting deadlines are promptly reported to the appropriate person
- Assistance is sought, where necessary, to meet specific demands and deadlines

Every organisation would like staff that are able to plan and organise their own work to ensure the most effective use of available time and resources. In every job there are tasks that need carrying out on a regular basis, routine tasks, and unexpected tasks that need to be fitted in around the routine tasks. The order in which you carry out the tasks will be your priority order, and this will depend on how urgent the task is and what is required.

There are a variety of planning aids available to help you plan efficient allocation of time and resources, so that everything is used as effectively as possible.

▶ *What aids are available?*

There are several aids available, some of the more popular in use in office are described below.

- **Desk diary**. A desk diary is normally A4 in size, although you may prefer to use a smaller one for your area of work. The layout may be one day per page or one week per opening and the pages may be subdivided into hours. The type of information that you write in this diary will include appointments, meetings and reminders. The reminders may be to yourself, to ensure that you remember to carry out a particular task. Quite often a whole section will share a diary and you will be able to find the availability or whereabouts of the people within your section by referring to the diary. Usually entries in diaries will be made in pencil to allow alteration at a later date.

- **Bring forward file** – also called a **reminder system** or **tickler file** (*see* Fig. 5.4 on page 123). This system can be used by individuals to remind them to carry out action on a particular date. Documents that need follow-up action can be placed in the file. The system you use need not be as detailed as the one described in Unit 5. Some people use an A4 ring binder with plastic wallets, each wallet having a document or reminder sheet with a date on it, the bring forward date. The wallets are filed in date order, next date on top, and the contents are removed on the due date. A similar system using index cards may be more suitable for your own arrangements.

- **Visual planners**. These are often made of plastic and allow information to be written on them using non-permanent marker pens. Items can be deleted by rubbing off the pen. It is usual for planners to be poster size and displayed on the wall so that they can be viewed easily (*see* Fig. 3.1). The type of information written on them will usually include holiday dates, meeting dates, special report dates, etc. Colour coding can be used to identify different members of staff or types of meeting. Confidential information should not, of course, be displayed on these planners.

- **Microcomputer or electronic diary**. Details of names, addresses, telephone and fax numbers, appointment and meeting dates can be entered into the computer. Some electronic systems with large memories can be used as a diary, address book, appointments schedule and itinerary. A printout may be obtained and used as an

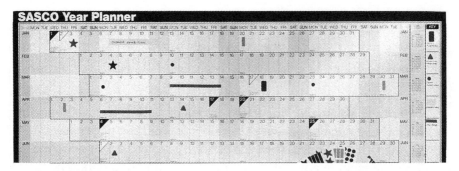

Fig 3.1 Visual wall planner

appointment card. Many people now have a hand-held electronic diary, no larger than a pocket calculator. These have limited memory space, but may be connected to a larger computer to access printing facilities.

● **Action plans**. These may be personal plans for individuals or plans for a section or department. It is useful to start the beginning of every week with an action plan. This is an opportunity to review the work carried out last week, identify any items left from the previous week that need completing, and to identify new items that need attention or completing this week.

■ DIY 3.1.1

Make several copies of the action plan shown in Fig. 3.2 on A4 landscape paper. Complete one action plan at the beginning of each week. Items brought forward from last week should be first on the action plan, followed by new items for the week.

Whether you use a diary, planner, computer or action plan it is important that the entries are:

● accurate – to avoid misunderstanding
● concise – include only the relevant information
● up to date – to ensure double bookings or too much work is not taken on

Always check to make sure that there is not a clash of requirements and that there is enough time to carry out the work scheduled.

Item No	Action Required	Deadline date	Dept/ Person to contact

Action Plan for . . . (insert your name) . . . . . . week commencing . . . .

Fig 3.2 Action plan outline

▶ *How can I allocate time effectively?*

You will need time to deal with your routine tasks such as post, photocopying, correspondence, filing and answering the phone. Additionally you may be receiving visitors, delivering and collecting items, keeping computerised information up to date, etc. You will need to organise your day so that you have time which is fairly quiet to carry out the unexpected duties that have arisen. Some of the more routine tasks may be quick to get out of the way and others may be left until later in the day. Remember that you will have deadlines to meet – one of which will be the last posting time to make sure your external correspondence is sent, otherwise the date typed on your letters will be incorrect.

■ **DIY 3.1.2**

Look at the following list of duties which you must carry out today, and put them in to a priority order.

1 Filing from yesterday.
2 Prepare envelopes for sending out the invoices.
3 Write a memo to Personnel about your holiday dates.
4 Get the end of month figures ready for your supervisor.
5 Update the database with the new customer information.
6 Photocopy the agenda for tomorrow's meeting.
7 Sort the post and distribute.

8 Read and respond to your correspondence.

9 Check the bring forward file.

10 Fax an urgent order for some A4 paper.

Regardless of the number and type of scheduling aids you use, you are likely to get unexpected demands on your time. This may be an urgent order or report that is suddenly required, someone in your section may go off sick – anything can happen to upset your intended day. When this happens you must be able to change your priorities without making a fuss, revise your schedule as quickly as you can and take on the extra duties required. However, if you have difficulties in meeting deadlines you must report this to your supervisor or appropriate person as quickly as possible. If the work you are carrying out is essential they may be able to arrange some assistance for you so that the deadline can be met. This change of priorities is all part of efficient time management – making the best use of an expensive resource. No matter how adaptable you are you should always ensure that you follow the health and safety requirements of your organisation and carry out the instructions of the manufacturer when using equipment. No shortcut should endanger you or your colleagues.

Completing Element 3.1

To complete this element on planning and organising your own work schedule you will need to put all the DIY tasks in your folder and carry out a final assessment. Competence must be proven in dealing with planning aids including diaries, schedules and action plans. Copies of notes and memos written to colleagues may also support your claim to competence.

Claiming credit

Once you have completed your final assessment, you will need to write in your record book or folder how, when, where and what you have done to prove that you are competent.

The following is an example of how one trainee completed this claim:

During my work at Natural Products I worked in a section of 4 people. I made sure that I completed an action plan every Monday (copies in my portfolio). This helped me to plan and organise my work for the week. Quite often I would be asked to carry out a job which had not been included in my action plan. I made sure that I included the new work with my existing work and rearranged my schedule as necessary. As well as my action plans I have also used a bring forward file. Copies of the notes and reminders used in this system have also been included in my portfolio. Sometimes I was unable to meet the deadlines set – for instance, when the monthly invoices needed posting, and my supervisor allowed one of the other juniors from another section to help me meet the post deadline. This was important otherwise a delay in the company receiving payments would have occurred. I always try to manage my time to suit the section I work in and the company. When I have finished my work and updated all my systems I offer to help others in my section – although this does not happen very often, as I always have plenty to do.

■ Element 3.2
OBTAIN AND ORGANISE INFORMATION IN SUPPORT OF OWN WORK ACTIVITIES

Performance criteria

- Up-to-date information, relevant to own area of responsibility, is obtained and maintained
- Information held is relevant and sufficient for work activities
- Sources of information are regularly reviewed for usefulness and relevance
- Information is organised into a suitable form to aid own work activities
- Confidentiality of information is maintained in accordance with organisational procedures

In order to carry out your work correctly and efficiently you will probably need to access information sources within your section. This may be price lists, catalogues, a database, a spreadsheet, customer records, telephone and fax directories, reference books, maps and diagrams – any information kept and stored in your section is a potential resource and information point for your work. It is therefore important that these resources are kept up to date, and have enough relevant information in them. If you are responsible for ordering stationery from external suppliers, you will probably keep more than one catalogue for information. You will also make sure that you obtain the new catalogue when issued, otherwise the codes and prices you have on record could be incorrect.

The information kept within your section should be reviewed on a regular basis. If it has not been used for some time, is it still required?

▶ *What kind of information am I likely to obtain and organise?*

There are 3 types of information that you will probably need to deal with at work.

1 **Technical** – this is anything that is relevant to your work or your section. Reference books needed for your work may include telephone directories (local and national), prices lists, filing systems, timetables (train, bus and air), etc.

■ DIY 3.2.1

Make a list of the technical information that you keep for your own work activities. This will include the files, books and computer records that you access to carry out your work. Next to each item, indicate how frequently you use the information – monthly, weekly, daily. Also state how you ensure the system is kept up to date.

2 **Organisational** – this will include company procedures, policies and objectives. Organisational information may be in the form of health and safety guidelines, quality standards and guidelines, internal organisation chart, staff locations and telephone extensions. Staff circulars, news sheets and magazines will all be treated as organisational information sources and should be kept up to date in the filing system.

■ DIY 3.2.2

Make a list of all the organisational information you need to keep within your area of work. State how frequently this information is received – yearly, monthly or weekly – or whether updates are sent periodically. Next to each item state how you keep this information filed, ie the type of system and classification used.

3 **Personal** – this information will be relevant to you and confidential, therefore it should be one of the files you keep in your own desk or cabinet. This information would include your job description, training action plan, personal agreements with your supervisor or trainer, pay scales and payslips, holiday entitlement, memos from you to Personnel and those received from Personnel.

■ DIY 3.2.3

List the types of personal information you keep on file at work. Do not include details of confidential information (unless you have discussed this with your supervisor and tutor). Which system do you use to keep this information and how do you ensure that it is kept confidential?

The technical and organisational information sources that you obtain and organise in your section may also be accessed by other members of staff, in which case they should also be kept up to date and the index system that you use should be easy to understand. In Unit 5 on page 113 there are details of the different types of filing systems and classifications. You should select the method which is best suited to the type of information being stored. If you intend changing a system, make sure that you discuss this with your supervisor and others using the system. It may be necessary to issue guidelines to the users once you have reorganised the system.

Completing Element 3.2

To complete this element on obtaining and organising information in support of your own work activities you will need to put all the DIY tasks in your folder and carry out a final assessment. Competence must be proven in dealing with information that is held which supports your own area of work. This should include information that is technical, organisational and personal.

Claiming credit

Once you have completed your final assessment, you will need to write in your record book or folder how, when, where and what you have done to prove that you are competent.

The following is an example of how one trainee completed this claim:

Whilst working in the reception area of Wallace & Warmer Ltd I made sure the information sources were up to date and relevant. These included the external telephone and fax directories and catalogues for our suppliers and customer information on the card index. When new directories or catalogues arrived I made sure the old ones were destroyed. The directories and files I use most are always kept in the middle drawer as this is easiest and quickest to access. Therefore I do not keep people waiting for longer than is necessary for information. I keep organisational material such as leaflets and promotional material, an organisation chart for this branch and for our Wandsworth branch, and the telephone extension list up to date. All the staff notices and circulars are displayed for one month on the noticeboard and then filed in the cabinet in the relevant file. Information on health and safety and the end of year/month reports are circulated and then returned to me for filing. My personal information I keep in my desk in a locked drawer. This contains my agreed training plans, memos and payslips.

■ Element 3.3
OBTAIN AND MAINTAIN PHYSICAL RESOURCES TO CARRY OUT OWN WORK

Performance criteria

- Resources obtained effectively meet requirements of own work
- Resources are stored safely and securely and are located to provide easy and quick access
- Resources are obtained in accordance with organisational procedures
- Damaged or unwanted resource items are dealt with in accordance with organisational procedures

Whatever your duties are within the organisation you will require resources to carry out the work efficiently. It may be your responsibility to ensure that there are sufficient resources for all of the section you work in. If not, you will certainly be responsible for ensuring your own supply of resources.

▶ *What type of resources may I need?*

Most people will need a supply of stationery – headed paper, memo paper, plain A4 and perhaps A5, envelopes, notepad, message slips, etc, and small consumables such as pens, pencils, staples.

■ DIY 3.3.1

Make a list of all the stationery and small consumable items that you use in your area of work. Next to each one write down how often you need to replace these items.

It is important that you identify when your supply of resources is getting low and reorder before it runs out completely. Depending on the type of reordering system you have, you may need to order a week or more in advance of wanting the item. It is also essential that you have the right equipment to carry out your job. For instance, a nylon ribbon in a typewriter is no good with a lift-off correction tape.

You may need to order items such as toner for the printers or photocopier, typewriter cartridges, staplers, hole punch or scissors. These items may not be kept as standard in your stores and more time may be necessary before replacement items can be obtained. You will need to know what your organisational procedures are regarding items that become damaged or are found to be faulty when you receive them. Quite often these are returned to the supplier – whether this is a central stores section or external supplier.

■ DIY 3.3.2

Write a memo to your new assistant informing her of the ordering procedures in your company. Do not forget to tell her how long it takes to get the items back to your section. Attach, if possible, a copy of the requisition form that is used.

Not only should you ensure that you have an adequate supply of resources you should also make sure that they are stored correctly.

▶ *How should the items be stored?*

Stock items are valuable as they are worth money to the company. Money tied up in stock cannot be used for anything else, therefore the stock should be looked after properly and kept secure. It is likely that you will only have a small area for storage of stock, but this should be suitable for the items you are keeping. Paper should be stored flat on shelves which are labelled so that replacement items are put away in the correct place. New stock should always be placed at the bottom or back of any existing stock so that the oldest items are used first. Any heavy or large items should be stored at the bottom of a cupboard or on the floor. Care should be taken when lifting and moving heavy items as many injuries can be caused by lifting items incorrectly.

■ DIY 3.3.3

Design a poster which can be displayed in your area of work or training room on the correct lifting procedure for bulky or heavy items. Remind colleagues of the dangers that they are exposing themselves to by not lifting correctly.

Hazardous stock should be stored carefully and preferably in a separate area, this may include correction fluids, cleaning materials and sprays, glues or duplicating fluids. All stock areas should be kept locked when not in use and access restricted.

■ DIY 3.3.4

Write a memo to all staff in the section in which you work informing them that the section's stationery cupboard will now be kept locked during the day due to items going missing. Outline the new arrangements you will make to enable them to get the items they require.

A small amount of stock is usually kept in direct access of the working area, either in drawers or special stationery trays built into the desk. Pens and other items are kept on the desk, usually in a caddy or other type of holder. This is to ensure that the working area is fully equipped with the necessary resources for carrying out the duties and time is not wasted in constantly leaving the desk to collect items. Within your own area of work it will be up to you to decide where items are placed, bearing in mind the easy access that you require for the items most often used. When organising your area take into consideration the placement of any computer equipment and printers as these items will be used constantly by you. You should also ensure that the location of the computer equipment meets the guidelines of the health and safety requirements for VDU and equipment. The telephone should be placed on your correct side to enable you to answer it, leaving your writing hand free to take any messages.

■ DIY 3.3.5

Draw a plan of your work area indicating where the physical resources are located when not being used. If you have to share resources show these on your plan and where your colleagues are located in relation to your work area.

Items such as hole punch, stapler, scissors, adhesive tape, etc, may be shared among several staff and would need to be located where all can see and obtain them easily.

Completing Element 3.3

To complete this element on obtaining and maintaining physical resources to carry out your own work you will need to put all the DIY tasks in your folder and carry out a final assessment. Competence must be proven in dealing with office consumables such as stationery, toner, cartridges and items of small equipment such as staplers, hole punches, binding equipment.

Claiming credit

Once you have completed your final assessment, you will need to write in your record book or folder how, when, where and what you have done to prove that you are competent.

The following is an example of how one trainee completed this claim:

During my work placement at Jenners I had an allocated work area that was next to the main secretary's desk. When I first started I had to identify the resources I needed (list in my portfolio). These were ordered and supplied from the central stores. Once I had organised my work area, I was able to carry out my duties efficiently and without unnecessary actions to use the resources necessary. I needed to share some of the resources with the Secretary and these were located on the top of the desks between us, as was the telephone. I used a typewriter for most of the documents I produced, although when the secretary did not need it I used his computer. It was necessary to order a new carbon ribbon and lift-off tape every 4 weeks; one was always kept in stock to ensure that we did not run out. We had a drawer in which a small supply of items were kept. One of the jobs I carried out was to sort out the drawer and I returned to the central stores many different items that had been kept for several years without being used (resulting in a waste of resources for the company).

I unfortunately dropped the stapler and this caused damage. I telephoned the stores department and they asked me to return it and order another one. The procedures were that any equipment that could be repaired would be reused, any that could not was disposed of. I needed to use a binding machine which was not kept in the secretary's office. I made some telephone calls to locate the nearest machine and then made arrangements to borrow it for a few days while I bound the reports for the secretary. The plastic spines had to be ordered from stores (see copy of stores requisition). During my time at Jenners we did not run out of any essential resources and I was able to carry out my own work without any problem.

UNIT 4
Create and maintain effective working relationships

- ### Element 4.1
ESTABLISH AND MAINTAIN WORKING RELATIONSHIPS WITH OTHER MEMBERS OF STAFF

Performance criteria

- Appropriate opportunities are taken to discuss work-related matters with relevant staff
- Essential information is passed to appropriate staff promptly and accurately
- Effective working relationships are maintained with individuals and teams
- Commitments to others are met within agreed timescales
- Methods of communication and support are suited to the needs of other staff

▶ *How can you establish and maintain effective working relationships with other members of staff?*

An effective association or relationship with other staff means that you are efficient, reliable, trustworthy, honest, competent and friendly. There are probably many more words you can think of to describe the things that make up a professional relationship.

In business it is important to get on with the people you work with. This may mean that sometimes you have to be nice to people you do not like, or put up with annoying habits of others. A successful business usually has an excellent working atmosphere and good teamwork. Working in a team is part of most businesses, and how you fit into the team will have a great effect on the business carried out. How you behave and work will depend on your attitude.

Fig 4.1 Which is the right attitude to work?

▶ *What kind of attitude should you have?*

Your attitude includes how you feel and act towards others – your interpersonal skills. Someone who has a 'good' attitude may be someone who

- always helps others willingly, even when doing jobs they do not like
- is always cheerful, and never seems unhappy or depressed
- has a good opinion of others
- does not gossip about others
- does not snoop on others
- has good presentation – clothes and hair
- shows interest when being spoken to

■ DIY 4.1.1

1 willing
2 cheerful
3 helpful
4 amenable
5 voluntary
6 co-operative
7 sympathetic
8 optimistic

9 supportive
10 useful

Write down the list of good qualities above and on the same line write down the opposite meanings. If you are unsure of a word, look it up in the dictionary or use a thesaurus. Tick the qualities which you posses. How can you improve the poor qualities that you have?

Part of being reliable means that you can be trusted to do something you have agreed to do. Once you have told your colleague at work that you will do a job – make sure you do. If you receive information from other departments or customers that your colleague needs, make sure you pass it on quickly. Any information you receive that needs to be passed on to someone else should be presented in a way that they can understand.

▶ *What ways are there for passing on information?*

You may pass on information verbally, that is by speaking to the person. If this is the case make sure that the information you are passing on is absolutely correct: check with the person providing the information that you have it right before they leave. If it is figures or there is a lot of information, it would be better to write it down.

Written information, to be passed to your colleagues, may be in the form of a memo or a note. If you handwrite it, make sure it is readable. Quite often when you are writing down information from a customer in front of you or on the telephone, the notes you make are messy and out of order. It would be better to rewrite the information in a form which can be easily understood by your colleagues.

Any information for colleagues must be passed to them as quickly as possible and without any errors. If your colleague is absent make sure that any urgent information is passed to someone else. Messages – especially urgent ones – should not be left on anyone's desk unless you know they will be returning shortly. You may need to telephone your colleague to pass on the information. Therefore you need to be able to use the telephone system properly, find telephone numbers easily and relay the information correctly. Planning and presenting information can sometimes be difficult. The way in which you choose to pass on

Fig 4.2 The case of the urgent memo

information to your colleagues may depend on the needs of your colleague. For example, if your colleague is continually busy and you need to pass on some detailed figures, it would be better to write them down, rather than verbally pass on the information. This is because if your colleague is busy, they will be less likely to remember figures as their mind will be on other things, or if they jot them down on a scrap of paper this may become lost in the rest of the work being carried out.

You may work with colleagues that have special needs, not only those with physical and mental disabilities, but also those that lack confidence, feel inadequate – people that need more support and understanding from you than colleagues who are fully able, competent and confident. When passing on information to these colleagues try to select the method that will best suit their needs.

▶ *Replying to requests for help*

If your colleagues ask you to help, what is your answer? No doubt it may depend on:

- who asked
- what they want you to do
- whether you are busy

- how you feel.

Who asked

If your manager or supervisor asked you to do something, no doubt you would do it. If you did not, the result could be losing your job, or harming the good working relationship you have been trying to build. Assistance should be given willingly: show that you want to be helpful. When you receive the request make sure you understand exactly what you have to do. If the request is unclear or puzzling, ask for an explanation. Quite often things can be ambiguous – that is, they can be understood in different ways. Do not put your own interpretation on the request – always check that you have understood correctly, otherwise you will waste your time, your manager's time and the company's time. Time costs money. In the same way, if you receive a written request, make sure that you can read and understand what it is asking. If you cannot – ask.

If you are asked by a colleague for help you may not respond in the same way as you do for a manager. You might argue with your colleague that you have more work than they do; that their work is boring; that they should work harder – as you do! How you respond to requests from your colleagues is just as important as your response to your manager. A helpful, willing response will strengthen your working relationship and make the office mood better. You should split work and responsibilities between you and your colleagues in the most practical and useful way. It should benefit the business and all of the workers equally; that is, one person should not have to do a great deal more than the others, or be left with all the jobs no one else wants. Quite often the 'new person' or 'office junior' gets all the 'grotty' jobs – for a while this may be you. It is still important to react in a willing manner – you may not be the office junior for long. Make sure that you treat any staff, especially office juniors, in the way that you would like to be treated.

What they want you to do

Quite often the jobs you are asked to do may be boring, routine and sometimes dirty. It is important to respond to these jobs as willingly as you would a more attractive job. It is usually easier to ask someone to help with a routine job as it needs little or no explanation. The more interesting jobs tend to be more complicated and take time to explain and understand. However, if you offer to help when your colleagues are not so busy, they will have time to explain some of the more interesting jobs and later, when they are busy, you may be able to assist with them.

Whether you are busy

It is sometimes difficult to juggle all the work you may have to carry out in one day. All work usually needs to be completed by a deadline, the difference being that the deadlines are unlikely to be the same. Some jobs can be left longer than others. How you organise your work will usually be up to you, but you should prioritise the work, that is, put in in an order where the most urgent jobs are done first. It is tempting to do the most interesting jobs first – do not be tempted; prioritise sensibly. If you are really too busy to help others when they ask, explain politely and try to tell your colleague when you think you will be free to assist. Do not carry out all your routine work before you help your colleagues with their urgent work. Prioritising includes deciding whether your colleague's work is more important and urgent than the work you currently have to complete.

How you feel

If you go to work feeling tired, irritated, annoyed or sick you may not feel like helping others. Sometimes you may genuinely feel ill, but feelings of tiredness may be the result of too many late nights. Keep your late nights for the weekends; make sure you follow a good routine of getting up in plenty of time for work. Avoid going to work feeling miserable or depressed – try to leave your problems and feelings at home. Sometimes it cannot be helped but you should remember to treat your colleagues courteously and not be rude. If you are ill, you should decide whether it is serious enough to go home; if so explain to your manager. Do not make a habit of taking time off for trivial illnesses; a few aches and pains should not stop you from working. On the other hand, if you have flu it would be unwise to work and pass your germs round the office. If you have a constant illness or one that keeps recurring you should see your doctor for advice. An employee with a poor attendance record is unlikely to be considered for promotion and may be the first in line for redundancy.

■ DIY 4.1.2

'There will be an emergency staff meeting at 4.00 today in the coffee lounge. All staff are expected to attend promptly.'

You need to pass this information on to your colleagues who have the following special needs:

1 One is deaf.
2 One is blind.
3 One is in a panic as they are behind with their work.
4 One is busy at other meetings all day.
5 One is out of the office visiting a customer and will not be back until 3.00.

State the method of communication you would use and why you chose that particular method.

▶ *Dress for the office*

Many offices follow a tradition for clothes to be worn in the office. Several businesses now supply a uniform to personnel. If you work in such a business you will not need to buy many items to wear to work.

Fig 4.3 Dressed for work?

When you first start work you may not have much money to spend on new clothes. It is therefore more important to select your clothes carefully. It is better to have a few suitable clothes than a lot of clothes that you cannot wear to several different places. Try to buy clothes that match and do not clash in colour or style.

■ DIY 4.1.3

List the type of clothes that you think would be unsuitable for wearing in an office where you are in contact with the customers. What type of image are you trying to show?

▶ *Apart from clothes, what else is important?*

Everyone sweats or perspires: *your* personal hygiene should not be a problem. If you wash daily and use deodorants, you should be all right. On the other hand, if you rely on a shower once a week, your hygiene could be a problem. You do not need to use expensive perfumes or colognes to hide smells. Any cologne or perfume used should be a light aroma and not too strong. It is important to wash your clothes frequently as the deodorants, perfumes and body smells will enter them and they will become foul. If you smoke the smell will stay in your clothes – no matter how much you try to blow the smoke away. The result will be an offensive smell which your colleagues should not have to put up with. Even if you wash yourself regularly, if you have unclean clothes the smell will be disgusting. Be aware of your smell; other people are.

Cleaning your teeth is as important as washing frequently. If you eat spicy foods, drink alcohol or smoke, make sure that your breath is fresh – use some breath fresheners or gum if necessary. Avoid strong-smelling food and drink if you know you will be dealing with special customers or have an important meeting.

Your shoes are also important. They should be regularly cleaned and repaired – there is nothing worse than a well-groomed person with 'tatty' shoes! Trainers are not usually acceptable for office wear. Your shoes should be comfortable to wear all day without tiring your legs. Girls should not have shoes with heels that are too high, especially if they are on their feet for much of the day. Constantly wearing high heels is bad for the legs and backache may occur. Girls should also make sure that their stockings or tights are free from holes and ladders. Keep a spare pair in the office – just in case. Worn-down heels and soles should be repaired as they may became dangerous if left. You may prefer to keep an 'office' pair of shoes to change into when you arrive and leave permanently in the office.

Hair should be washed regularly. Most people use some kind of spray, gel or mousse, as well as shampoo. If you suffer from dandruff you should use a special shampoo to deal with the problem: simply brushing your shoulders clear is not enough. Dirty, dull hair or shoulders full of dandruff may be offensive to your colleagues and workmates. Unusual hair colours – blue, purple, pink or green may also be unacceptable. They may not fit the image your company is trying to convey.

If you wear make-up, do not use too much, or get it on your collar or clothes. Nails should be kept clean and in shape. You do not need professionally manicured nails; if you cut them to a shape that follows the curve of your fingers, they should look good. If you file and paint your nails, always make sure your nail polish is unchipped. Keep a bottle at work to 'touch up' chips, in case you break a nail or catch it during work. Handcream or barrier cream should be used if you suffer from dry hands. Wash your hands frequently if they tend to get hot and sticky – especially if you shake hands with colleagues, customers, clients and visitors to the company.

Jewellery worn should be reasonable, so as not to interfere with the work you are doing. Large items may be unsafe: bracelets, chains and pendants may be caught in machinery or drawers; rings may catch in equipment or damage the glass of a photocopier. Any scratch on the glass of a photocopier will leave marks on the copies made.

▶ *Health and safety at work*

When working with others, you should be aware of your duties under the Health and Safety at Work Act as well as the legal responsibilities your employer has. When carrying out tasks for others you should take care not to break any of the rules of the Act and report any faulty equipment or hazards found.

Health and Safety at Work Act 1974 (HASAWA)

This Act brings together many of the previous health and safety laws. The basic idea of the Act is that there should be a joint effort by employers and employees to provide a safe and healthy working environment.

The employer has to provide safe:

- equipment and systems of work
- working conditions, and adequate arrangements and facilities for welfare
- use, storage, transport and handling of substances and articles
- means of access to and from work

If an accident occurs the employer must investigate it fully and all staff should be fully informed, supervised and trained in accordance with their work rule.

Employees have the responsibility for:

- taking care of their own safety
- safety of other people affected by their actions
- co-operating with employers and any other people involved in carrying out duties under this Act

When working in a company or training centre you should know:

- names and location of trained first-aid staff
- location of accident report form, record or book
- location of first-aid box
- what to do if you discover a fire
- where fire-fighting equipment is kept
- how to select and operate the correct equipment

This information should be included in any training or induction you receive when starting work.

▶ *Other legislation*

Other legislation that you should be aware of is that which deals with Equal Opportunities. Many employers have Equal Opportunity statements and guides for their staff to follow. This legislation makes it unlawful for anyone to treat a person less favourably than they would otherwise simply because of their race (nationality), sex, age, religious belief or marital status.

■ DIY 4.1.4

You notice the following advertisement on the noticeboard.

A vacancy has arisen in the word processing department for an assistant to the supervisor. Qualifications required are WP Stage 2, English GCSE and at least 2 years' experience in the company. Any female staff interested in applying should do so by the end of the month. Applications from those with an ability to speak Welsh would be favourably considered. Please apply in writing to Dai Williams, Supervisor WP Dept.

Rewrite the advert so that it reflects an equal opportunity for qualified staff to apply.

▶ *What should you do if difficulties arise at work?*

What you do about difficulties at work will depend on the type that occur. Some you will be able to deal with yourself, others you may discuss with a colleague or with your supervisor.

If you find that a difficulty arises at work which you cannot discuss with your colleague or supervisor, try to find someone outside work you can confide in. Someone in your family may listen and make some suggestions for solving your problem or you could talk to someone at an advice bureau. Quite often someone who is distant from the problem can see the possible solutions.

If you discuss a problem with a colleague or supervisor it is important not to exaggerate any of the difficulties, but to report the matter exactly as it is. If you make up details it is likely to create further difficulties and other people involved may not trust or rely on you in the future.

Completing Element 4.1

To complete this element on establishing and maintaining working relationships with other members of staff you will need to put all the DIY tasks in your folder and carry out a final assessment. Competence must be proven in dealing with line managers, immediate colleagues and other members of staff with related work activities.

Claiming credit

Once you have completed your final assessment, you will need to write in your record book or folder how, when, where and what you have done to prove that you are competent.

The following is an example of how one trainee completed this claim:

When working for J Boyce & Sons, as a part-time administration assistant, I assisted with all tasks when requested. I made sure that the information that I passed on to the manager and the other staff was correct and in a suitable form. For instance, I made sure that I wrote down any necessary information for the manager as she was usually busy. I put the notes or memos in her pigeonhole, if the information was urgent I passed it direct to her secretary. The staff working in the office sometimes shared the work, especially when it was busy. We all helped out to make sure that we finished on time to catch the post or to meet the deadlines. Some of the most important information to pass on quickly were requests and complaints from customers. I made sure that I got the name and telephone number right before passing it on to the correct person. I always made sure that as well as writing the name and number down, I told the person about the complaint. This was so that my note did not get left without attention for too long.

Although we do not have many difficulties with relationships in the office, there is one person who I do not get on with very well. They tend to be very fussy about the work I do for them. I try to make sure that the work I do is in the exact way that it was requested and check carefully for errors. If changes are needed I do not get cross or upset.

I have attached copies of memos and notes that I have written when passing on information to some of my colleagues.

■ Element 4.2
RECEIVE AND ASSIST VISITORS

Performance criteria

- Visitors are greeted promptly and courteously
- The nature of the visit and the needs of visitors are identified and matched to the appropriate products, personnel or services of the organisation
- Reception and directing of visitors is in accordance with established procedures

- The structure, products or services of the organisation are accurately described and promoted to the visitors as appropriate
- Methods of communication and support are suited to the needs of the visitor
- Communication difficulties are openly acknowledged and appropriate help sought to ensure understanding
- Difficulties in providing support to visitors are acknowledged and appropriate help sought
- Records are complete, legible and accurate
- Established procedures are followed for dealing with awkward or aggressive visitors

When a person enters a building or office the first person they will see is the receptionist. The receptionist represents the organisation and has the responsibility of presenting themselves according to the impression the organisation wishes to give. Large organisations will employ reception staff who take full responsibility for receiving and directing visitors, whilst a smaller organisation will combine the receptionist's responsibilities with telephone and general office duties.

▶ *What skills and qualities do you need?*

It is essential that the receptionist knows what the organisation expects, in terms of dress, attitude and responsibilities. An advertising company would probably have a modern, lively approach to its business and expect the receptionist to reflect this in dress and attitude. A solicitor's office would be more likely to want the receptionist to present a more formal and conservative image. It is important to get it right.

A good receptionist should have the following:

- neat appearance
- pleasant manner
- clear voice
- helpful attitude
- tact and diplomacy
- calm and polite nature
- positive image
- organisational skills
- first-aid knowledge

- knowledge of the company and its products
- knowledge of staff and their responsibilities.

All visitors must be greeted promptly and courteously. The reception desk should never be left unattended – an unanswered telephone call or a caller kept waiting could result in valuable business being lost.

▶ *How should you deal with a visitor?*

There will generally be 3 types of visitor:

1 Visitors with appointments:

- job applicants for interview
- sales representatives
- visitors attending meetings
- visitors from other organisations.

2 Visitors without appointments:

- sales representatives selling goods
- people enquiring about vacancies
- people enquiring about goods/services
- people asking directions
- general enquiries.

3 Regular visitors without appointments:

- delivery people from other organisations
- postal deliveries
- service/maintenance engineers
- cleaning/display contractors
- family/friends of staff.

Greet visitors promptly, do not keep them waiting. If you are in the middle of doing something that cannot be left, smile at the visitor to show you have seen them, tell them you will only be a second and remember to apologise for keeping them waiting. Ask visitors for their name, how you can help them or the name of the person they wish to see (write this down so you do not forget it) and if they have an appointment. You may be able to help the visitor yourself; contact somebody in the organisation who can help them; or book an appointment with the person they need to see.

Visitors may arrive without an appointment, but may need to be seen urgently. The receptionist will need to contact the person or department concerned to explain the problem and find out whether the visitor can be seen immediately.

Always be courteous and helpful. If there is a delay explain this to the visitor: never leave them waiting not knowing why their appointment is running late. Offer a cup of coffee and a newspaper, magazine or some of the organisation's literature to read. If the visitor arrives early for their appointment make them comfortable and inform the person they have come to see that they have arrived. If the visitor is late, deal with them quickly and find out if it is still possible for them to be seen; if not, offer another appointment.

The visitor may need directions to the person or department they are visiting, or they may have to be escorted, depending on the organisation's security arrangements. It may be the case that they are collected from reception or left to find their own way if they have visited the person/department before. They may need to be issued with an identity badge for security reasons and may need information regarding car parking facilities. You may also be required to care for their baggage, which for security reasons should be labelled with their name and kept in a safe place ready for collection.

■ DIY 4.2.1

You have been asked by a visitor for directions from your work to the nearest office employment bureau. If you are unsure, use a directory to find the nearest one and then write down the instructions on how to get there. The visitor is walking, make sure you give details of any road names or landmarks to look out for.

▶ *How do you deal with difficult visitors?*

Occasionally there may be some unwanted callers. Always be firm but polite, never lose your temper and do not aggravate the situation. If you need help, contact the nearest supervisor or a security guard if there is one. If you are alone and feel threatened, be prepared to call the police.

If a caller is angry, try to find out why, and what you can do to help to relieve the situation. A senior member of staff may have to be contacted to deal with the situation and will need to know all the details first. The caller should be asked to wait in another room, rather than discuss their complaint in front of other people who may be sitting in the reception area.

▶ *How do you receive deliveries?*

The reception is the central area of an organisation or department, and it is likely that all deliveries including mail will be received there. The receptionist may have to sign a receipt or delivery note as confirmation that the delivery or special mail has been received. A delivery note (*see* Fig. 4.4) will contain details of goods being delivered. This should be checked, and signed by the receptionist only if everything is in order with no omissions or damaged goods.

If a delivery is received for a specific department or person the receptionist may telephone the department and ask for someone to come to reception to check the goods and sign for them. When deliveries are received they should be passed on to the relevant person or department as soon as possible.

If you are too busy to check the goods ask for assistance, or sign the delivery note as 'Received but not examined'. If you sign the delivery note and then discover omissions or breakages or that incorrect goods have been delivered, time will have to be spent contacting the suppliers to report the problem. Remember that the suppliers will have a signed acceptance note and may, if they choose, refuse to correct any errors.

▶ *How do you take messages?*

If a visitor wishes to leave a message make sure you write it down and check all details. It is vital for names, addresses, telephone numbers and so on to be written down correctly and legibly. A message that is unreadable or contains incorrect information is of no use to anyone. The organisation may use telephone message slips (*see* Fig. 4.5) or general message slips that can be used for visitors and telephone

DELIVERY NOTE			No 346	
TWYFORD CARRIERS LIMITED				
Southdown Road, Twyford, Westshire TD4 8AR				

Delivered to:
OP Electronic Services
OP House
PO Box 19
Bracknell
Berkshire RG21 3PT

By order of:
Systems Furniture plc
Brookfield Industrial Estate
Twyford
Westshire TD3 2BS

Date despatched: 9 March 19—

No of packages	Description	Order	
		No	Date
3 3	Desks Pedestals	489	2.3—

Received in good order and condition

but not examined

Customer's signature .... *T Parrick* ....

Fig 4.4 A delivery note

messages. A pad of these should be kept on the reception desk and near to the telephone switchboard.

When a message is taken it should be passed on to the correct location as soon as possible. This may involve telephoning the member of staff and giving details verbally over the telephone, for example to return a call, or simply leaving a message slip on a desk or in a pigeon-hole – this will depend upon the organisation's policy.

MESSAGE FOR

M _____

WHILE YOU WERE OUT

M _____

Of _____

Telephone No _____

Telephoned		Please ring	
Called to see you		Will call again	
Wants to see you		Urgent	

Message: _____

_____

_____

_____

_____

_____

_____

_____

Date _____ Time _____

Received by _____

Fig 4.5 A telephone message form

■ DIY 4.2.2

A visitor comes into your office and asks for Jayne who works with you. Jayne is not available and the visitor, who you do not recognise, asks you to take a message.

'Can you tell Jayne that I called. I need to know whether she will be free to visit Jones and Son with me on Friday morning. I want to leave at about 10.00. It is important that I know by 4.00 today at the latest whether she can make the appointment. Have you got all that?'

Write out a message slip for Jayne. What other information would you needed to have asked the visitor?

▶ What records are kept on reception?

There are 3 kinds of records:

1 **Visitors' register**. All visitors to a company sign the register (*see* Fig. 4.6), with the exception of services such as postal or goods deliveries. The completed register shows the name of the visitor, company or home address, time of arrival, name of contact and action taken. The receptionist may also be required to include time of departure to show the visitor has left the premises together with details of their security badge number.

2 **Appointments book**. The appointments book records all future appointments and is used by the receptionist to see who is expected to visit. Future appointments for visitors who arrive without an appointment can be made in this book. Information detailed in the 'action taken' column of the visitors' register can be written in the appointments book if it concerns future appointments that have been made. A simple diary can be used for this purpose.

3 **Staff in and out book**. This is used to record the whereabouts of staff working for the organisation. If a member of staff has to leave the premises, the book (*see* Fig. 4.7) is completed with details of name, date and time of leaving. Upon their return they sign the book and make a note of the time.

It is essential that all records are kept up to date, legible and accurate. Unreadable writing, an appointment that has not been entered and staff leaving the premises without telling the receptionist create confusion and a bad image of the organisation.

VISITORS' REGISTER						
DATE						
Identity Badge No.	Time in	Time out	Name	Company	Appointment with	Action Taken

Fig 4.6 Visitors' register

STAFF IN/OUT BOOK				
DATE				
NAME	DETAILS OF ABSENCE	DEPARTMENT	TIME OUT	TIME IN

Fig 4.7 Staff in and out book

■ DIY 4.2.3

Draw up a page from a visitors' register. Keep a record of everyone you receive during your work for the next week. Visitors may be internal or external to your organisation, expected or unexpected. You may not need the Identity Badge Number column – it will depend on your organisation's procedures.

▶ *What do you need to know about the organisation?*

The answer to this question is 'just about everything'. During the course of the day you will be asked a number of questions; only with experience will you learn all the answers. When you first join an organisation you should be shown round the building as part of your induction training, be introduced to members of staff and the staff you will work most closely with. At first it will be impossible for you to remember all the names and duties each person performs, but in time this information will come to you easily.

In time you will be expected to answer questions on the whereabouts of staff, details of goods and services offered by the organistion, full address, telephone/fax/telex numbers, postcode, and be able to identify different staff and their responsibilities. If you are unable to answer a question you should know enough about the organisation to know who can. Useful information sources are:

- organisation charts
- internal telephone directories
- national/international telephone directories
- *Yellow Pages*
- company brochures
- price lists
- and most importantly, the people you work with.

■ DIY 4.2.4

Where would you find the following information?

- The company's fax number
- The senior manager's name
- The company's VAT registration number (if it has one)

- A local photocopying bureau
- The international dialling code for Muscat in Oman
- The name of the person responsible for health and safety
- The name of the person who deals with ordering supplies
- The location of the nearest first-aid box
- The fax number for Heathrow Airport, British Airways reservations
- The name and address of your main competitor

The receptionist must have available all esssential directories, such as internal, local and national ones, so that time is not wasted looking for information required on a regular basis. Also, details of the most frequently used suppliers and clients should be kept at hand so they are easily found when needed. Reference books such as *Kelly's Business Directory*, rail and airline timetables and AA/RAC guides may also be required.

The receptionist must keep a record of all visitors to the organisation, however small in number, using either a visitors' register or reception diary. A staff list defining responsibilities should also be kept so that the receptionist is able to see at a glance who should be contacted in connection with different areas of work.

■ DIY 4.2.5

Draw up a checklist similar to the example in Fig. 4.8. Look round a reception area in your workplace or training centre and write in the right-hand column details of materials available. Make a note of any books, posters, etc that you think should be included. Do you think the reception area is attractive? Do you think information is displayed attractively? Give details of your recommendations at the bottom of the list.

The receptionist is seen as a source of information. Therefore, information at hand must be up to date and correct. Organisations have staff joining and leaving employment regularly; they may also move from one department to another. Details must be inserted on the organisation chart and changes made in the internal directory. Incorrect information will create bad feeling between staff if they have been given the wrong name or extension number, and create a poor image of the reception staff.

RECEPTION AREA AT	
VISITORS' REGISTER	
DIARY	
PUBLICITY DISPLAYS	
ORGANISATIONAL NOTICES	
READING MATERIAL	
INTERNAL DIRECTORY	
LOCAL/ NATIONAL DIRECTORIES	
STAFF LISTS	
FREQUENT SUPPLIERS LIST	
HEALTH AND SAFETY INFORMATION	
ORGANISATION CHART	
REFERENCE MATERIAL	
COMPUTER HARDWARE	
RECOMMENDATIONS	

Fig 4.8 Reception checklist

If a visitor is given wrong information it will reflect badly on the receptionist and the organisation itself. Therefore, organisation charts, staff lists and internal directories must be amended regularly so that the information they give is at all times correct.

It is likely that the receptionist will have to request stationery, leaflets or posters at times. It is normal practice to complete a stationery requisition form (*see* Fig. 4.9) and send this to the person in charge of stationery, or to a Stores Department in a large organisation. The requisition form may have to be authorised with the supervisor's signature. It is important not to over-order stationery – you will only cause storage problems in reception if you do – but it is more important to make sure you never run out of anything. Items of stationery that you are likely to need are:

- telephone message pads
- pens and pencils
- rubbers and rulers

STATIONERY REQUISITION	
No	
Date	
Quantity	**Description**
Signed	Storekeeper's initials
Department	
Authorised	....

Fig 4.9 Stationery requisition form

- lined, rough paper
- bond paper
- scissors, staplers and staple removers
- sealing tape and glue.

Other items needed would depend on the work carried out. For example, headed business paper would be needed if the receptionist was responsible for typing business correspondence, as well as memorandum paper and items such as typewriter ribbons and correction fluid.

▶ *What about confidentiality?*

It is very important that you understand the kind of information you are allowed to give to visitors. You will be expected to find and give information readily one moment, and protect sensitive or confidential information the next. Make sure you know what information you can and cannot give to visitors by asking your supervisor. If you are ever in doubt, ask the visitor to wait a moment while you check with your supervisor.

General visitors should never be given personal information, such as the home telephone number of a member of staff. The receptionist must be polite, informative and friendly, but must never give out unauthorised information to anyone.

▶ *What about health and safety*

The organistion is responsible not only for its staff but also for its visitors. The receptionist must inform visitors of unauthorised or dangerous areas and whether protective clothing, shoes or headgear is needed.

In the event of an evacuation, for example a fire alarm or bomb scare, the visitors' register can be used to make sure all visitors are out of the building. The register must therefore be kept up to date to prevent risks being taken to locate a visitor who may have left the building some time ago.

If the switchboard is on reception it may be the receptionist's responsibility to contact the emergency services. Details of what to do in an emergency should be displayed next to the switchboard as there is no time for panic or confusion in an emergency. You are much more likely to have to deal with emergencies if you work in a main reception, as this area acts as the central point for the organisation. It is useful to have a first-aid box available and know who to contact in the event of an accident. The names and extension numbers of qualified first-aiders should be kept next to the telephone.

■ DIY 4.2.6

Answer the following questions as fully as possible:

1 Why should visitors be greeted promptly and courteously?
2 Why do you need to know the nature of the visit?
3 What is your organisation's procedures for dealing with external visitors to (a) main reception and (b) a departmental office?
4 What records should be kept in a main reception?
5 How would you deal with an awkward or aggressive visitor?

As the receptionist you will be required to use a variety of equipment, for example word processor, typewriter, switchboard, franking machine and so on. It is your responsibility to ensure all machinery and equipment is used in accordance with the manufacturer's handbook. If you have never been shown how to use a piece of equipment, ask your supervisor to show you.

Make sure plug points are not overloaded and leads are not left trailing. Deliveries and boxes should never be left where someone can trip over them and items such as empty milk bottles should never be allowed to build up waiting for the milkman's collection.

Completing Element 4.2

To complete this element on receiving and assisting visitors you will need to put all the DIY tasks in your folder and carry out a final assessment. Competence must be proven in dealing with visitors both expected and unexpected, and those internal and external to the organisation. The needs satisfied must include routine enquiries, complex enquiries and directions to other parts of the organisation.

110

Claiming credit

Once you have completed your final assessment, you will need to write in your record book or folder how, when, where and what you have done to prove that you are competent.

The following is an example of how one trainee completed this claim:

During my training course I learnt how to deal with different types of visitors. This included foreign visitors, visitors with special needs such as deafness or blindness and difficult visitors, both expected and unexpected. A video was made of me receiving visitors with different problems. The video has been kept by my tutor.

During my work experience at Jacob, Reeve and Partners I greeted visitors and kept the visitors' book up to date. Each visitor had to write their name, company, car registration, time of arrival and person they wanted to see. I then rang through to the person or their secretary to let them know the visitor had arrived. If the person was not ready I asked the visitor to take a seat and apologised for keeping them waiting. Sometimes callers just wanted information about the cost of advice. I gave them leaflets that were available and the name of a partner they could telephone for further information. I kept a record of the number of people that asked for this information but we did not need to keep their names. On one occasion we had a visitor who was in a wheelchair. It was difficult for him to get to the partner's office because of the stairs. I informed the secretary about the problem and the partner came down to reception and spoke with the client in a side office. If I was unsure of information or whether a person should be sent to an office I checked with my supervisor. I did not receive any visitors that were aggressive, although some got a bit annoyed when they were kept waiting. I apologised and let them know that I was trying to find someone to help them.

I have kept a log of the visitors received which has been signed by my supervisor. I have also photocopied a page from the visitors' book, although the names had to be blocked out due to confidentiality. The entries I made when visitors left were accurate and neat.

UNIT 5
Store, retrieve and supply information

■ Element 5.1
MAINTAIN AN ESTABLISHED STORAGE SYSTEM

Performance criteria

- New information is put into the storage system following organisational procedures
- Stored material is maintained in good condition in appropriate location
- Item movements are monitored and recorded accurately
- Overdue items are identified and system for return implemented
- Out-of-date information is dealt with as directed
- Opportunities for improving established systems are identified and appropriate action taken
- Work practices conform to organisational requirements

Most business transactions involve keeping records usually in written or printed form – letters, minutes, memoranda, reports, buying and selling documents are all examples of records kept in an office. If an office is to run efficiently, documentation must be stored using a quick and reliable method of classification. The method used will depend on the type of documentation being stored, it is vital that members of staff understand the classification in use so that all documents are stored in their correct sequence.

Filing is used for a number of reasons:

- to **preserve** information so it is readily at hand when needed
- to **protect** information so it is safe from damage or loss
- to **sequence** information in a logical order so it is easy to locate.

In general terms there are 6 commonly used classifications:

1 **Alphabetical**. Material is filed according to name in alphabetical order. This classification is very popular and relatively easy to use, provided all users abide by agreed rules – or files will be misplaced! British Standard BS1749 gives details of the current conventions, or if in doubt, look in the telephone directory.

2 **Numerical**. Material is filed in numerical order according to its reference number. This classification does not require a list of rules and as numbers are infinite so is the filing system. However, it is not always easy to match a customer with their reference number and it may be necessary to use an alphabetical index system as well, to enable quick retrieval of information.

3 **Chronological**. Material is filed according to its date, with the most recent at the front. Dates can be combined with other methods: for example, correspondence would be classified alphabetically but within each file it would be placed in chronological order.

4 **Geographical**. Material is filed according to the location it refers to, for example town, area or country. This system is useful for a company operating on a regional basis, but within each area one or more of the other methods is needed. An example of a combined numerical, geographical, alphabetical system would be the postcode.

5 **Subject**. Material is filed according to subject in files kept in alphabetical order. This method would be used by teachers to keep all information on one subject in the same place, and ease of retrieval would be assisted by placing all files in alphabetical order.

6 **Alphanumeric**. Files are arranged in alphabetical groups and are numbered within these groups. In some systems, each letter has a guide card which also gives an index of the numbered files in that letter group. For example, a guide card covering Aa – Ak would be numbered A1 and the first file in this group A1/1, the second file would be A1/2 and so on. This classification's primary division is alphabetical, but files within the division can be positioned in any order providing they are given the next number in the sequence for reference purposes. This system therefore provides each file with a reference number that can be used for correspondence. Files containing similar material can be grouped together and new files are simply placed at the back of the relevant division rather than having to be slotted into sequence as with alphabetical filing.

No one classification is better than another – the art is in finding the best method to suit the type of documents to be stored. All classifications do have one thing in common, however – they all allow documents to be stored in *logical* sequence. Remember that it will not always be the same person putting files in or taking files out of a filing system. Therefore, a logical sequence is necessary if files are to be retrieved quickly and efficiently when needed and not lost in the system.

■ DIY 5.1.1

In your own words explain how the alphabetical, numerical and alphanumeric classifications work. Give examples of the type of material that would be classified and what kind of offices or department you would find each classification used in.

The most important classification to understand is alphabetical. If filing in subject or geographical order, the sequence of your documents will still be alphabetical. For example, English will always come before Mathematics in a subject classification, and England before Scotland in a geographical one.

Numerical classification depends upon having quick access to a file number; therefore, it is usual practice to keep a small alphabetical index to back up a numerical system. If the file number is lost or forgotten the surname or company name can be looked up in the index, which will give details of the file number you require.

▶ *What is an index?*

An index can be used as a key to the file. With numerical filing, for example, you would be unable to find a customer's file if they had forgotten their account number, and so the alphabetical index becomes the key to help you find the file. However, indexing systems are also used independently to store a variety of information.

Card indexes are usually kept on the desk top and contain a number of postcard-size, lined cards. Each separate card will contain information such as name, address, telephone number, account number and so on. The index will be divided by guide cards such as A, B, C, so that the correct card can be found quickly.

Rotary indexes work on the same principle but are round and can be rotated to find the correct card.

Strip indexes are made up from narrow strips of card slotted into a holder; strips can be removed easily and additions slotted into the correct sequence.

■ DIY 5.1.2

Prepare a set of index cards, one for each student named below. Place the student's surname in block capitals in the top left-hand corner of the card, followed by a comma and the student's forename. Arrange the index cards into correct alphabetical order. (Ignore the figures in brackets for the moment.)

(1) JULIE HARTOPP	(2) STUART SMITH	(3) JAMIE HIGGS
(4) SARAH FOSTER	(5) JOHN O'MALLY	(6) ABIGAIL SMITH
(7) MARC POWELL	(8) JO WHITE	(9) FAYE DUNN
(10) PAUL RIDER	(11) KAREN KHAN	(12) NOREEN PATEL
(13) RUSSELL WINTER	(14) TYRONE CHAN	(15) RICHARD AHMED
(16) JEREMY ISSACS	(17) IBRAHIM ALI	(18) FAYE O'BRIAN
(19) KAREN DAVIS	(20) JENNA VANDY	(21) KELLY SAYERS
(22) EVA DACOSTA	(23) NATALIE CHUBB	(24) LEILA SCOTT
(25) SONIA GONCALVES	(26) JO BILLAM	(27) JENS SKINNER
(28) TRACEY WINTER	(29) JADE PROTHEROE	(30) SCOTT ROSE

▶ *What filing methods are there?*

The term 'methods' refers to the manner in which the information is stored. This may be **vertical, lateral, horizontal** or **computer-based**.

Vertical filing cabinets are normally made from metal and can be bought as one-, two-, three- or four-drawer systems. They can be arranged in an office to offer extra worktops or as room dividers. Modern cabinets have metal runners along each side that support suspended pockets into which information is placed and held vertically in the drawer. Folders can slide backwards and forwards (if the drawer is not overloaded) to aid retrieval of information.

Lateral filing is similar to the storage of books in a library. This system saves space as no drawers have to be pulled out and it can be fitted from floor to ceiling (although you will need a ladder to reach files at the top). Shutters can be added for security and to prevent files becoming dusty or damaged. Pockets are hung from runners and folders are slotted into each pocket in a vertical position. Electronic lateral systems are also available that rotate shelves at the touch of a button.

Horizontal filing allows information to be stored flat. It is used for large documents such as maps, drawings and plans as it allows storage without creasing. This method is most likely to be found in areas such as architects, or planning offices.

Computer-based filing uses a database program that is designed to store and sort information. Files are produced by keying in the information and can be sorted easily using simple instructions. The database is set up using fields such as name, date of birth, account number and so on. The computer can be instructed to sort records alphabetically by name, or numerically by account number, or chronologically by date of birth. Computerised filing saves space and time and is particularly useful for personnel records, wages records and stock records. Files cannot go missing, are easy to update and you can request as many copies of the file as you wish.

▶ *What is microfilm used for?*

There are 3 main systems that produce miniature copies of documents on to film for easier retrieval and less bulky storage.

1 Microfiche – consists of a sheet of microfilm, usually 105 mm x 148 mm that can hold up to 100 photographed pages.
2 Microfilm – consists of strips of film stored on reels or cassettes.
3 Aperture card – individual images are photographed and placed into a cardboard frame.

All of these systems require the use of a reader to view the film; some readers incorporate a printer so that a hard copy can be printed. The systems save a great deal of space and it is now possible to print direct from mainframe computers on to microfilm. However, companies without this facility will need to purchase their own microfilm processing unit or send their records away to a processing company who will transfer them onto microfilm.

▶ *What other methods of storage are available?*

There are also smaller types of storage equipment that can be used to protect and keep documents in a logical sequence.

1 **Box files and lever arch files**. These files are often used in offices to keep 'pending paperwork' that is waiting for a decision to be made on it. A box file or lever arch file will keep paperwork neat and secure for short or long periods.

2 **Concertina files**. These files are also referred to as expanding files as they open out into separate compartments, often labelled with the letters of the alphabet or numbers. These files are useful for pre-sorting documents prior to filing and are often used for storing domestic paperwork such as electricity, gas and telephone bills.

3 **Ring binders**. These binders require holes to be punched into the paperwork, or the use of plastic wallets into which paperwork can be inserted. Guide cards can divide the information into sections. It is likely that you are currently using such a folder for your evidence portfolio.

4 **Pocket folders**. These folders are often used to carry paperwork that is stored in a filing cabinet. The flap on the folder helps to keep the contents secure, and the folder can be labelled to indicate its contents. These folders are particularly useful if storing confidential information as they can be clearly marked 'CONFIDENTIAL' and their design helps to keep the paperwork enclosed secure.

5 **Manilla folders**. These folders are brown in colour and consist of one piece of folded card. The card can be labelled and the contents sit inside. When information is required the whole folder can be removed or just the required paperwork.

▶ *How do you sort, handle and store documents?*

You should always pre-sort documents before going to the filing cabinet. Organise all your filing into sequence while at your desk, using either the desk top or a concertina file divided into the same sections as your filing cabinet. The advantages of doing this are:

117

- pre-sorting can be done when you have time to spare
- paperclips can be removed and any damage repaired at your desk
- all documents for one file can be put away together
- correspondence for the same file can be sorted chronologically
- all files for one drawer can be filed at the same time
- time spent at the cabinet, preventing others' access, is reduced.

When documents have been pre-sorted, go to the filing cabinet and insert paperwork neatly into the file. Make sure documents are placed into the correct folder, not sticking up or slipping out between dividers. If you find the file is full, insert another section or folder, but remember to label this first.

You should always file daily and never let a backlog build up. If you are ever unsure of where to put a file, do not guess. It is far better to ask your supervisor than to place a file out of sequence – never to be seen again! If you are unsure where to place or find a file or document, look for clues in and around the area of the number or name to see if there are similar files. A cross-reference card, 'absent' folder or 'out' card will tell you where the file is, if it is missing. Only ask for help when you have looked thoroughly yourself.

▶ *What is a cross-reference card?*

This is used to direct staff to another file. It may be the case that a file could be placed in a number of different locations – a cross-reference card in each location will direct the person to where the file is actually held. A company's name may change or a female member of staff may marry and change her surname – both situations require a cross-reference card (*see* Fig. 5.1) under the old name to direct the person looking for the file to the right place.

▶ *What is referenced and non-referenced material?*

Referenced material contains some form of identification that indicates where the document, file or even book has to be placed. When dealing with correspondence such as business letters you will normally see a reference using the initials of the person who typed the letter and the initials of the person for whom the letter was typed, for example

CROSS-REFERENCE CARD
For correspondence in the name of:
....
Refer to:
....

Fig 5.1 A cross-reference card

AB/PJB. The letter or document itself may have a reference number to identify its contents, or may, for example, have a customer reference number.

When you look at the books on a library shelf notice how each book has its own reference number. This number can be looked up using a microfiche or database program and gives the exact location of the book. In the same way, business documents can be referenced so that they are easy to find and can be placed into a logical sequence in the filing system. Look at the following example of a reference number:

UK/ST6/GOODS/9

In a sales department this could mean that correspondence refers to a client in the United Kingdom, dealing with Sales Team number 6 who has purchased goods with an identity code 9. The reference number can be used on all correspondence relating to the same order so that when it is filed it is always placed in the correct place.

Non-referenced material may be used in smaller offices where staff are familiar with the paperwork coming into and going out of the office. Files would be kept using a simple classification system, such as alphabetical or numerical filing, into which correspondence and business documentation could be classified without confusion. However, this system does not allow for any newcomer to the office who is unsure of how the business works.

■ DIY 5.1.3

Here are the student enrolment numbers for each of the students sorted alphabetically in DIY 5.1.2.

1)	178412	2)	985453	3)	472649	4)	827308
5)	1042292	6)	879740	7)	087736	8)	199428
9)	234226	10)	376747	11)	0775367	12)	896752
13)	762990	14)	178768	15)	298176	16)	344698
17)	907587	18)	908465	19)	124856	20)	987384
21)	980584	22)	198028	23)	127389	24)	198309
25)	1874038	26)	783092	27)	18739	28)	191912
29)	1984872	30)	0019871					

In the top right-hand corner of the index card place the student's enrolment number. You can match students and their enrolment numbers by following the bracketed numbers. For example, (1) refers to Julie Hartopp whose enrolment number is 178412. Place the index cards in numerical order.

▶ *How do you trace overdue files?*

Keeping track of files is an important responsibility. Efficiency in an office will be affected if files are not readily at hand or if no record is kept of where they have gone. Some organisations state that staff are allowed to keep files only for a set period of time, for example no longer than 2 days, before they have to be returned. Several methods can be used for keeping track of files:

● allow only one person to take/return files to a cabinet
● keep a file book next to each cabinet so staff can write in details of the file they have taken
● use an 'out' card to indicate where a document has been taken from and by whom
● use an 'absent' folder to indicate where a file has been taken from and by whom

The last two tracer systems give the added advantage of being placed in the cabinet in the exact position of the document or file that has been taken. When the file is returned it can be replaced easily by looking for the out card or absent folder.

▶ *What is an absent folder?*

An absent folder is used to keep track of who has a file, their department and the date the file was taken. Most organisations use a printed form, similar to the one in Fig. 5.2 which is glued to an empty folder. When a file is removed the absent folder is completed with the relevant details and is put into the filing cabinet in the place of the removed file. When the file is returned the absent folder is removed and can be used again. If, in the meantime, the file is needed it can be easily located by reading the information on the absent folder.

ABSENT FOLDER			
Date taken	Name/Number of file taken	Name and Department of Borrower	Date returned

Fig 5.2 An absent folder

▶ *What is an out card?*

It may be the case that a person does not require the whole file, but only a document from it. It is important that a record is kept of who has what, and where the document has gone. If a separate document is removed from a file it should be replaced with an out card similar to that in Fig. 5.3. The out card will sit in the file and will only be removed when the document is returned.

OUT CARD				
Document title	Borrower	Department	Date borrowed	Date returned

Fig 5.3 An out card

Some organisations use absent folders and out cards, some use one or the other and some will not bother with either! If you are responsible for the filing, you will be expected to know where files have gone and who has taken missing documents. By keeping absent folders, out cards, or both, on top of the filing cabinet you can encourage other staff to keep track of files.

■ DIY 5.1.4

Your filing classification system needs to be updated so that it can be extended more easily. Your boss has asked you to go through the enrolment numbers and add a letter to each indicating the course to be followed. Use the following information to help you:

- All enrolment numbers beginning with 0, 1, 2 or 3 should have the letter A placed before the number to indicate the Administration course.
- All enrolment numbers beginning with 4, 5 or 6 should have the letter B placed before the number to indicate the Business course.
- All enrolment numbers beginning with 7, 8 or 9 should have the letter C placed before the number to indicate the Clerical course

For example, Julie Hartopp's enrolment number should now read 'A178412'.

You must now re-sort your index cards into alphanumeric order by dividing the 3 alphabetical classifications, A, B and C, into separate groups. Each group should then be filed numerically according to the rest of the enrolment number.

▶ *When and how would a bring forward system be operated?*

This is also called a reminder system or tickler file (*see* Fig. 5.4) and is used to remind staff that a certain task has to be completed on a particular day. A simple desk diary can be used and entries made for dates in the future. However, a filing cabinet drawer or a concertina file can be used; both are able to hold correspondence relevant to the task that has to be done on the day.

The file is divided into months and days of the month. When letters are received or appointments made that require some future activity, a dated reminder or the letter itself is placed in the appropriate dated compartment of the file. At the end of each week and again at the beginning of each day the file would be checked to make sure nothing has been overlooked.

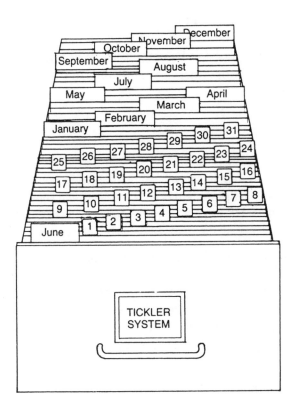

Fig 5.4 A tickler system

An example of how this system would be used can be seen in a travel agency where copies of invoices are placed in a file in date order two weeks before a customer's payment is due. When this date arrives a reminder can be sent to the customer so that they are able to arrange payment on time in readiness for their holiday.

▶ *How do you open a new file?*

In some organisations the job of opening new files is the responsibility of the office manager or supervisor. If you are asked to do this make sure you follow the system already in use. Firstly, check to see if there is a file already in the system and never automatically open a new file. If the customer is a 'one-off' the paperwork is likely to be placed in a miscellaneous file to save room in the filing cabinet. It is usual practice to type or write the name of the file directly on to the folder or on a sticky label. This information should always be placed in the same location on each folder. You may also require a title strip to be completed and placed in the correct position in the filing system. An index card may also need to be completed. When you have done all of this report back to your supervisor and confirm that a new file has been opened.

■ DIY 5.1.5

Your classification system has now been rearranged to alphanumeric. To retrieve index cards in this system is easy providing you know the full enrolment number of the student. If you only have the name, or numerical part of the enrolment number, finding the card will be quite difficult in a large system.

In order to make your system more efficient it is necessary for you to compile an alphabetical visible index system. This system will list the students alphabetically by their surname, followed by their forename and then their full enrolment number. Design your own index system (a strip index would be the best) that can be used to look up a student's name alphabetically in order to find their enrolment number so that their index card in the main system can be found.

Remember your strip index should be kept in alphabetical order but your main index cards are in alphanumeric order.

CIRCULATION SLIP		
Please read and pass on:		
NAME	DEPARTMENT	INITIAL/DATE
Please return to: By:		

Fig 5.5 A circulation slip

▶ Circulation slips

A circulation slip (*see* Fig. 5.5) is used if information needs to be seen by a number of staff. Slips that list the names of all staff in a department can be prepared, and one is attached to the information, for example a price list, business journal, internal memorandum or perhaps a piece of correspondence. When each member of staff has seen the information they cross their name from the list and pass the information on to the next person. When all staff have seen the information it is returned, usually to the person named at the bottom of the list, ready for filing.

Blank circulation slips can also be prepared and used when only a small number of staff need to see a piece of information. Staff names are inserted and the slip attached to the information with details of the department if necessary. When each member of staff has read the information, they initial and date the slip and pass it on to the next person. The last person on the list will pass the information and completed slip back to the person named at the bottom.

▶ How do you deal with confidential files?

All company files could be classed as confidential. Personal information, company reports, financial accounts or minutes from a business meeting should never be discussed with people outside the company. It is important to recognise that information dealt with on a daily, routine basis may be of interest to a rival company. A member of staff may be interested in a colleague's salary or perhaps their home address and telephone number. Therefore, it is important that you do not leave paperwork lying round the office, however innocent you may think it is.

If you do deal with confidential material make sure all files are kept in one place under lock and key. Folders should be clearly marked 'CONFIDENTIAL' and not be left on a desk or lent to an unauthorised person, however nice and friendly they may seem. Dead files should never be put in a bin or skip, but should be shredded or incinerated so they are unreadable.

Confidential information held on a computer database must also be protected. Use passwords or keywords to restrict access and protect information. Only authorised staff should know the password or keyword, which should be changed regularly and never written down. Printouts should be kept in a folder marked confidential and disks should be kept locked away in a cupboard, not just in their disk box. Information stored on a computer database will be covered by the Data Protection Act (*see* page 161).

▶ *How do you destroy files?*

Confidential files should be destroyed by putting them through a shredder (*see* Fig. 5.6) or burning them in an incinerator. Electric shredders simply need the documents to be fed through and they will be automatically cut into long thin shreds. Remember to remove staples and paperclips first, as these can break the machine if passed through the cutters! Manual machines are also available that require you to turn a handle and feed the document through. The result is the same – an unreadable piece of paper.

▶ *What about safety?*

Modern, vertical filing cabinets have an anti-tilt device that prevents more than one drawer being opened at a time, which could easily lead

126

Fig 5.6 A shredder

to the cabinet toppling over. Cabinet drawers should always be closed after use, never left open for someone to bump into or fall over. If you keep files on top of cupboards or use a floor-to-ceiling lateral system it is essential that climbing stools or ladders are provided. Never balance on a chair, particularly one with wheels!

When using a shredding machine make sure you keep your fingers, hair and dangling jewellery out of the way. When you have shredded documents bag them up and remove from the office, do not leave them lying round for people to fall over or create a fire hazard. Above all, keep your office and desk area tidy and free from hazards. A desk full of filing looks untidy, creates a bad image of yourself and the office and can be a safety hazard.

■ DIY 5.1.6

Add the correct address and telephone number to each student's main index card (not the strip index). To do this, match the numbers in brackets. For example, the address and telephone number for Julie Hartopp is number (1) in the list below. Place this information in the middle of the index card.

(1)	19 Landers Way, Poole	786578
(2)	12 Tring Place, Bournemouth	789567
(3)	23 Urwin Crescent, Bournemouth	767584
(4)	89 Grenville Road, Poole	765356
(5)	98 Shore Road, Poole	789056
(6)	94 Britannia Road, Poole	734867
(7)	3 Glen Road, Poole	–
(8)	34 Wellington Road, Wareham	680745
(9)	16 Saltash Way, Dorchester	563425
(10)	1 Union Street, Weymouth	234156
(11)	9 Union Street, Weymouth	231769
(12)	56 Oxendon Way, Bournemouth	768598
(13)	76 Somerly Close, Parkstone	764983
(14)	89 Connaught Crescent, Poole	761098
(15)	77 Sunnyside Road, Poole	709164
(16)	1 Salisbury Road, Wareham	680356
(17)	143 Binley Road, Weymouth	–
(18)	19 Penn Hill, Poole	–
(19)	76 Rosey Road, Dorchester	563782
(20)	56 King John Ave, Bournemouth	571880
(21)	11 Yelland Close, Porchester	–
(22)	89 Park View Road, Christchurch	674838
(23)	99 Seaview Crescent, Poole	564983
(24)	1 Selby Rise, Dorchester	674837
(25)	4 Wytch Avenue, Southampton	892758
(26)	37 Bay View, Porchester	487591
(27)	88 Yardly Way, Bournemouth	647837
(28)	19 Albert Square, Weymouth	783987
(29)	77 Sunrise Crescent, Southampton	–
(30)	9a Glen View Road, Christchurch	674910

1 You have just been informed that JULIE HARTOPP has recently married and her surname has changed to WRIGHT. You will need to amend Julie's main index card so that the surname reads 'WRIGHT'. The main index card will remain in the same place as this is filed numerically and this order will not have changed.

To prevent any confusion it is also necessary to insert a cross-reference under 'H' in the visible strip index so that anyone looking for her details under the surname of 'Hartopp' will be directed to the correct location, ie 'Wright'. This is called cross-referencing. You will find an example of the information required for a cross-reference in Fig. 5.1.

2 Prepare 2 spare index cards to be used as 'out cards'. These cards should be kept at the back of your system and placed in the position of cards that have been removed. You will find an example of the information required on an out card in Fig. 5.3.

■ DIY 5.1.7

You have dealt with manual files so far in this element. Have you noticed how long it has taken you to prepare the cards and organise them alphabetically, numerically and then in alphanumeric order? How do you think you could improve this system? The whole process would be much easier and efficient if carried out using a database program. Set up a database using the fields:

SURNAME:
FORENAME:
ADDRESS: (You will need 2 lines for this)
TELEPHONE NUMBER:
COURSE CODE: (This field should only accept A, B or C.)
ENROLMENT NUMBER:

1 Sort your records alphabetically by surname and do a printout.
2 Sort records numerically by enrolment number and do a printout.
3 Sort records to show students that are on course 'A' only, course 'B' only and course 'C' only. Do 3 separate printouts.
4 Insert details of the following new students:
Michael Bardy, 27 Union Drive, Swanage, Telephone: 379498.
Enrolment: 859875. He is on a clerical course.
Martin Taylor, 88 Heslop Road, Swanage. Telephone: 379459.
Enrolment: 389587. He is on a business course.
Do an alphabetical printout.

5 These students have left and their details have to be deleted from the database:

(a) Sarah Foster; (b) Paul Rider; (c) Kelly Sayers.

Do an alphabetical printout.

You should have 7 separate printouts when you have completed this DIY.

Completing Element 5.1

To complete this element on maintaining an established storage system you will need to put all DIY tasks in your folder, and carry out a final assessment. You must prove competence when dealing with methods of classifying information alphabetically, numerically and in alphanumeric order.

Files, books, reference material or computer data can be used to prove competence. Information must be stored promptly and in the correct location in an undamaged, safe and secure state. Opportunities for improving the system should be identified and appropriate action taken. Systems used must be up to date, accurate and in the requested form. Overdue or out-of-date files should be dealt with in accordance with organisational procedures and relevant legal requirements, eg the Data Protection Act, should be followed.

Claiming credit

Once you have completed your final assessment, you will need to write in your record book or folder how, when, where and what you have done to prove that you are competent.

The following is an example of how one trainee completed this claim:

I have filed all personnel documents in the right place as quickly as possible. I made sure all damaged paperwork was repaired, paperclips removed and I placed paperwork flat and square in the folder. I always closed the cabinet drawer when I had finished. I used an alphabetical system in the personnel department and a numerical in the accounts. I set up an alphanumeric system for student record cards. I always made sure files were put in the right place.

The personnel records were kept in alphabetical order because this was the best classification as the surname could be used. In the accounts department they used numerical filing according to the customer account number. When using the numerical system we had to refer to the alphabetical index if a customer did not know their account number. The index was kept in alphabetical order by company name and each card contained details of the customer account number. In order to improve the student index card system I transferred it to a database. Data protection laws were adhered to.

Element 5.2
SUPPLY INFORMATION FOR A SPECIFIC PURPOSE

Performance criteria

- Information requirements are understood
- Information sources are correctly identified and accessed
- Where available information does not match requirements, options and alternatives are identified and offered
- Information is correctly transcribed and compiled
- The information supplied is in an appropriate form
- Essential information is supplied within required deadlines
- Confidential information is disclosed only to authorised persons

No day will go by without you being asked for some kind of information. You may immediately know the answer to the question being asked, or you may have to refer to reference material as a source of information.

Your first problem may be finding the correct reference material for the information required. The following list gives details of common reference books and the information they provide.

Book	Information
Telephone directory	Local telephone numbers and addresses.
Yellow pages	Local business telephone numbers and addresses.
Business Pages	Local business telephone numbers and addresses (excluding retail outlets).
Thomson Directory	Local business telephone numbers, addresses and postcodes.
Mail Guide	Information on all Post Office services.
Dictionary	Spelling and meaning of words and abbreviations.
Thesaurus	Different words with the same meaning.
British Rail timetables	Train times and destinations.
ABC Guide	Information on air travel, shipping and coaches.
AA and *RAC Guides*	Details roads, towns, routes, hotels, garages, etc.

Whitaker's Almanack	Information on world affairs, calendar year, statistics, prizewinning authors, plays, films, music, details about United Kingdom and a wide range of other topics.
Who's Who	Biographical details of famous people.
Debrett's Peerage	Details correct forms of address.
Good Food Guide	Information on places to eat.

Other sources of information that you may also need to use are:

Directory Enquiries
Newspapers
Road Maps
A–Z street guides
Internal telephone directories
Company organisation chart
Company computer files
Company paper-based files
Company database
Prestel, Teletext, Ceefax
Library or company microfiche.

People and organisations who are there to help you are:

AA or RAC
Local authority
Chamber of Commerce
Citizens' Advice Bureau
British Telecom
Post Office Customer Service
English Tourist Board
Inland Revenue
The Department of Trade and Industry
The Consumers' Association.

Locating information may be a simple process of knowing 'who' to ask – your supervisor, boss, colleague or library staff may know the answer to your question, or they may be able to tell you from where you can get the information.

During the course of a day you may be called upon to access information either:

- orally over the telephone or face to face
- using a computer, eg Prestel or database
- using a paper-based source, eg files or reference books.

If you do need to ask for information make sure you are polite and know exactly what information you require – remember, you are asking someone to spend their time helping you! If you use the telephone to contact a person or organisation, be prepared with notes of the information you require and use the correct telephone manner.

It is important that when you are asked to find information you are aware of when the information is required. If the request is urgent you must prioritise it accordingly and fit it in with your daily tasks as quickly as possible. If the request is not urgent, wait until you have time to spare. All staff have to work to deadlines – remember that if you are late in obtaining information for a colleague you affect their deadline as well as your own.

■ DIY 5.2.1

Prepare a table like the one in Fig. 5.7. Each time a colleague, supervisor, customer or client asks you for information make a note of the date, details of information required and the source you used to obtain the information. You will have to design the table so that there is enough room for your entries. It should fill at least one sheet of A4 paper.

DIY 5.2.1 – Supply information for a specific purpose		
DATE	INFORMATION	SOURCE

Fig 5.7

In an office environment you will find information from paper-based files, microfiche or files held on a computer database. Some organisations provide computer and/or television access to information – this is called Viewdata. You may have already used Prestel, Teletext and Ceefax.

Prestel links television screens or personal computers to a large computer via BT lines. Information is updated every 24 hours and includes:

- company information
- directories
- market research
- business news/services
- share prices
- government statistics
- travel information
- weather information
- sport and entertainment
- banking and investment
- mailbox
- customer guide

This service allows the user to actually make bookings using their keyboard, for example, for theatre tickets and air tickets. The user is charged according to how long they have used the line, in the same way as a telephone. In addition, a registration charge is paid to Prestel.

Teletext and **Ceefax** give similar information as Prestel. This information is often available at no additional cost on television screens, but does not allow users to make bookings. Information services such as the speaking clock are also provided by BT, and 0891 numbers, advertised in newspapers, can be used for information such as weather reports and traffic news.

▶ *What is microfilm and microfiche?*

Microfilm is used to store reduced, photographic copies of documents. Each document is photographed on to strips of 16mm film, to nearly a twentieth of the original size. A special reader is used which enlarges the document on screen back to its original size. Some readers will allow a copy of the document to be printed.

Microfiche works on the same principle but documents are photographed on to single sheets of microfilm measuring 150 mm × 100 mm. Each sheet can be labelled with details of its contents and is placed on a reader when information is required. This system is most commonly used in libraries – if you look up an author name or book title on the microfiche you are able to see if the library has the book and, if so, where it is located.

■ DIY 5.2.2

Sources of information we have spoken about include:

- databases
- viewdata
- microfiche

You will be able to find at least one of these information sources in your workplace, training centre or local library. Write an information sheet giving details of the advantages and disadvantages of each of these sources of information.

▶ *How do I extract the information required?*

When you are first asked to find information, write down details of what is required, use questions to make sure you are clear in your own mind exactly what you are looking for. When you have found the information it is likely that your source will give more than is required. It is your responsibility to go through all the information and pick out only the relevant points.

If, for example, your boss asked you to find the train times for London to Dover, the first questions you should ask is: 'What day and between what times?' It is unlikely that your boss will need the time of every train for that day, only a train to get to/from an appointment or meeting. You may be able to photocopy information directly from the source you have found, but make sure that the information is not protected by copyright.

It is useful to underline or highlight information to pick out the important points. Make notes as you read through information and always remember to say from where the information was taken. Your boss may want to get further details from the same source or you may be asked to find the same or similar information again. If you have kept a note of your source this will be an easy process.

▶ *What is copyright law?*

The copying of documents is controlled by the Copyright, Designs and Patents Act 1988. It is illegal to copy documents that are protected and the symbol © is printed, normally on the first page or on the back of the first page of the document. If you look at the front pages of this book you will find the symbol as well as a statement that copying is not allowed. However, some documents may be copied if it is for educational purposes and others may be copied if the author's permission is obtained first. You should always check before copying that the document you wish to copy is not protected. Obviously if the document has been written by someone in the office it will be all right to copy it. The Act also covers copyright in music and video tapes, records, TV and radio programmes and computer programs.

▶ *How should you compose notes?*

You should make notes of the information you find as you go along. Always use a note pad, never scraps of paper than can be easily lost. Leave plenty of room between notes so that additional information can be slotted in if necessary. A wide margin will also allow space for insertions or markers for important facts. Try to number the information so that is can be read back in a logical sequence. Leave out unnecessary words and use abbreviations to cut down on time. If you are unsure of standard abbreviations you can find these listed in your dictionary.

Write up notes as you find each piece of information and when your research is complete, transfer the notes to your chosen form of presentation as soon as possible. It is better to present your information whilst it is still fresh in your mind. When taking notes from speech, edit any irrelevant information and listen for key words. Factual information such as times, dates, etc, should be noted in full.

136

■ DIY 5.2.3

You work in a Travel Department and have been given the following statistics regarding newly appointed couriers.

First name	Surname	Passport?	Languages spoken	Age
Amanda	Blacker	Y	GERMAN	19
Sally	Sager	Y	FRENCH	20
David	Presley	Y	FRENCH	24
Mark	Harrison	N	ITALIAN	18
Rachael	Miller	N	SPANISH	19
Jade	Chandris	Y	GERMAN	28
Perri	Scott	Y	FRENCH	29
Leila	Scott	Y	HINDUSTANI	19
Crystal	Harper	Y	FRENCH	18
John	Emrie	Y	HINDUSTANI	23
Lynne	Patience	N	GREEK	19
Shervin	Patel	N	SPANISH	28

The Travel Manager has asked you to prepare a bar chart showing the range of ages. He would also like the table rearranged and typed in alphabetical order and two different coloured highlighter pens used to indicate who has and who has not got a passport.

▶ What do you do if you cannot find the information?

First make sure you have looked everywhere you can think of. Your supervisor will not be pleased if you are constantly asking for help instead of looking for yourself. Your supervisor may be able to point you in the right direction, or they may not know either! Once you have tried everyone and everything you can think of report back to the person who requested the information and explain your actions to date. This is particularly important if the person needs the information for a specific time or date.

In your search for the information you should identify other options and alternatives that may be of help. For example, your boss may request the name and number of a local stationery suppliers. It is sensible for you to supply 2 or 3 alternatives in case the first one cannot be contacted. Likewise, alternative hotels, venues, restaurants, travel times and so on will provide a wider selection to choose from.

■ DIY 5.2.4

You work for Coopers & Co, Chartered Surveyors, 15 Westmead Road, Basingstoke BA12 8BB. The Sales Executive, Lorraine Harvey, has been invited to visit the London Branch of the company based at 113 Leicester Square, London. She will be travelling from the office and wishes to stay overnight in a 4-star hotel.

1 Look through the extract from her diary for the week (given in Fig. 5.8) and decide what day she should attend the meeting.

2 Check BR timetables and find the best times for her to travel by train to/from London.

	DIARY
Monday 9 Feb	Meeting with Managing Director 12.00 – 3.00 pm Dentist 4.00 pm
Tuesday 10 Feb	Sales meeting – Room 66 9.30 – 3.30 pm (working lunch) Need sales figures for 1993/94
Thursday 12 Feb	Presentation at the London Chamber of Commerce, Queen Street, London 10.30 am – 2.30 pm Dinner with Michael – La Jardin (pick up at home 9 pm)
Friday 13 Feb	Lunch with Purchasing Manager 12.00 – about 2.00 pm Take dog to the vet – 4.00 pm
Saturday 14 Feb	Write up Sales meeting report

Fig 5.8 Diary extract

3 What underground tube(s) will get her from the BR station to Leicester Square?

4 Select a 4-star hotel within walking distance of Piccadilly Circus.

5 Write to Mrs J Derham, Sales Director at the London Branch to inform her when and how Lorraine will be travelling. Give details of what time she should arrive at her office (it's about 5 minutes walk from the underground station). Also give the name and address of the hotel you have selected and ask her if she would like to join Lorraine for dinner.

6 Prepare an itinerary for Lorraine's trip to London.

▶ *What methods can be used to present information?*

There are a number of ways in which information can be presented. If you have spent time searching for information it is important that when passing on your findings you do not confuse the person who asked for the information. You should choose a method of presentation that displays the information in an easy to understand format.

You must always remember to give a heading to your information and if necessary provide a key. A key is used to explain colour codes or small indicators on a plan or graph. Look at the key used for the London Underground – this identifies each line by colour.

Look back at the 4 DIY tasks you have already completed. You will have already presented information using a table, text (in a memorandum, itinerary and a letter) and a bar chart. Other methods available to you are:

- diagrams
- graphs
- pie charts
- pictograms
- flow charts

Diagrams

Diagrams are useful for showing a layout or how something works. You could use a diagram to show the directions of how to get from A to B, or to show what something, such as a piece of equipment, looks like. A map, as in Fig. 5.9, is also an example of a diagram.

MAP OF SALES AREA

Fig 5.9 An example of a diagram

Graphs

Line graphs, as shown in Fig. 5.10, are used to show a set of figures. Different lines indicate different figures that can be compared against each other if plotted on the same graph. A line could be used to show sales figures and another to show staff wages in comparison.

■ DIY 5.2.5

Look at the following information. Read it through and then prepare a line graph to present the information so that each year's figures can be compared.

The amount of A4 paper being used at Collier Insurance Services is getting out of hand. The boss, Mr Chris Collier, has asked you to present a chart showing a

QUARTERLY SALES

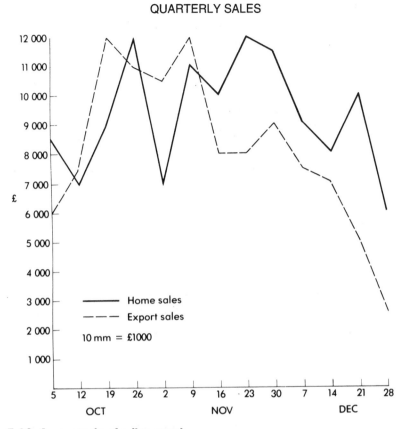

Fig 5.10 An example of a line graph

comparison of paper usage over the last 3 years. The figures you need are as follows:

1991 – 40 reams in each of the first 2 months of the year, 45 in March, 40 again in April, and 37 in each of the last 2 months of the half year.

1992 – 52 reams used in each of the first 3 months, following 3 months dropped to 48, 45 and 40 respectively.

1993 – first 3 months of the half year 38, 36 and 34 reams respectively, and the last 3 months levelled out at 33 reams each.

1 In which year was there maximum paper usage?
2 In which year was there minimum paper usage?

UK SALES

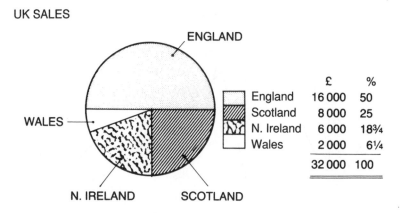

	£	%
England	16 000	50
Scotland	8 000	25
N. Ireland	6 000	18¾
Wales	2 000	6¼
	32 000	100

Fig 5.11 An example of a pie chart

Pie charts

Pie charts, as in Fig. 5.11, are used to show figures as a percentage of the whole. The circle (pie) measures 360 degrees and is divided up into segments to show the different percentages, like the slices of a pie. The larger the slice, the larger the percentage in relation to the whole.

Pictogram

Pictograms, as in Fig. 5.12, use symbols or pictures to represent approximate figures. If the symbol or picture is cut in half so is the amount it represents.

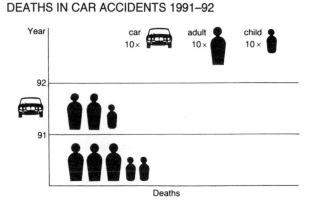

Fig 5.12 An example of a pictogram

142

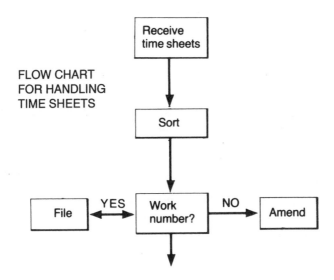

Fig 5.13 An example of a flow chart

Flow charts

Flow charts, as in Fig. 5.13, are used to show steps through a process in the order they occur. By answering yes/no questions you are given the next stage in the process.

■ DIY 5.2.6

Prepare a flow chart showing the steps of a process. Computer programmers often use flow charts when designing programs, although for the purpose of this DIY you should choose something a little easier. Making a cup of tea, completing an assignment or how to deal with incoming mail are ideas you may wish to use.

Completing Element 5.2

To complete this element on supplying information for a specific purpose you will need to put all the DIY tasks in your folder, and carry out a final assessment. This must show that you are able to identify and access correct sources of information, and if the information you find does not match requirements, that you are able to provide options and alternatives. When you find information you must transcribe and compile it correctly, using a presentation method that is appropriate. You must prove that you can work to deadlines and treat confidential material correctly. The information sources you use must include internal and external sources, paper-based information, computerised data and information given person to person.

Claiming credit

Once you have completed your final assessment, you will need to write in your record book or folder how, when, where and what you have done to prove that you are competent.

The following is an example of how one trainee completed their claim:

In the training centre I used internal, national and international telephone directories to find numbers for my supervisor. I also used PO leaflets for mail costs and the library microfiche for book details. I only took relevant information, eg when I was asked for a telephone number I did not give the address as well. When my supervisor asked for details of the nearest stationery suppliers I gave the nearest plus 2 other alternatives. I gave coach as well as train times, if these were suitable alternatives. I have used graphs, charts, pie charts and text to present information (see work folder).

I made sure all information was correct before presenting it. I proofread all material and checked it against my notes and made sure I followed the copyright law. I always asked if there was a deadline for information required. If there was I made sure I met the deadline; if not, I still tried to present the information as soon as possible.

UNIT 6
Maintain data in a computer system

■ Element 6.1
INPUT DATA AND TEXT INTO A COMPUTER SYSTEM

Performance criteria

- Suitable computer software is used
- Data and text are correctly entered
- Where the source data is incomplete, clear directions are obtained from the appropriate person
- Where the source data is unauthorised, clear directions are obtained from the appropriate person
- Errors in inputting and coding are identified and corrected in accordance with organisational procedures
- Reference codes are generated as necessary
- Where work is not achievable within specified deadlines reasons are promptly and accurately reported
- Work is achieved within agreed deadlines
- Organisational procedures for storing source material are followed
- Equipment and data are safeguarded against damage
- Confidentiality and security of data are in accordance with organisational requirements
- Safe working practices are followed

Data, or information, may be stored manually, in a filing system or in a computer-based system. There are 2 main parts to any computer system, the hardware and the software.

▶ *What is hardware?*

The hardware includes the actual machinery (*see* Fig. 6.1): the screen (or VDU – visual display unit), keyboard, mouse, processor (or CPU – central processing unit), drives and a printer.

The CPU is the part of the machine which reads the information (data); the drives store the information. The CPU will contain a hard disk (also called a fixed disk) which cannot be removed from the machine, and it will also have 1 or 2 slots in the casing to insert floppy disks to store the information externally. The drives that contain the disks are usually called C for hard drive and A and B for disk drives. Other drives may be created but this is not important for this unit (you only need to go into making extra drives if you intend being a computer technician or programmer).

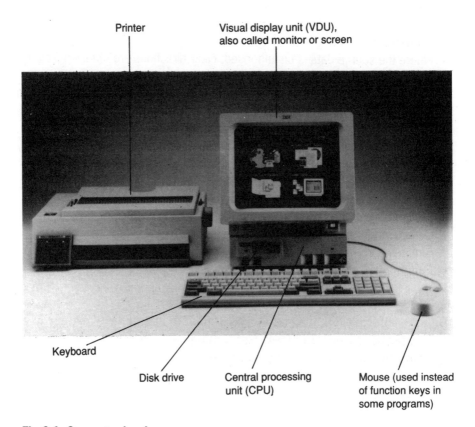

Fig 6.1 Computer hardware

▶ *What is software?*

Software is the programs that make the hardware work. They are supplied on floppy disks, which are usually 3.5 or 5.25 inches in diameter and are protected by a cover, either hard or soft plastic. The disk itself is visible and looks like a dark brown, smooth circular piece of plastic – it should not be touched or it will be damaged. Programs are written in languages that the CPUs can understand. The most common are BASIC (**B**eginner's **A**ll-purpose **S**ymbolic **I**nstruction **C**ode) and COBOL (**CO**mmon **B**usiness **O**rientated **L**anguage). You will not need to understand these languages unless you intend to become a computer programmer. Most of the people who use computers do not understand how they work, only the programs they use.

■ DIY 6.1.1

The parts of your computer will include a VDU, CPU, keyboard, drives and printer. First list the type of equipment you are using, including the make, model, size, etc. Secondly, list the software, or applications, that are run on the machine you have access to. Next to the name of the software list the type of package it is, eg word processing, database, spreadsheet, accounts, graphics, desk-top publishing, etc.

Most of the programs used in a business or college are loaded from the floppy disks to the hard drive. This is called installing a program. The program can then easily be used on a daily basis without having to reload every time. Each time a program is loaded on to the hard drive, it uses up space and, as a hard drive has a limited amount of space, it can only hold so many programs at one time. The number of programs held depends on the size of each program and the size of the hard disk.

▶ *Looking after the equipment*

You should check the screen is placed at a comfortable distance from the keyboard, to make sure you do not suffer from eyestrain. Alter the brightness of the screen to suit you, using the brightness control and the contrast control. The screen should be facing away from windows, or direct artificial light, to reduce the glare. If this is not possible, an anti-glare screen may be attached. There should be sufficient space around your keyboard to place your work or to use a mouse or joystick.

▶ Which parts of a computer can be cleaned?

Very few. On switching off and unplugging from the mains, you can clean the screen with an anti-static spray (recommended by suppliers or local stationers); the casing can also be wiped clear of dirty fingermarks and dust. You will need to use a brush or small vacuum to remove dust from between the keys. **Never** remove the casing from computers. The screen is sensitive and should not be left on when not in use as static from the screen will also attract dust. If the machine will not be used for a while, turn the screen brightness down or off.

Keep food and liquids away from all computer equipment. If an accident should occur, disconnect from the main supply immediately and call your supervisor.

▶ What precautions should you take with computer equipment in the office?

Switch off all machinery at the end of the day (the only exception may be the telephone answering machine, which will take telephone calls in your absence, and the fax machine, which may send and receive messages during the night). Make sure that any connecting wires are not trailing across the floor – they should be taped under the desk or placed close against the walls. Do not overload sockets; multi-extension leads should be used when several items need to be plugged in at the same time. Alternatively extra sockets should be installed. Check the leads regularly for fraying or broken connections. New regulations under the Health and Safety at Work Act (HASAWA) and the Electricity at Work Regulations state that all electrical equipment must be regularly checked to confirm it is safe to use. Consult your tutor or health and safety representative if you are not sure about the state of any of the equipment you use.

▶ *What is good posture?*

To make certain you do not suffer from strain and injury, you should sit in the most comfortable position for typing. Strain can occur to the neck, back, arms and legs, and on occasion can lead to serious complaints. To reduce the risk of injury, or RSI (repetitive strain injury), you should use a chair that can be adjusted to suit you. It should allow you to sit with your feet flat on the floor (use a footrest if necessary), and have an adjustable back-rest to support your lower back. Desks for typing are generally lower than normal desks, to allow the keyboard to sit at the correct height.

Your head should be upright, otherwise you will find your neck will ache from constantly looking down at the desk. This means that the document you are working from should be placed on a document holder, either to the right or left of your keyboard, whichever you find more comfortable (*see* page 354).

▶ *How should you look after your disks?*

Floppy disks are fragile and can easily be damaged – and damage may result in you losing all the information stored. The information is stored on the disks in tracks, (*see* Fig. 6.2) which are similar to the grooves on a record. Each track has a circle which can hold a certain amount of information. Disks may be single or double sided – double sided means that disks can store information on both sides, and therefore store more information than can single sided. They can also be single, double or high density. The density of the disk refers to the amount of information that can be stored: a double-density disk can store twice as much information as a single-density disk; high density stores the most. The speed at which the CPU runs will depend on which type of disk you can use. It is similar to video recorders that can run at different speeds. If you halve the speed of the tape through the machine you can store twice as much.

As mentioned earlier, disks are protected by a plastic cover. The 5.25" covers are flexible, but should never be bent. The top of the disk is smooth and has no edges, whilst underneath you will find that three edges have been folded over and electronically 'stapled' in place. The exposed parts of the disk should be in the middle, with an oval slot on

149

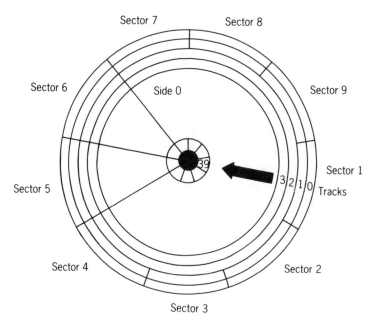

Fig 6.2 Disk track diagram

the side. This oval slot is pushed first into the disk drive in the casing of the CPU. A 3.5" disk is protected by a hard plastic cover which has an arrow printed on the front indicating which way it should be inserted into the CPU. It also has a metal protection cover over the exposed part of the disk – slide one back carefully to see the disk. Both these disks may also be called diskettes.

Before any disk can be used for storing information it will need to be formatted (sometimes called initialising). Formatting a disk prepares it to accept information from the system you are running on your computer. It is usually done by using the 'format' command, but you will need to check with your supervisor or tutor before you carry out a format on equipment you are unfamiliar with. If you format an existing disk all the information stored on it will be lost, as formatting cleans the disk completely.

Protecting the information on your disk

On the 5.25" disk you will see a small rectangular cut in the side of the disk. This is the write protection notch. If you do not want to put any

150

further information on the disk or you want to make sure you do not delete any of the information you can stick a label over the notch and the CPU will then stop you from storing or deleting any further information.

On the 3.5" disk at the bottom right-hand corner at the back of the disk you will see a small plastic square that will slide up and down. In the up position, the disk would be write protected. It is the same process as protecting a video at home: when you break off the plastic square from the front of the video, it stops anyone from recording over your favourite film.

Another way of protecting information stored on disks is to save the file, with a password or keyword. Before the CPU will allow you to look at the information stored or to delete the file it will be necessary to type in the password. If you use passwords, make sure you remember them and if you write them down make sure it is somewhere that is not easily found by everyone else in the office. Check that your company does not have regulations regarding the use of passwords before starting your own system.

Labelling your disks

To protect the exposed areas of the 5.25" disk you should place it in a paper cover and store all disks in a disk box. This may be a small box which can store 5–10 disks or a desk-top box which can store many more. Each of the disks should be labelled, and it is useful to put the label in the corner which is held while placing the disk into the CPU (see Fig. 6.3). When placed in the disk box the labels should be in the top left-hand corner.

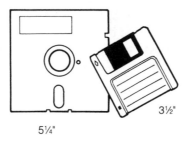

3½"

5¼"

Fig 6.3 Labelled disks

Always write on the label before you stick it on to the disk. If you need to change what is written on the label of a 5.25" disk at a future date, you can use a fibre-tipped pen. Do not use biro or pencil as the pressure of writing on the label may damage the disk.

Using your disks in the CPU

To insert a 5.25" disk into the CPU hold the label, insert it into the slot and push the lever down into position. To insert a 3.5" disk hold it in the right-hand corner and push it into the slot until it clicks down into place.

Protecting your disks from damage

The disk box should be kept in a dry place which does not become too hot or cold and should not be exposed to intensive light. The disks should also be kept away from the top of the CPU, telephones, electrical equipment, steel or any magnetic surface as these may corrupt your disk (even a steel knife and fork could corrupt a disk!). A corrupted disk may mean that you will be unable to get your data back, but you should check with a computer technician as they may have access to special programs that can retrieve data or repair damaged disks. Data could also be lost through accidentally deleting a file, handling or overloading the disk: again, check with a computer technician as deleted data can usually be retrieved, as long as you have not reformatted the disk.

■ DIY 6.1.2

Answer the following by completing the sentences.
1 A formatted disk is one which ...
2 If a disk becomes corrupted it cannot ...
3 The drives are called A, B and C. A and B refer to ... C refers to ...
4 A floppy disk can be protected by ...
5 VDU stands for ... and it is the ... part of the hardware.

To reduce the chance of losing your data through a corrupted disk, it is usual to make 'back-up' copies. This means that you keep a copy of the data on a second disk. Some businesses have a set procedure for making back-up copies. Check with your supervisor at work or discuss with your tutor how frequently you should make back-ups. Even hard disks may be corrupted so do not rely on keeping all your data on hard disk only. For this reason some companies change their hard disks and have back-up copies of them, especially when they are dealing with millions of pieces of information every day.

Saving your data

It is important to save your data regularly. If you are working all day on the same file, you may save it every half hour or so, just to make sure you do not lose all the work through someone accidentally switching off your computer or an electrical power cut. Some programs remind you to save your work by flashing a message at you while you work and slow the system down, which generally annoys you so much you save quickly to enable you to get on! Some programs will create a back-up for you and save automatically every 20 minutes or so.

To save a file it is necessary to give it a file name, which is used to recall the file when you wish to edit or change the information. The names you choose for files will depend on company policy or may be entirely up to you. However, if the choice is yours try to have a system that is logical.

The file name will usually indicate the content of the file. It cannot contain more than 8 characters (preferably only letters, as in some programs numbers and other characters have special meanings to the computer). Some databases are also particular about whether small letters or capital letters are typed. If you decide to call your file 'STOCKJAN', but when you want to call the file back you enter 'stockjan', it may not be able to find it. This is called 'case specific', which means the computer is looking for a particular 'case', ie lower- or upper-case letters (also called 'shift sensitive').

The second part of the file name is called an extension, and your computer will automatically issue an extension to your file. For your database files the .DBF extension will be used – you should keep a record of the file names you allocate to your data.

▶ *What does a database do?*

A database package is similar to a filing system, in that it stores information and allows you to retrieve it later. You can add a new file or delete an old one. You may already have filed items in alphabetical order, but the computer can sort information by itself. This means that you can put the information into the computer in any order, and when you add a file it does not have to be at a particular place. Many different organisations use databases to store all sorts of information such as customer names and addresses, staff or patient information, stock records, properties for sale, membership records, etc.

The type of information needed for each database will vary and you will need to look carefully at the information to be stored before you create a database. Each piece of information needs to have a line of its own, called a **field**. For example, if you were creating a database of your relations' birthdays you would probably want one field for name, one for the day, one for the month, and another for the year – 4 fields altogether. If you wanted to include the address you may wish to have further fields for street, town, county and postcode (see below).

Name
Day
Month
Year
Street
Town
County
Postcode

The computer is able to sort out for you the files stored with a common field. For instance, if you wished to have a list of all the relations who had birthdays in May, you would be able to **list** these by requesting the computer to **sort** out all the files that have May in the field called month.

The fields will be listed on the screen in the shape of a **form**. The information for the relations' birthdays would therefore look like the form shown here:

Name..
Day................
Month............................
Year ....

The space you need for each field will depend on the information you intend putting in it. For the name field you will have to make sure that it is long enough to type in the longest name; the date would need a maximum of only 2 spaces as the numbers would be between 1 and 31; the month field would require a maximum of 9 as September is the longest month (or only 2 spaces if the month were typed numerically, eg September would be month 9 and October 10) and year would require only 4. Usually the database program will indicate, by dots, dashes or a block, how much space has been reserved in a field.

You will also need to tell the computer the type of information you will be putting into the field, ie alphabetic letters, numbers or a combination of both. In our example the first field, name, would be alpha, the second field, date, would be numeric. The street field would be alphanumeric, as it would probably have the number of the house and the name of the street.

■ DIY 6.1.3

Design a database which will contain fields to hold information on youth club members. Select suitable fields (such as name, address, etc) and then work out how much space you need in each field. Design the form required on a piece of paper by writing the field names and indicating the space allocated to each field. State which would be alpha, numeric or alphanumeric data.

You may find that once you start using your database the space allocated to a field is not enough. Most programs allow you to change the space, even after you have started saving information.

▶ How do you access a database program?

The database may be on your computer only or it may be connected (networked) to another or several hundred terminals (machines). Networked systems are used in large companies and allow many users to access the same information. The networked system would share the same CPU and all the information would be saved centrally on the CPU, although it may be possible to save your particular information separately on a floppy disk.

Access to your database will depend on which program you are using and how the computer has been set up. Some computers will have been set up with a menu (a list of items from which you can choose a program) which appears when you switch on, others will just have a prompt, such as c:\>, which is waiting for you to enter a command. Find out from your supervisor or tutor how to access the database program installed on your machine and make sure you write it down, so you do not forget.

Your files in the database program will have different names; if you save your family information as 'FAMILY.DBF' you would not use this name for another file. A file with information on the 3rd Division football clubs might be called FOOTBALL.DBF (remember the file name cannot be more than 8 characters and the .DBF is the extension automatically allocated by the computer, and indicates that the file is a **D**ata**B**ase **F**ile).

If you were looking at information in the FOOTBALL file and you wished to look at the FAMILY file, usually you would have to close one file and open the next; in most database programs, you cannot jump from one file to the other and have both open at the same time. To open and close files you will select the correct option using the cursor keys and then press the return key or, if you are using a mouse, click on the option required.

When you enter information (text or numbers) into the database it is important to be accurate, otherwise you may have problems when

156

selecting or looking for particular files. If you wanted to look at all the family records of people who lived in **London** and you had typed **Londen** in some of the records, the computer would not be able to find them. Therefore you should always proofread on screen after entering text before going to the next record or saving the file. If you have made an error it is easy to correct it by using the cursor keys: go back to the field where the error is, delete it and type in the correction.

■ DIY 6.1.4

You have been asked to help your friend's sister, Carly, with her homework. She wants you to explain what the following terms mean in computing. Write down a short paragraph on each, in simple language, to explain to her what they are.

- Field
- Form
- File
- Network
- Terminal
- File name
- Extension

▶ *Searching, sorting and retrieving information*

You may be asked to search through the records to find a particular form. If so, you can use the 'page down' key or 'next record' option on the database menus. This will allow you to look at each file. If you wanted to look at a particular set of records you could get the computer to 'sort' the records for you. You will need to tell the database what you need. To do this you will choose a particular field, such as month, in the family file. The computer will need to know what you are looking for: you could say all the forms that have 'May' in the month field.

Once set up the computer will search for all the records that have **May** typed in the month field and it will show you on screen how many forms it has found. You can then look through these records on screen or take a printout of them. If you wished, you could choose 2 fields for the computer to sort at the same time: all the records that have **May** in the month field and also have **London** in the address field. The computer will again show how many records it has found for you to look through. Once you have found (retrieved) the forms you need, you can write the details down from the screen or take a printout.

▶ *What organisations may use databases?*

Being able to sort forms is one of the main advantages of a database record system over a paper-based system. An estate agent, for instance, could record all the details of the properties for sale. When a customer is looking for a 4-bedroomed house in Erith, priced at £80,000, the office clerk could easily find the correct forms by stating the 4 special fields (type of property, price, bedrooms, location) and the details. A printout of all the houses available could then be made to give to the customer.

A club could use the computer to find out which members need to renew their subscriptions each month. Businesses may use it to select the customers located in the Lewisham area, to enable their representatives to call and inform them of a special offer. Travel agents use databases which are linked nationally to one another and to the main providers of flights and holidays. They can find a holiday in a certain country or for a certain price or date in a few seconds, and inform the customer of the options.

Colleges can keep details of their students on a database and are able to print out all those attending on Tuesday evening for Law, or any other options required.

The use of databases are many and, in particular, the financial world uses databases to make sure it has the most up-to-date information about stocks and shares. The stock exchange computer system is called SEAQ, Stock Exchange Automated Quotations system. Each marketmaker (dealer in stocks and shares) has a terminal connected to the central computer and business is carried out via the computer. The main computer is updated every minute by agencies such as Reuters, Topic and Telerate, who have the latest information on the market movements. The uses of a database are many – no doubt you can think of several more.

■ DIY 6.1.5

A local hairdresser has asked you to help them design a database which will keep details of their regular customers. Some of the customers prefer to have special shampoos, colours and perms, etc. Others like particular staff to do their hair. The owner of the shop wants to be able to write to the customers and keep them informed of new products and special offers. Design what you think would be an acceptable form, including the name and size of the fields.

▶ *How do you add new records to the database?*

To fill out a new form, or to add a record, you should open the file in the normal way for sorting or looking. You will find that your database menu will have an option called 'append', 'add record' or something similar. Select this option and a blank form will appear on the screen; complete the fields with the necessary information and save the file again. Your new record will then be added to the file. You will need to look at your own database to see the exact procedure to add forms, but generally databases are very similar.

▶ *How do you delete a record?*

To delete a record you can either go to the form you wish to delete and delete the page/record. Or you may be able to specify a particular field, for example delete all the records that have London in the town field. The computer will mark the records ready for deletion and when you save and exit the program these records will not be saved. The computer may give you an opportunity to change your mind when you are exiting, and a message may appear on screen such as 'DELETE ALL RECORDS MARKED?'

In reply to this you can answer Y/N. If you reply Y the file will be saved without the marked records; if you reply N you can continue to work in the file and the records will not be deleted.

▶ *Should you back up database files?*

Most certainly, all your records created on the computer should be backed up for the reasons discussed earlier. The database will have an option to allow you to do this. Make sure that you back up regularly, or every time you finish entering new text, or deleting files. The back-up files should be stored safely and, if they are confidential, in a locked cabinet. Some companies delete all the records from the hard disk at the end of each year and keep a copy of all the records on floppy disk (such as a college, so that all the new students for the year can be entered on to the system). It is important to remove old files from the computer system and keep as much space free as possible for your new files.

▶ *Planning and organising your work*

You should make sure that you have all the necessary information before starting to update your database. The information may be supplied to you in different ways. It could be that the company has a form which is completed by hand and the information is taken from it and typed into the correct file, form and field. On the other hand, you may be taking information from customers or clients verbally and entering direct on to the database whilst on the telephone. If this is the case you must make doubly sure that the information you have entered is correct before your customer hangs up the telephone: always read back to them the information you have entered.

The database is only as good as the users make it. If the information is out of date and inaccurate it will be of little use to anyone. It is very important to update your database regularly with information as it is received, new telephone numbers, changes of address, new requirements of customers, etc.

The information stored may be confidential, in which case access should be restricted to those people authorised to use it. This can be achieved by using passwords to gain access: each department may be allocated a password, or each separate user. Some systems will also allow users to look at the information but not change any of it or delete it. This system is sometimes used for students' records, where the tutor enters all the information regarding assessments and the student is allocated a password which allows them to access their record and look at the results or make a printout of them. Only the tutor can amend the record, and access by other students is restricted as they will not know the password.

160

Floppy disks can be copied or stolen, so make sure they are kept in the disk box and then locked in a cupboard or drawer. Again there should be restricted access to the disks. A booking out system should be introduced when confidential disks are taken away from the office by authorised users.

▶ Legal requirements for databases

If you set up a database which has personal information on individuals it must be registered with the **Data Protection Registrar**. The records should not be kept longer than is necessary and proper security procedures should be introduced to make sure only authorised staff have access to the information stored. The information should also be kept up to date, accurate and never be passed to anyone who may use it for other purposes, eg a list of doctors' patients being passed to a mail order firm to allow it to send sales material. Further information regarding registration can be obtained from the Post Office or direct from the Data Protection Registry.

■ DIY 6.1.6

The Data Protection Act is very important to all users of computers. Find out more about the Act and write a letter to your friend, the local hairdresser (DIY 6.1.5), about how the Act will affect him. Give as many details as possible, but make your explanation clear.

▶ What is a spreadsheet?

A spreadsheet is a table which has 'cells' made up from horizontal and vertical lines. These are called 'columns' and 'rows'.

In the example shown in Fig. 6.4, the spreadsheet has 5 columns and 5 rows. Each box is one cell, therefore this example has 25 cells. To locate particular information in a spreadsheet you would state the column letter and the row number, eg A3, B4, C2, D5 and E1 all have the word 'cell' printed in them (similar to the game of battleships). Which cells have a * in them? The number of columns and rows you can have depends on the software program you are using, but most

161

	A	B	C	D	E
1					cell
2		*	cell		*
3	cell				
4		cell	*		
5				cell	

Fig 6.4 Example of a simple spreadsheet

can go up to at least 100. When you are working on a spreadsheet you will find that the cell you are currently using will highlight, in a similar way to the cursor in a word processing package. You can move round the cells by using the cursor arrow keys or a mouse. If you wish to go to a particular cell you will be able to instruct the cursor to go to it, rather than using the cursor to find it. This facility is particularly useful if the spreadsheet has several hundred cells. Cell size can be changed, if you need to enter a particularly long figure. You will need to consult your manual to see how to use these facilities.

▶ *What uses do spreadsheets have?*

Most spreadsheets are used for presenting, analysing and planning financial information. For instance, a petty cash account, sales achieved by different sales representatives, expenditure of the department under budget headings, etc, could all be kept on a spreadsheet. Once the information is entered it can be saved, recalled later, updated, deleted, moved or copied. It is also possible to make calculations using formulae. A formula is a set of instructions that you type in, which makes the computer perform a particular task. An example would be an instruction to add up a column of figures.

■ DIY 6.1.7

1 The following terms are commonly used when dealing with spreadsheets:

- column
- row
- cell
- formulae

Explain each one, in your own words, giving examples.

2 Give 3 situations in which a spreadsheet may be used.

▶ *Entering data*

When you enter figures you will move to the cell required and key in the necessary information. If you are using dates or times you will need to check the spreadsheet manual to see which format is acceptable. For instance, to type in 3 June 1994 you may need to key in one of the following:

030694   03-06-94   3-6-94   03/06/94   3/6/94

or the package may accept one of the following:

3 June 94   3-Jun-94

If the format is 060394, this means the information needs to be put in month, day, year order. This is the accepted layout for international use and may be due to the fact that the program you are using was designed abroad or is intended for use across more than one country. America, for instance, uses this format most of the time.

For time, the options for 2.30 pm would include:

2.30 pm   02.30 pm   14.30   1430   14:30

Seconds are sometimes added:

14:30:10

You may use some of the cells for labelling columns or rows, and a heading may also be typed at the top. If using calculations (formula) these will also be contained in a cell.

In the example shown in Fig. 6.5, a formula would have instructed the computer to add the columns down and put the total figure in row 6, and to add the rows across and put the total in column G.

	A	B	C	D	E	F	G
1		SALES	FOR	1994			
2	£	SE	SW	WALES	NE	NW	TOTAL
3	ITEM 1	140 000	142 000	20 000	90 000	75 600	467 600
4	ITEM 2	20 900	12 000	49 000	35 000	26 900	143 800
5	ITEM 3	36 800	46 800	26 900	50 000	60 000	220 500
6	TOTAL	197 700	200 800	95 900	175 000	162 500	831 900

Fig 6.5 Example of completed spreadsheet

■ DIY 6.1.8

Which cells in Fig. 6.5 contain the following data?

1 50 000
2 831 900
3 SW
4 TOTAL
5 60 000

▶ *How is the formula entered?*

A formula always begins with = .

You will need to tell the computer exactly what you want to do. In the example above we wanted to add B3, B4 and B5 and put the result in B6. The type of formula for this would be =+B3:B5 which would mean B3, B5 and all the cells in between should be added together. The formula would be in cell B6, which is where the total would be entered by the computer. What formula do you think is in C6, D6, E6, F6 and G6? To make the calculations across the rows, a formula would have been placed in G3, G4, G5, and G6. For G3 this would have been =+B3:F3.

■ DIY 6.1.9

1 Find out from your supervisor or tutor the name of the spreadsheet package you are using.
2 By consulting the manual find out what formulae would be needed to make the calculations for the spreadsheet in DIY 6.1.8.
3 What would the formulae be for adding B3 to G3, missing out F3?
4 What would the formulae be for adding E3 and E5, missing out E4?
5 What would the formulae be if you wanted to increase all the figures in row G by 25 per cent?

A spreadsheet program will also allow you to 'project' figures. This means that if your spreadsheet has figures for sales for 1993 in column B and your company wants to know the expected increase in sales if there is a 5 per cent increase each year, a formula can be entered which will increase all the figures in the column by 5 per cent for 1994, 1995, 1996, 1997, etc. This facility is called projections and is used to estimate income and expenditure, sales and profits, growth and decline of products, etc.

▶ *Can you increase or decrease the size of your spreadsheet?*

If you wish to increase the size of your spreadsheet after you have already entered data, there will be an option (like adding a record in a database) for you to do this. In the same way you can reduce the number of columns and rows selected and delete data from the cells. Data in a cell can also be moved or copied to another cell. Information can also be sorted alphabetically and numerically. However, you will need to consult your manual to see what instructions your computer needs to do this.

■ DIY 6.1.10

By consulting your supervisor, tutor or manual find out how to do the following.

1 Insert an additional row.
2 Insert an additional column.

3 Widen a column.
4 Delete a column.
5 Delete a row.

▶ *What happens if mistakes are made?*

The spreadsheet information will only be of use to you and your company if the data is 100 per cent correct. This means that the information you enter must be checked when you are entering, before saving and again in a printout. It is crucial that any errors are corrected immediately, preferably before you save the file. If errors are identified afterwards, however, you will need to call the file back and make the correction, remembering to save the file again before exiting from the program. Not only must the data be correct but the formulae must also be doubly checked, because if these are wrong it could lead to important decisions being made on incorrect figures. Many programs have 'fault' messages that appear if you have entered the incorrect formulae and will not allow you to proceed until the problem is sorted out.

If a fault occurs on the program or with the system it should be reported to your supervisor. Always save your information before leaving the machine unattended.

▶ *Presenting information*

Many companies use spreadsheets for regular reviews of sales, stocks, etc, and these may be discussed at a weekly or monthly meeting. If you are producing spreadsheets on a regular basis you should ensure that the style used is consistent. If the managers wish to compare one month's printout with another the information should be in the same place and the headings the same. The style of type used and the size of print should also be consistent. Nearly all the spreadsheet packages allow printouts not only of the spreadsheet itself, but also in the form of bar charts, line graphs, pie charts and scattergrams. Quite often a diagram, such as a bar chart, is easier to understand than information in the form of a spreadsheet. If you use these facilities the printouts may be used for evidence in Units 13.2, 14.2 and 15.2.

▶ *What measures are used for ensuring security and confidentiality?*

Much of the information used in spreadsheets is likely to be highly sensitive, that is, confidential. It should not be taken out of the office or shown to anyone who is not involved with the work. Passwords or keywords can protect files and back-up files should be made in case files become corrupted – do not rely on your hard disk. Never leave your office with information displayed on the screen, as you do not know who may enter. Always save it, and either exit the program (if you are going to be quite a while) or cursor to another part of the spreadsheet which has empty cells (if it is only for a few minutes). You could also turn the screen down, so that the information cannot be seen.

▶ *Other computer packages*

Apart from using a computer for database and spreadsheet work, you will probably spend most of your time using a word processing package to create correspondence, reports and perhaps record keeping. Further information and DIYs are included in Unit 13 on page 350.

There are many other types of computer package available, some of which you may use in your job. These may include desk-top publishing, route planners, design and specification packages, accounts, diary systems and many others. It is possible to gain credit for this unit with any software package as long as the performance criteria and range statements are met. If you are unsure discuss it with your supervisor.

Completing Element 6.1

To complete this element on inputting data and text into a computer system you will need to put all the DIY tasks in your folder and carry out a final assessment. Competence must be proven in dealing with data which is complete and incomplete, with text and numerical processing, and with adding, amending and deleting data and text.

Claiming credit

Once you have completed your final assessment, you will need to write in your record book or folder how, when, where and what you have done to prove that you are competent.

The following is an example of how one trainee completed this claim:

I have been carrying out a training course and have worked part time, for the last 3 months, in an estate agent office at the weekends. During my training and at work I have used a database, spreadsheet and word processing package. I know which software to use for a particular job; for instance I have carried out work in a spreadsheet for petty cash, used a database file of customers and created letters and memos using a word processing package. If I was unsure of the writing or exactly where to put the information I checked with my supervisor or trainer. I read through my work before resaving it to make sure there were no errors. When saving information during my training course, I used my own file names. At work, however, we have a book and anyone saving information has to use the next number. If the file we are using has already been used then it would keep the same number. Occasionally I have been unable to complete all the updates that I needed to before we closed. I told my supervisor how far I had got and left the remaining work for the other staff to complete on Monday. I always left a note for the other members of staff as well as telling my supervisor.

I did not drink or eat around the computer equipment. All the leads were positioned so that no one would trip over them. At the beginning of the day and at the end I set up and closed down the equipment as requested. At no time did I leave confidential information lying about for clients to read, nor did I leave information on screen that was confidential. I have used passwords to access some of the packages but do not use passwords on my own disk. At the training centre all the trainees have their own allocated password to enter the computer system.

■ Element 6.2
LOCATE AND RETRIEVE DATA FROM A COMPUTER SYSTEM

Performance criteria

- Suitable computer software is used for location and retrieval of data
- Requested data is correctly located, accessed and retrieved within specified time constraints

- Search methods are appropriate and effective
- Confidential data is disclosed only to authorised people
- Equipment and data are safeguarded against damage
- Safe working practices are followed

Most of the criteria for this unit will be completed while carrying out the tasks and duties necessary for Element 6.1. However, it is important that you demonstrate competence in being able to find and retrieve particular files and documents.

There will probably be many occasions at work when you are requested to find a particular file on the computer system. At first this may be confusing, but once you are familiar with the procedures it will become an easy task for you to complete.

You must be able to identify in which of the software packages the file is likely to be saved, eg a database record, spreadsheet file or word processing file. Your computer screen may have a menu system which enables you to access the package or it may need you to type in the correct package file name at the C:> prompt. When you first start work, it is best to write down the instructions and the type of files kept on the packages. You will not need to ask unnecessary questions of your colleagues and staff if you keep a record yourself.

When you are trying to find a particular file, the package you are using may allow you to type in the file name and the computer will locate it. The command given to the package will depend on what you are trying to find. There is usually a 'find', 'locate' or 'goto' command. You will need to be familiar with the package to know how to use these particular facilities. When using database packages it is possible to find a record using a search condition of more than one field. For instance, in your DIY 6.1.3 you designed a database which included information on club members. If you wanted to find all the members named 'Smith' that lived in a particular area eg 'Woodstock', it would be possible to list these 2 conditions as part of the search. The computer package will then search for all the records that have 'Smith' as the surname and 'Woodstock' as the town.

In the previous element of this unit we discussed how to keep safe confidential information, by protecting your disk and your files. You will need to know about your organisation's procedures for keeping information safe and secure.

■ DIY 6.2.1

Make a list of the packages you have used at work or at your training centre. These should include a database, spreadsheet and word processing package. Write out instructions on how to locate and retrieve a file or record from the package. Make a printout of the directory for each package and cross-reference this to Element 6.3.

Completing Element 6.2

To complete this element on locating and retrieving data from a computer system you will need to put all the DIY tasks in your folder and carry out a final assessment. Competence must be proven in dealing with the locating and retrieving of files and records with reference codes and particular details. The methods of finding files must include automatic searching, manual searching and multi-field searching. The packages that you use should include at least one containing text and one containing numerical information.

Claiming credit

Once you have completed your final assessment, you will need to write in your record book or folder how, when, where and what you have done to prove that you are competent.

The following is an example of how one trainee completed this claim:

During my training course of 6 months (May–October) I have used the following computer packages: Works (spreadsheet, database and wordprocessing), Wordcraft 6 and Sage Sterling Accounts Package (which included stock control and payroll). I have located files using automatic and manual search commands. In the database package I have found files using 2 and 3 search conditions. The printouts are in my evidence portfolio. I know the type of information that is kept in these packages and in which package to look for a particular file. I have my own system of storing information on my disks. To make sure that the information on my disk (and on my section of the hard drive) is secure I keep the write protect notch on and use keywords (passwords) for confidential information. I always make a back-up of all my files at the end of each week.

I make sure that I follow the safety procedures of the centre at all times. I also make sure that the equipment is used so that damage is not caused to the hardware or software.

■ Element 6.3
PRINT DOCUMENTS USING A COMPUTER SYSTEM

Performance criteria

- Printed document is correct and complete
- Hard copy is clean, clearly printed and aligned correctly
- Efforts are made to minimise the wastage of paper
- Printer area is kept clean and tidy
- Where work is not achievable within specified deadlines reasons are promptly and accurately reported
- Work is achieved within agreed deadlines
- Documents are correctly collated and distributed as directed
- Equipment and data are safeguarded against damage
- Safe working practices are followed

It is quite likely that you will be using several different packages on your computer when working: not only databases and spreadsheets, but word processing packages, accounts and financial applications, diary reminder (time management) systems, stock control systems, desk-top publishing and graphics. In all the applications you become familiar with you should be careful when selecting an option to print that you have selected the correct file and that, if necessary, the printer has been given the correct instructions. If you make a mistake, the instructions to the printer can usually be cancelled (either through the package being used or on the printer direct). Always cancel an instruction if it is wrong as this will save paper and ribbon, ink or toner.

▶ What options for printing are there?

You may be asked to print a document in 'draft', which would normally mean one-and-a-half or double line spacing, to allow for corrections and changes to be written in the spaces. On some packages you will also have a 'draft' option on the printer instructions, which means that a dot matrix printer will only print the characters once instead of twice, and the laser printers will print lighter characters. By setting the graphics quality on 'medium' instead of 'high' you will also save ribbon, ink or toner.

171

Draft quality documents and graphics are not usually suitable for sending to customers and clients outside the organisation. Many companies will also produce extra copies on the printer instead of using a photocopier. Which works out the most cost-effective will depend on the type of printer you have, the number of copies being made and the type of photocopier you have. You will need to do some research to come up with a genuine comparison of cost. For the majority of letters that need one copy an extra copy is likely to be printed; with some printers carbon paper can be used.

Documents that have more than one page must be collated in the correct order and suitably fastened before distribution.

▶ *What is collating?*

This means putting the documents in correct page order. If you have 25 copies of a 30-page report it will take some time to put the pages in the correct order. You will need to have a work area where the 30 pages can be placed in separate piles; alternatively, you will have to sort the first 10 pages (or however many you can lay out) followed by the second and third, then the 3 sets need to be collated into the final sets. You will need to lay the documents out in a logical sequence, either in page number order or – to speed up the process – an order where both hands can work at the same time. For example, a 10-page document could be laid out as shown in Fig 6.6.

The left hand would pick up one page 10 and place it in the space in front, the right hand one page 9, and place it on top of page 10. Both hands can move at the same time and the document is collated from back to front. Complete sets can be stacked at right-angles to each other. Try it – it does work!

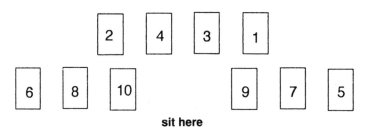

sit here

Fig 6.6

If you need to collate large documents frequently, it may be worth investing in a collating machine. The pages are placed in order into sections of the machine and a rubber roller pushes one sheet from each section out ready for stapling. It is also possible to have automatic stapling and folding machines attached to the process.

Once the documents have been collated they will need to be distributed correctly through the internal and external post systems. Do not forget to enclose confidential documents in a sealed envelope when circulating through the internal post.

▶ *What types of printer are there?*

There are 2 different types of printer, one called impact (where contact is made with the paper) and the other non-impact (where contact is not made with the paper). Examples of impact printers are dot matrix and daisywheel. A dot matrix printer creates the letters and other characters by printing dots in the shape of the character – the more dots the better the printing quality as there is less space between the dots. The printer head is rectangular in shape and is made up of pin heads – the pins are pushed forward and form the shape of the character. Dot matrix printers can print up to 200 characters per second and can also produce diagrams and graphics.

A daisywheel printer is the same as the daisywheel on a typewriter, where the spokes of the printing wheel have characters on the end and it turns to allow the correct character to touch the paper. A daisywheel can print at up to 70 characters per second but cannot produce diagrams and graphics.

Both these types of printer are widely used, and if you have a computer at home with a printer it is likely to be one of these (*see* Fig. 6.7). They are fairly inexpensive to buy but are quite noisy and because of this they tend not to be used very much in large offices. To reduce the noise, some companies cover the printer with an acoustic hood or screen, or when possible the printer may be located in a separate room.

Examples of non-impact printers are ink jet and laser (*see* Fig. 6.7). An ink jet printer squirts tiny jets of ink on to the paper to form the characters and the quality is very good. An ink jet printer can type up to 5 pages a minute. It is also able to form pictures and graphics. A

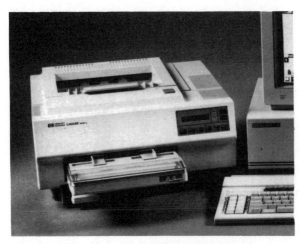

Fig 6.7 Dot matrix, ink jet and laser printers

laser printer uses laser beams to transfer the characters from the screen on to a drum, which turns and transfers the characters on to the paper. Lasers can produce a page of A4 typing in about 6 seconds. They can also produce excellent graphics.

Ink jet and laser printers are quiet to run but are more expensive to buy than impact printers. Laser printers can also be quite expensive to maintain as they require toner and parts to be changed when high numbers of copies are made. Colour printing is possible but may not be good enough for business letters.

▶ *What type of faults may occur?*

The most common type of fault is a paper jam. You should read the printer manual to see how to remove the paper. Be particularly careful with laser printers. Printers that rely on ink or toner powder will need new cartridges, but an indicator will usually let you know in good time when the cartridge is getting low. Graphics, spreadsheets and bold typefaces (especially large fonts), in particular, use the toner of a laser much quicker than the normal print of letters, memos and reports – so do not use these unless you need to.

If the printer is not receiving information check that the cables are securely connected between the computer and the printer, and that the printer is plugged in and switched on. If a printer is being shared, ensure that any switch box being used is also connected properly and switched on. Any other electrical faults or definition faults will need to be reported to your supervisor or tutor.

▶ *How can you maintain your printer?*

There are several maintenance procedures you can carry out which will help your printer stay free from problems. Before carrying any out, however, you should consult your manual and any computer technicians who may assist your department. Through ignorance you may cause more damage than remedy potential problems.

1 Keep the printer free from dust; keep the guards on when in operation.
2 No liquids should be allowed near the printer.
3 Brush out any excess paper dust or toner dust that collects inside

175

the printer.

4 On laser printers there are parts which can be cleaned with special tools supplied by the manufacturer.

5 Switch off at the end of the day.

6 Do not use creased or poor quality paper.

Completing Element 6.3

To complete this element on printing documents using a computer system you will need to put samples of your printouts obtained from databases, spreadsheets and word processing in your folder and carry out a final assessment. Competence must be proven in dealing with text and numerical processing (ie word processing, database and spreadsheet – although other packages may be acceptable as well). The documents in your folder must include text and tabular examples.

Claiming credit

Once you have completed your final assessment, you will need to write in your record book or folder how, when, where and what you have done to prove that you are competent.

The following is an example of how one trainee completed this claim:

During my course and my work experience I was asked to print many documents from the software packages. I made sure that I used recycled paper for 'test' printouts. This was old headed paper and reports that were no longer required. I made sure that I did not smudge the ink (as the printer was ink jet) by allowing the pages a few seconds to dry before handling them. Any messy copies were not used. The printer was kept clear of used paper and the cables were kept to the back of the table.

If I was unable to complete my work by the time required I spoke to my supervisor to tell him why, otherwise I left the work on the desk of the person that needed it. On some occasions I had to put the work in envelopes (internal and/or external) and put the work in the post.

When I had documents that had several pages I made sure they were in the right order before stapling or clipping them together. This was important when the pages were not numbered.

At all times I made sure that I followed the right procedure when setting up and closing down the equipment. I did not have fluids or other dangerous things near the equipment that may cause damage.

UNIT 7
Prepare documents

■ **Element 7.1**
RESPOND TO CORRESPONDENCE

Performance criteria

- Correspondence received for own reply is correctly identified
- Correspondence received outside own responsibility is routed promptly to correct person
- The speed, mode and cost of the reply reflect its urgency and importance
- The correct meaning and tone of the response are accurately conveyed by the language and grammar used
- Response is accurate, clear and in the style of the organisation
- Copies of correspondence and replies are stored in accordance with organisational procedures
- Procedures for the security and confidentiality of data are in accordance with organisational requirements

In any organisation there is a necessity to prepare correspondence both within the organisation and for sending outside. It is usual to send a memorandum to people within the organisation and business letters to people outside the organisation. In Unit 13 on page 360 you will see how to set out a memorandum and on page 359 how to set out a business letter. It will be necessary for you to be totally familiar with the layouts of these business documents before you are able to complete this unit.

Whatever job you hold it is likely that you will need to write your own memos and letters. A valuable member of staff is one who can recognise and carry out the tasks within their area of responsibility without constant reference to supervisors and managers. Therefore if you are able to recognise which items of correspondence, received in your section, can be dealt with by you without reference to your supervisor, you will be assisting the work flow of the department and easing the workload of others in your section. It is unlikely that you will be able to do this until you are totally familiar with the work of the section. At first you will need to ask your supervisor whether you are able to answer the correspondence, then draft the reply and check with your supervisor that it is correct before sending it. After a while you will able to recognise which correspondence you are able to deal with on a regular basis, without reference to your supervisor. However, if you are ever in doubt, it is always best to check rather than get something wrong.

When sorting the incoming post, you should identify which of the correspondence you are able to deal with and which needs to be directed to others in your section. It is important that post received for others is passed on quickly, so that the necessary action can be taken and replies sent as promptly as possible.

Correspondence may not only be received through the post, but also through the fax and electronic mail systems (if your organisation has them). When replying to correspondence you will need to decide whether you will use electronic mail, fax or post. Obviously it will depend on the urgency of the matter, the cost involved, the importance of the matter and the content. It is unlikely that you will send a confidential letter through the fax as anyone receiving it can read it. Although some faxes have confidential mailbox receivers not many companies actually have these in use.

▶ *How do you decide which correspondence you can deal with?*

It is with experience that you will get to know which documents can be dealt with quickly and easily by you. Your supervisor may delegate a particular area of work for you to deal with or you will start to want to carry out more tasks with responsibility. At the beginning of any job you should receive a job description and this will tell you what responsibilities are included in your position, but as your knowledge of the organisation and its personnel increase, you will find yourself better able to reply to correspondence or enquiries without having to ask your supervisor. This knowledge, together with getting to know how your section works, will also help you to recognise correspondence you are unable to deal with and should pass on to someone else.

■ DIY 7.1.1

You work as a clerical assistant to Mr Sam Ewart, Personnel Manager, and have received the post from the mailroom. You are responsible for keeping all the salary details, holiday information and details on new jobs. Sort through the mail and make 2 lists, one of items you are able to deal with and the other of items that need to be passed to Sam.

1 Letter asking whether you have any vacancies for receptionists.
2 Letter asking for an application form for a vacancy that you are currently advertising.
3 Memo from a member of staff asking if he can take 5 weeks' holiday at one time.
4 Letter marked confidential for Mr Ewart.
5 Invitation to Mr Ewart to attend a presentation at a local school.
6 Letter addressed to personnel and marked 'Private'.
7 Memo from a member of staff asking for a copy of the latest pay scales.
8 Letter from a member of staff who is unhappy in her job.
9 Box of stationery received from central stores with a form that needs signing and returning to confirm receipt of the items.
10 Letter from a bank that is asking for confirmation of an employee's salary for a mortgage application.

▶ *How should you deal with the correspondence yourself?*

In order to help you deal with the correspondence your organisation will have a selection of stationery, such as letter headed paper and memo paper. Once you have sorted out the items you are able to deal with it is important that the replies are sent as quickly as possible. However you must make sure that the presentation, grammar and spelling are all correct. Correspondence sent out with errors will only give the receiver a poor impression of you, your department and your organisation. It could even result in a loss of business for your company.

Most organisations have a particular way in which they lay out their correspondence. This is called 'house style'. The company may want a particular style of presentation, type of punctuation, typeface and size, the way in which enclosures are indicated, etc. Regardless of how you are taught to lay out correspondence at school or college for your examinations, or how you did it at a previous company, the organisation's own house style must be followed.

There are a few basic rules that may help you when preparing correspondence:

1 Presentation should always follow house style – if you do not know what your organisation's house style is, find out! If there is not one, use one which is used by the majority of people in your section.
2 Use the right piece of paper for the job. Letters should always be typed on letter headed paper. The organisation may have many different types of headed paper, for instance with different departments or directors' names on. Memos should be typed on memo headed paper.
3 Never allow your correspondence to be sent out with spelling, grammar or printing errors. Make sure that when you print on headed stationery the paper is placed straight in the printer, otherwise you will end up with a crooked letter or memo.
4 Make sure all facts and figures such as dates, times and amounts of money are correct.
5 If errors are found, the correction should be unnoticeable. Use a suitable method of correction according to the paper used and error made.
6 Always mark the correspondence to show enclosures and continuation pages to avoid confusion. Remember to enclose all the contents in the envelope.
7 Make sure that you sign all your correspondence before posting it. Memos are not usually signed in the same way as letters but can be initialled. This indicates to the reader that it has been read and checked by the writer.
8 Prepare the envelopes and address packages according to Post Office regulations (*see* page 240). Indicate in pencil on the envelopes which class of post you wish the post room to use and if a special service is required.
9 Letters which are confidential, private or personal should be marked with the appropriate word on the correspondence and on the

envelope. Memos with these markings should be placed in a sealed envelope as well as any internal circulation envelopes used.

■ DIY 7.1.2

Collect samples of letters and memos that have different styles of presentation. Indicate which style your organisation uses, or if they do not have a house style, the style you normally use.

▶ *How do you write your own correspondence?*

Correspondence will either give information or ask for it. The message should be clear and not confuse the reader. There should be no vagueness or confusing language. The correspondence should be to the point without being too brief, blunt, impolite or too vague. Tact must always be used particularly if dealing with a complaint or problem. The material should be carefully organised and all points covered while keeping a pleasant tone. In general, correspondence should be:

● concise and to the point
● written in straightforward language
● easy to understand
● accurate and tactful
● courteous in tone
● in a logical order
● follow house style.

The opening paragraph should indicate what the correspondence is about, the middle paragraph(s) should contain the information being requested or given, the last paragraph should bring it to a polite close. Words should never be used unless you are absolutely sure of both their meaning and their spelling. Avoid words that might confuse the reader or be misinterpreted.

When you first start to write your own correspondence, it is useful to make a list of all the points you need to cover in a logical order – refer to any previous correspondence which will indicate the information being requested or given. If you use a word processor then, with time, you may find that you are able to create your correspondence directly on to screen, without needing to draft it by hand first. When using a word processor, always spellcheck your work and use a thesaurus to broaden your vocabulary (while remembering the rules on using straightforward language – do not use complicated words for the sake of it).

■ DIY 7.1.3

Your company has advertised a vacancy for a telephonist and applications have started to come in. Draft a letter that would be suitable for sending to the applicants. An application form will need to be enclosed with the letter and it will be signed by S Ewart, Personnel Manager. Write a memo to Sam Ewart, informing him that you have received 12 applications to date and that you have drafted a letter to the applicants. Ask him to approve the letter so that it can be sent out.

▶ *Why and how should you proofread?*

Proofreading is usually thought of as a tiresome, tedious job. However, the quality of your work, and the impression you and your organisation wish to give both internally and externally, should mean that errors in correspondence are simply not acceptable. Proofreading is time consuming but if a customer or client were to receive correspondence with errors, particularly in figure work, this could lead to a loss in confidence and possibly business.

Practice makes perfect. The more proofreading you do the better you will get at it, although when you have an important document or one with a lot of figures in it, it is useful to get someone else to read through the document as well – providing of course that it is not so confidential that another member of staff cannot see it.

When writing correspondence always use a dictionary if you are unsure of the meaning or spelling of a word – keep a list of commonly misspelt words at hand for easy referral. If using a word processor use the spellcheck as a matter of routine – it will save time and help you towards error-free correspondence. However, do remember that a spell-check may not identify:

● grammatical errors

- words that have been double typed
- incorrect information or figures
- words, lines or paragraphs that have been missed out
- word substitutions
- incorrect punctuation
- inconsistent presentation.

Correspondence will still need to be checked by you to make sure that any errors are made unobtrusively.

▶ *What is an unobtrusive correction?*

You will find a number of methods and materials can be used to make corrections. The choice will depend on the type of error and the equipment you are using. The method should be one that suits the type of correction to be made – it should not be seen easily by the eye and not draw away the reader's attention from the content of the correspondence. Large blobs of correction fluid smudged over the paper or holes made with rubbers are not acceptable, and typed correspondence with incorrect words crossed out and rewritten in pen, however neatly, should never be allowed out of the office.

The type of correction chosen will also depend on the equipment used. Word processors have the advantage of allowing you to key text in, proofread on screen and correct errors as you go along, and the document can then be finally spellchecked. An error-free document can then be printed. Draft copy may be printed first. For example, a long report or correspondence with many figures will need to be carefully checked.

Do not get into the habit of printing all your documents to proofread – this is a waste of time and materials. Many sheets of paper may be used in an attempt to get a correct copy when careful screen proofreading could result in getting it right first time. If you do need to print to proofread a document, use the back of previously wasted paper.

Modern typewriters normally offer a correction facility and/or a display to help proofreading and error correction. Correction tapes can be used with many typewriters. There are two types. One uses a sticky tape which lifts the error from the paper and needs to be used with carbon-based cartridges. The other type is made from a chalky substance and is used with nylon ribbons and cartridges. The error is corrected by covering it up with a white impression. Both types of correction ribbon can only be used for small errors of a few letters and should not be used for whole sentences or paragraphs.

■ DIY 7.1.4

You have been given the following memorandum to proofread. Check it and retype. There are a total of 12 errors. Can you spot the errors that would not have been identified by a word processor spellcheck facility?

MEMORANDUM
To: Sara Lippett
From: Kris Bourne
Date:

CHANGE OF COMPUTOR SOFTWARE
As I mentioned to you earlier this month, we have ordered new software for the computers in the sales Department. We would now liek you to install it during the next 2 week's. staff are on holiday and the machines are not being used as as much as they would normaly be.

Please let me no if you are able to do this, you can contack me on egstension 243 anytime this week.

Apart from producing memos and letters you may also need to produce form letters.

▶ *What are form letters?*

A form letter is one which has the majority of the information prepared, but needs a date, name, address and salutation. Form letters are business letters sent from one organisation to another. The advantage with this type of letter is that it saves time having to retype the contents each time. Form letters can either be printed by a duplicating process (offset litho, photocopying, etc) or word processed. The missing information can be added using a typewriter, but care must be taken to make sure that the letter is inserted correctly and the spaces lined up before typing the information.

Organisations may have a series of form letters that are used. They can also be stored on disk. The correct letter can then be retrieved and the information added before printing off.

DIY 7.1.5

Design a form letter that could be used by an accounts department reminding their customers that payment of their account is outstanding and should be made within 7 days. Leave a space for the date, name, address, salutation, account number and the balance outstanding.

▶ *What type of response will you make?*

The type of people that you will write to will be:

1 people internal to the organisation
2 people external to the organisation

This may include:

● your own boss and more senior staff
● regular clients or customers
● first-time enquirers
● occasional contacts
● overseas contacts

The type of reply you make to these contacts will depend on the nature and size of your organisation and will be based on your duties and responsibilities. You may find that you will be responsible for writing standard replies, such as the form letters mentioned above, or individual replies that may require you to carry out some investigation, letters of apology or to explain things. Your correspondence may take the form of oral or written responses, depending on the type of correspondence received, the person involved and the equipment available to you. If you make an oral response it is important to make a note of it for the file.

For instance, an emergency order may be taken verbally over the telephone or face to face, but will need to be followed by a written

185

confirmation on headed paper. A written invitation from a boss or someone making a complaint may require initial verbal contact for confirmation followed by a written response. Correspondence requesting information may require a brief verbal or written acknowledgement to allow you time to find out the necessary information. The use of a fax machine will allow typed correspondence to be sent quicker than post and may be used when the matter is urgent.

■ DIY 7.1.6

You have received the following telephone messages. Reply to them in writing.

TELEPHONE MESSAGE

To: From: Jayne Swaffield
Date: 10 May   Time: 9.05   Organisation: Accounts
                                                                          Department
Tel No: Ext: 4839   Fax:

Message

She has received the stationery supplies that were sent yesterday. The order has been put together incorrectly. There are 2 items not ordered and 3 that were requested are missing. She is definitely not very happy and wants an explanation.

TELEPHONE MESSAGE

To: From: John Prior, Manager
Date: 12 May   Time: 12.00   Organisation: Haven Hotel,
                                                                          Burbidge BH21 03H
Tel No: 0422 492041   Ext: 124   Fax:

Message

He would like confirmation that the meeting on Wednesday of next week of the northern sales reps will take place. He wants to know numbers (last figures I had were 30) and the time that coffee is to be served in the morning.

TELEPHONE MESSAGE

To: From: Jenny Small
Date: Time: Organisation: Canteen Assistant
Tel No: Ext: 235   Fax:

Message

Jenny has heard that other staff in the canteen section are being paid more than she is. She would like you to send details of what the others are receiving.

▶ *Will you sign all the correspondence you write?*

This will depend on the rules of your organisation. In some cases the company will be quite happy for you to sign all the correspondence you write. However, it may depend on the content of the letter or memo. At first always check with your supervisor whether you can sign the correspondence or not – you will soon get to know what the regulations are.

▶ *What should you do with the copies of correspondence kept in the department?*

These should be filed in the appropriate place. This may be the customer record files, personnel files, your own filing system or a correspondence file. Correspondence files are usually kept in chronological (date) order with the most recent on top. This makes it easier for people using the file to find the most recent letters. It is important that you file away the copies of the correspondence as quickly as possible in case anyone else wishes to use the file. If a telephone query comes in to the office when you are not present and someone tries to answer the query without having an up-to-date file, incorrect information may be given. This will leave the customer or client with a poor impression of the organisation and you will not be respected by your colleagues for putting them in that position. All the records and files should be treated as confidential and you should not disclose to one customer any information on another customer – for instance, what they have purchased or the current state of their account. All companies have different procedures for confidentiality and security. This may include certain files being locked with restricted access, keywords and passwords on computer files and word processing files, restricted copies in circulation and keeping your own files out of sight of others in the department. It is important that you find out what your organisation's policies are regarding confidentiality and security and stick to them. In some organisations (eg banks and building societies) you may be required to sign a declaration that you will not discuss or disclose any of the information you have access to, especially outside the company. These rules would apply whether you worked for the organisation full time, part time or for a short period on work experience. Breaking these rules could result in losing your job.

■ DIY 7.1.7

One of your friends has asked you for help in writing a report on security and confidentiality of correspondence. List down the systems and procedures you are familiar with and write a short paragraph on each. Do not include any reference to your organisation or mention systems used at companies you are familiar with.

Completing Element 7.1

To complete this element on responding to correspondence you will need to put all the DIY tasks in your folder and carry out a final assessment. Competence must be proven in dealing with replies to correspondence that has been received from people both internal and external to your organisation. The type of replies must include standard and individual.

Claiming credit

Once you have completed your final assessment, you will need to write in your record book or folder how, when, where and what you have done to prove that you are competent.

The following is an example of how one trainee completed this claim:

During my course and my work experience (Sept–June) I have written many different letters and memos for my own signature and for that of my boss. The copies are in my portfolio and I have kept a log of correspondence that I have written. I was unable to keep copies as the content was confidential to the organisation.

When writing the correspondence I made sure that the grammar, spelling and layout were correct before signing. I made corrections on screen before printing out. I carefully checked figures against the original draft. I had to use catalogues and price lists to find the figures. All the copies were filed in the customer records and I kept copies of the non-confidential ones for my portfolio.

I always made sure that the tone of my correspondence was friendly but carried the correct message; the language I used was simple but clear. My supervisor checked several of my first attempts and then I was allowed to write and sign the documents myself. If the matter was urgent I made sure that the correspondence was hand delivered internally and went first-class post externally. On some occasions the letter was faxed as well as posted. This made sure that the person receiving it had the facts in front of them in the shortest possible time.

Element 7.2
PREPARE A VARIETY OF DOCUMENTS

Performance criteria

- Instructions are understood
- Completed documentation meets the requirements of the workplace
- Layout, spelling, grammar and punctuation are consistent and in accordance with conventions and house style
- Corrections, when appropriate, are unobtrusive
- Security and confidentiality of information is maintained
- Copies and originals are correctly collated and routed, as directed
- Where work is not achievable within specified deadlines reasons are promptly and accurately reported
- Work is achieved within agreed deadlines

▶ *Apart from correspondence what other documents may you need to prepare?*

It will depend on the type of organisation and the type of department you work in. Each department has documents that are specialist documents; for instance, a Purchasing Department will prepare orders, a Wages Department will prepare payslips. The work of the department will determine the type of document produced in addition to the usual memos and letters (*see* Fig. 7.1).

DIY 7.2.1

Match the documents with the departments.

orders	sales
payslips	training
invoices	salaries and wages
publicity material	purchasing
vacancy advertisements	marketing
sales reports	personnel

In addition to the departmental documents there will also be general documents that need to be prepared. These may include reports, statements, end-of-period figures, meeting documents, articles,

189

Fig 7.1 Examples of business correspondence: an enquiry, a quotation and other documents

advertisements, notices, invitations, etc. Some of these documents will be typewritten, some may be handwritten – it will depend on the instructions you have received.

▶ *Which documents will you be responsible for?*

At first you will probably have to prepare figures or reports for your own area of work or section. This could be a report on how many orders have been placed in the last month, what is their total value, how many are new customers, etc. To find out this information you will need to access the files and other information sources within your department. The directors or managers of your organisation will hold regular meetings and will need to discuss the progress of each of the departments. It is quite likely that your organisation will have an aim or plan of work for the year, and the managers will want to monitor progress in line with this plan. If progress is slow then explanations and corrections will need to be made.

The report that you make will be submitted to your supervisor, who will also be receiving reports from other individuals. It will then be your supervisor's turn to write a departmental report for submission further up the line. Your supervisor will not have time to check that the content and figures of your report are 100 per cent accurate – it is your responsibility. However, if mistakes are submitted to the managers, it will be your supervisor's responsibility – as their name will be on the final document submitted and they will be accountable for any errors made.

Make sure that you fully understand any instructions given to you by your colleagues or supervisor before starting the task. If you come up against a problem, inform the correct person and agree what action you will take.

▶ *Does all documentation have a house style?*

Not always, but some organisations will want the same layout, typeface and typesize used. This is especially the case where documents are being submitted to a meeting of the managers or directors. This ensures that all the documentation submitted to the same meeting has the same appearance. Documents such as enquiries, orders, acknowledgements, invoices, statements, etc, are likely to be on pre-printed stationery and therefore have a set layout which will include the organisation's details such as name, address, telephone and fax numbers, VAT number (if any), etc.

■ **DIY 7.2.2**

Research and present the following information in the most suitable form.

1 Exchange currency rates for all the European Union countries.
2 The names and addresses of 3 local senior schools.
3 The organisation of your section within your company, listing the names and the titles of the people concerned.

▶ *Should you still proofread all documents?*

In Element 7.1 we discussed how important it was to ensure that the correspondence you produced was error-free, proofread and accurate in content. It is just as important for any other documentation. The documents must be error-free and any corrections made should be unobtrusive. Quite often standard documents such as delivery notes, invoices, etc, are printed on NCR (no carbon required) paper. The sets of sheets may also be numbered which means that you cannot just keep using a new set when making a mistake. The different sheets will usually be on different coloured paper – pink, yellow, blue as well as white. If an error is made on these sheets it will be necessary to use coloured correcting fluid, making sure that it is quite dry before typing the correction. The NCR paper will not work twice, therefore it will be necessary to correct each sheet individually.

■ DIY 7.2.3

List the different types of correction method you are aware of and give a situation where each method is best used.

You may find that when you create a report or a long document it will be necessary to include a chart or diagram. This may be done by 'cutting and pasting'. This means that you leave a space or cut the paper where the diagram needs to be inserted and tape the parts together. The sheet can then be photocopied to give a good master copy, ready for recopying or circulation. However, you must make sure that the amended sheet is collated correctly with the remaining pages.

▶ *What is collating?*

This means putting the documents in the correct page order. Pages will usually be numbered using arabic numbers, eg 1, 2, 3, or small roman numerals, eg i, ii, iii. You should be familiar with both. If you have 25 copies of a 30-page report to make, it will take some time to put the pages in the correct order. You will need to have a work area where the 30 pages can be placed in separate heaps. Alternatively, you will have to sort the first 10 pages (or however many you can lay out)

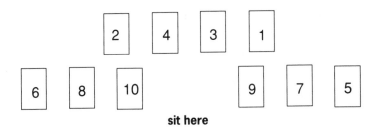

sit here

Fig 7.2

followed by the second set of 10 pages and then the third. These three heaps would then have to be collated into the final sets. You will need to lay out the documents in a logical sequence, either in page number order or, to speed up the process, an order where both hands can work at the same time. For example, a 10-page document could be laid out as shown in Fig. 7.2.

The left hand will take one copy of page 10 and place it in the space in front, and then the right hand will take one copy of page 9 and place it on top of page 10. Both hands can move at the same time and the document is collated back to front. Complete sets can be stacked away from the work area.

Collator. If you are lucky, your organisation may have a machine to do this job for you, called a collator. If you are asked to carry out a lot of collating, it may be worth investigating the cost of a collating machine. Machines are also available that automatically collate, staple and fold documents.

Jogger. Another machine which helps in a print room is a jogger. The photocopied documents are placed in the jogger and it shakes them together so that the corners are neatly together before the document is stapled.

Stapling may be an automatic process in some photocopiers. If you do the stapling, you may use a manual stapler or an electric one – take care with an electric one as it is fast and likely to make you jump when you use it, so keep your fingers out of the way!

Duplexing (back-to-back copying) can be carried out on a basic machine by feeding the same sheet of paper into the machine again. This reduces the amount of paper used, so is cost-effective. It also reduces the amount of paper that has to be circulated, which may reduce postal costs (if the document is to be posted to customers, for example), or reduce the amount of space required for filing (if the document is being distributed to staff).

Computers. The most intelligent photocopiers combine computing with copying. Information can be entered on to a computer and stored, and this can then be recalled and automatically printed directly by the copier without having a 'hard' copy (original copy) to print from. It is also possible to network a photocopying machine to allow it to receive and send information to and from distant computers.

▶ *How is a multi-page document held together?*

There are many different methods of securing documents apart from stapling them. Some need special equipment but others are cheap and as efficient as stapling.

Paperclips

Paperclips come in different sizes, from quite small to huge (up to 50 mm–75 mm long). They are quick and easy to use and fairly cheap to buy. The disadvantage with them is that they tend to pick up other documents when they are kept in a pile.

Treasury tags

To use tags, holes need to be punched in the document, either in the top left-hand corner or half-way down the left-hand side. The treasury tags have plastic strips at each end which are threaded through the holes. Tags are available in different colours and lengths, with longer ones for the bulky documents. They are quick, cheap and efficient to use, but are not really suitable for sending documents externally.

Ring binders

Once again, the document would have to be hole punched. Ring binders may have two or four rings and come in different sizes. They are quite expensive and would not be the normal way of securing everyday documents. However, they are extremely useful for items such as staff handbooks or a set of instructions.

Spiral binding

This process needs a special machine which is used to punch oblong holes along the edge of the document, and to open up the teeth of the plastic spiral. The pages are fed carefully on to the open teeth, and when the last page has been positioned the teeth can be closed, securing the document. Metal continuous spirals are also used in this way, except that the spiral is pushed on from the bottom to the top of the document. Electric machines are available that will carry out the whole process and would be a useful piece of equipment to any office that regularly produces booklets requiring binding. The result is a professional look to the document which is suitable for internal and external use.

Flat comb binder

This is a similar process to the spiral binding, the difference being that two plastic strips are used, one with spikes and one with holes. Holes are punched in the document and the spikes are pushed through the holes. The holed strip is then pushed over the spikes and is heat sealed, the document being secured between the two plastic strips. Again a professional look is obtained but special equipment is required that is quite expensive to purchase (*see* Fig. 7.3).

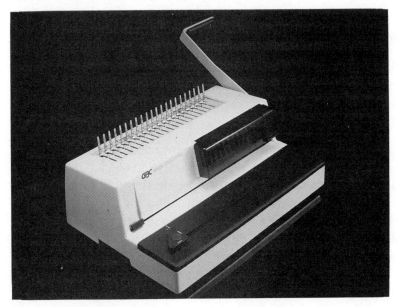

Fig 7.3 A comb binder

Slide binder

A slide binder is the easiest to use, and is quite cheap, but is not so useful. The binder is made from solid plastic and is slid along the edge of the document (no hole punching is needed). The pages are held firmly but they can be difficult to keep open when reading, as the book would not stay open flat on a desk. Although this is not essential, a plastic tray with guidelines is available, which helps to get the binder on easily and in the correct place.

Heat binding

This gives the document a professional look, similar to a paperback book. The document has a gummed strip placed along the edge and this is put into a heat machine which locks the strip into place. Once cool, the document can be handled without fear of losing the pages. Special equipment is required and this is expensive, so it would not be worth buying unless a lot of binding is required.

If you meet any problems in collating and securing your documents, make sure that you inform your supervisor. You should also tell your colleagues of the delay that will occur in getting the finished work back to them.

▶ *How to circulate documents*

If a document requires the attention of more than one person or department, you will need either to make the number of copies required or attach a routing slip, sometimes called a circulation slip (*see* Fig. 7.4).

This slip should be attached to the document needing circulation detailing the names and departments who need to see it. Once the document has been seen by the named person they will cross out their name from the list and pass the document on to the next person. The last person named will return it to the person identified at the bottom of the slip. This method should only be used when a document is not urgent as it may take some time for it to circulate. Even if 'Urgent' is written on the routing slip it will still take several days to circulate and may lay in someone's tray if they are out of the office.

ROUTING SLIP

Read or copy and pass on in order shown below:

Name	Department	Initial/Date

Please return to:

By:

Fig 7.4 Routing or circulation slip

■ DIY 7.2.4

Type or write the following information in a suitable format. Add a circulation slip listing the people detailed.

We need to update our records and check that the information we have on file is correct, as new car permits will be issued at the end of next month. Please read and make any necessary alterations. When complete the document should be returned to me in Personnel. Thanks Sharon Mackett.

Simon Purkiss, Sales, Fiat L130 JJK; Peter Grimes, Dispatch, Skoda YAP 412R; Stanley Benson, Personnel, Jaguar, Xl 34; Eric Young, Sales, BMW K927 JLS; Gill Davis, Purchasing, Metro J938 NKS; John Spracklin, Sales, Escort K238 NSO; Micky Eldicott, Director, BMW L098 AND; Simon House, Purchasing, Granada H523 NOW; Keith Spalding, Director, Rover L739 BOW.

▶ *What if you cannot get all the work done on time?*

You will need to start estimating the time it takes you to carry out tasks. Routine tasks are fairly easy to estimate as you will be doing these all the time. Special jobs or tasks that are only carried out every so often are more difficult to estimate and it will depend on how much information needs to be researched and collated before you can start. Your supervisor may set a deadline for you – 'I need it for Friday' or 'I need it yesterday' may be the type of deadline that you are familiar with. Obviously you cannot produce something yesterday, but the supervisor is indicating that it is urgent and should be a priority for you. If you have any difficulty in completing the work you should keep your supervisor informed – a decision may need to be taken on whether more people should be allocated to the task or whether others should be advised that the information will be late. There will always be busy and hectic times at work, and it may be necessary for you to work extra time to complete the work in hand. If it becomes common practice that you are working extra time, you may need to discuss this with your supervisor. Either you are not organising your work as well as you could, or your workload has increased and another pair of hands is necessary.

Wherever possible, though, work should be completed to the agreed deadlines. You will then become a valuable, reliable member of staff. The more work you carry out, the more responsibility you will be given, which will make the job more interesting. This may result in you being given a better job with more pay!

■ DIY 7.2.5

Prepare a notice for your organisation's noticeboards. You need to inform staff of a Dinner & Dance that will be held on 20 December, tickets will be £5 each for staff and £10 for guests. It will be held at the Pavilion, starting at 7.30 till 12.30.

Completing Element 7.2

To complete this element on preparing a variety of documents you will need to put all the DIY tasks in your folder and carry out a final assessment. Competence must be proven in dealing with documents which includes text, tables, lists and numbers.

Claiming credit

Once you have completed your final assessment, you will need to write in your record book or folder how, when, where and what you have done to prove that you are competent.

The following is an example of how one trainee completed this claim:

Whilst working with Cold Co Ltd I have been responsible for preparing different documents. The instructions I received from my supervisor were sometimes verbal and sometimes written. If I was unsure of what was required I checked with the person wanting the work carried out. The documents that I have prepared include orders, statements, payslips, reports, agendas and minutes. Where possible I have included samples of these documents in my portfolio. However, some of the information is confidential and I am unable to provide copies. I have kept a record of the number and type of documents prepared which has been signed by my supervisor. The agendas that I prepared were circulated to all the managers. A routing slip was not necessary as individual copies were made. All the documents were kept confidential and secure, and copies were filed away as quickly as possible.

I made sure that the documents I prepared were accurate and that any errors found were corrected. I followed the house style for the documents by looking at the files to see how they were laid out before I typed them. On some occasions it was necessary for me to draft the documents first. If it was difficult to get access to a word processor I hand wrote these for my supervisor.

Most of the time I was able to meet the deadlines required by the staff. Occasionally when I was very busy I had to inform people that I would not be able to carry out their work for 2/3 days. I made sure that the most urgent work was completed first. (See also my claim under Element 3.1 – Plan and organise own work schedule.)

UNIT 8
Receive and transmit information

■ Element 8.1
RECEIVE AND TRANSMIT INFORMATION ELECTRONICALLY

Performance criteria

- The most appropriate transmission system, in relation to urgency, cost and security, is selected
- The equipment selected is correctly used as laid down in operating instructions
- Material is prepared accurately and correctly for transmission
- Information is transmitted to correct location within required deadlines
- Outgoing and incoming communications are dealt with in accordance with approved organisational procedures
- Incoming information is promptly routed to correct location
- Security and confidentiality procedures conform to organisational requirements
- Any faults are promptly rectified or reported

Modern telephone systems have been designed to meet the needs of an organisation of any size. A switchboard may be used that allows a number of incoming calls to be connected and then transferred to the relevant person or department. Internal telephones allow members of staff to contact each other direct using an internal telephone extension number. They also allow contact with the main switchboard, which may have to be used to request an outside line in order to make an external telephone call.

You will find that all organisations, whatever their size, depend upon telephone contact. Some conduct a major part of their business over the telephone, for example orders for goods from a mail-order catalogue. They rely on well-trained members of staff to answer and

200

Fig 8.1 An office telephone

record information quickly, efficiently and accurately. Mistakes cost time and money and will not be tolerated by a business organisation. In an emergency situation, mistakes might even cost lives.

When members of staff answer the telephone, they act as representatives of that organisation and therefore must create the right impression. Staff have a responsibility to communicate information accurately and clearly, using an appropriate style, tone and vocabulary. Good communication skills are essential if this is to be achieved. A member of staff who sounds competent, efficient and gives a good impression of the organisation over the telephone is a valuable addition.

▶ What equipment are you likely to use?

There is a range of telecommunications equipment available to suit the demands of each organisation. This depends on the size of the

201

organisation and the department in which you work. You may find yourself using a telephone switchboard with up to 10 incoming lines and numerous internal extensions, or you may be responsible for using an office telephone using a single, direct line out or linked to a main switchboard.

▶ *Telephone*

Modern telephones offer numerous additional facilities, such as last number redial, memory, selective call-barring and secrecy. They also offer diversion services, such as no-reply diversion or engaged diversion, 3-way service and call waiting. There are other facilities and services available, some of which are free although others will be charged for. It is important that you understand the facilities available on the telephones you use at work (and at home) and appreciate how these might be used to improve your efficiency when at work.

■ DIY 8.1.1

In your own words explain how the telephone system is used in your workplace or training centre. How do you answer the telephone? What special facilities does your telephone system offer? What methods are used to reduce telephone charges?

▶ *Switchboard*

A switchboard is used to accept incoming calls, allow them to be answered and then transferred to the appropriate person or department. Calls can be held or 'parked' while the switchboard operator deals with other calls, locates a particular person or finds out information. Switchboards can be used to monitor all outgoing external calls made by members of staff. They will need to request an outside line from the switchboard operator before they can dial out. Some switchboards require the operator to dial the number and then transfer the call to the member of staff once it is connected. Other switchboards can be set up to allow extensions to have direct access to an outside line by dialling a number, eg 9.

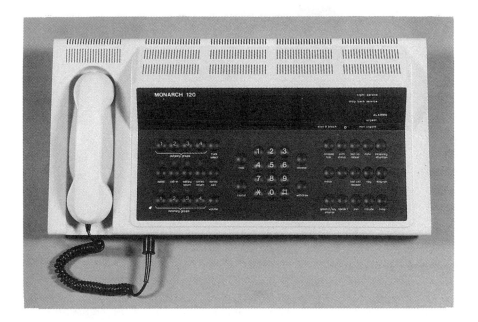

Fig 8.2 An electronic switchboard

Switchboards can be programmed to prevent long-distance calls being made. BT National Standard rate calls can be made between 0800 and 1800 hours. However, calls made using BT Chargecard and mobile telephones are charged at peak rate between 0800 and 1300 hours. Cheap rate calls can be made from 1800–0800 hours. Saturday and Sunday are also charged at cheap rate. Internal calls made within an organisation are free of charge as they are operated through the organisation's own switchboard.

▶ *Answering machines*

These machines are used to answer the telephone when no one is available, ensuring that no calls or messages are missed. An announcement is recorded which invites the caller to leave a message after the 'bleep'. Answering machines allow the office to be unattended whilst orders and messages are left, recorded on the machine, during any time of the day or night.

203

Fig 8.3 An answerphone

If you are answered by an answering machine, do not be frightened. Speak slowly and clearly, stating your business and remembering to leave your name and telephone number. It is also wise to state the date and time of day that you are calling. If you do find yourself surprised by an answering machine, replace your receiver, write down your message and call back when you have prepared yourself.

The first person in the office in the morning should play the recorded messages to find out if there is anything important that needs attention straight away. When the tape is played back it is wise to have a pen and paper ready to jot down all information and telephone numbers.

▶ *What codes of practice and legal requirements should you follow?*

In addition to basic telephone services BT offers telephones and other telecommunications apparatus for sale or rent together with a range of other services including apparatus repair, data communications and services such as recorded information and electronic mail. Any apparatus approved by law for connection to BT's network can be used in conjunction with BT's services, whether supplied by BT or not.

The government's marking orders make it easy to see whether or not equipment has been approved for connection to BT's network. The

APPROVED for connection to tele-
communication systems specified in
the instructions for use subject to the
conditions set out in them.

S/1016/3/L/501938

Fig 8.4 Example of BT approved label

'approved' or 'prohibited' marks as shown in Fig. 8.4 should be clearly
visible on the outside of the equipment. Approved equipment is
identified by a green circle and prohibited apparatus by a red triangle. It
is unlawful for unapproved apparatus to be connected to a BT network.

BT detail their Code of Practice for Consumers in the Consumer
Advice section of the *Phone Book*. The code of practice gives details
regarding:

Telephone service	Telephone bills
Fault repair	Network faults
Operator services	Payphones
Phone Books	Telex
Message (Callstream) Service	Complaints
Services for disabled customers	Arbitration
Telemessages and international telegrams.	

If you do have cause for complaint you are advised to contact your
local BT office first so that they may have an opportunity to put right
any problems. Refer to the Customer Advice section of the *Phone
Book* for details regarding claims and refunds under BT's Customer
Service Guarantee. If this action does not resolve your problem, obtain
independent advice from a local Telecommunications Advisory
Committee, Citizens' Advice Bureau, Consumer Advice Centre or
Trading Standards Department, or one of the telecommunications
organisations recognised by the Secretary of State.

As a last resort, you can contact the Office of Telecommunications
(OFTEL) which was set up as a government department under the
Telecommunications Act 1984 to regulate telecommunications within
the UK. Names and addresses of independent and advisory bodies can
be found at the back of the *Phone Book*.

▶ *How should a telephone be answered?*

1   A ringing telephone should be answered as quickly as possible. (Some organisations guarantee that your call will be answered in no more than 4 rings!)

2   Identify the organisation and yourself clearly. (Organisations will have an approved method of doing this.)

3   Use a pen and paper to note all information.

4   Identify the caller and either deal with the call yourself or transfer the caller to someone who can help. (Announce the name of the caller before transferring the call to the other person.)

5   Always remain courteous, polite and, above all, helpful.

6   Keep the caller informed of your actions so they are aware of any delay and never tell a caller to 'hang on'.

7   If the call is for someone who is not available, ask if anyone else can help; if not, take a message.

8   Do not give confidential information – pass the call to your supervisor.

9   If you do not have the information requested at hand, offer to ring the caller back.

10 Before ringing off, make sure you have recorded all the information required, including the caller's telephone number. (You may also have to complete a log book of all incoming calls.)

▶ *How would you deal with a wrong number?*

First try to help the caller. Give your own organisation's number again to clarify where the mistake has been made. If your number is different to that required, the caller can ring off and dial the correct number. If the caller has been given your organisation's number by mistake, ask for more details about the enquiry and see if you can find the correct number.

If you find that you regularly receive calls for another organisation, keep a note of their number so that it can be passed on to the caller quickly and efficiently. Never be off-hand with a caller who has the wrong number, but be polite and helpful as this will create a good impression of your own organisation. You may find that you receive a lot of wrong number calls because your number is similar to that of another organisation, or above or below their number in the directory. If you greet callers correctly and give a good impression you may attract additional business.

▶ *How would you ensure a message is taken accurately?*

Firstly, remember to keep pen or pencil, scrap paper and telephone message pad next to the telephone. You will need to pass on the following information:

1 Name of caller and organisation/department
2 Caller's telephone and extension number
3 Details of message
4 Name/department/room number of person for whom the message is intended
5 Date and time of call
6 Your name as the receiver of the call

You may prefer to write information received over the telephone on to scrap paper and then transfer this neatly to the message pad. If you are busy, however, it may be safer to write directly on to the message pad so that you do not forget the call. It is vitally important that messages are passed on promptly to the correct person so that the call can be returned. Do not leave messages lying around your desk. A lost message to return a call could mean a lost order for business and a very angry colleague.

When you have taken a message, you should always confirm the details back to the caller. Repeat the name and contact number to ensure that mistakes have not been made. One wrong digit in a telephone number will cause confusion and create a bad impression of your organisation if the call cannot be returned. Messages must give full information. It is not acceptable to write that 'a man called ...', or, 'I think her name was ...'. If you are ever unsure of what a caller has said, do not be afraid to ask him/her to repeat details or spell out words you do not understand.

■ DIY 8.1.2

1 Find the operating instructions for the answering machine used in your organisation or training centre and write up an information sheet that could be used by other members of staff.

or

2 Write an information sheet on the switchboard or multi-line telephone system used at your workplace or training centre.

Your information sheet should cover at least one side of an A4 piece of paper. Remember to include details of the type and make of equipment you are describing.

and

3 Prepare another information sheet giving advice on how to compose messages. Attach to your sheet examples of completed message forms such as that shown in Fig. 8.5 indicating what information should go where.

▶ *What information can be given over the telephone?*

The amount of information you are able to give over the telephone will increase as you get to know the organisation for which you work. It is important, however, that you recognise occasions when information should or should not be given out. You have already been told that you must be polite and helpful at all times, but this does not mean giving out any information you can lay your hands on in the name of helpfulness.

If you are ever unsure, tell the caller that you do not have the information and that you will transfer them to your supervisor. Alternatively, offer to call them back later to give you time to check. It is important for you to realise that limitations governing disclosable information are there to protect the organisation, its business and its employees.

You will learn from the organisation's literature, such as house journals, organisation charts, internal telephone directories, catalogues, price lists, etc. You will also learn by talking to members of

MESSAGE FOR

M _____
WHILE YOU WERE OUT

M _____

Of _____

Telephone No _____

Telephoned		Please ring	
Called to see you		Will call again	
Wants to see you		Urgent	

Message: _____

_____

_____

_____

_____

_____

_____

_____

Date _____ Time _____

Received by _____

Fig 8.5 A telephone message form

staff about their role and duties in the organisation. With experience, you will know about the products or services offered by the organisation, which departments deal with different areas of work and who to contact if a person is not available.

■ DIY 8.1.3

What information do you deal with that could be classified as confidential? Explain why this information is confidential and the procedures you follow to ensure it is not passed on to unauthorised people.

▶ *How do you make an outgoing call?*

We all think we know how to use the telephone, but it is surprising how easily mistakes can be made. By following a few simple rules, you can avoid making mistakes and help build your confidence.

1 Write down the number and dialling code (check these are correct) and the name or department you require.

2 Make a list of questions or notes needed for the call.

3 Lift the receiver and listen for the dial tone (you may have a hands-free button that allows you to talk into a small speaker and keep both hands free).

4 Key in the full number carefully at a steady rate (a beep will be heard each time a number is accepted).

5 If you make a mistake, replace the receiver, wait a couple of seconds and try again.

6 When the call in answered, ask for the person or department required, and/or the extension number, if known; give your own name and/or the name of your organisation, and say on whose behalf you are calling, if relevant.

7 When you are connected, be prepared to repeat the same information again.

8 Talk clearly and concisely, using your notes as a reminder to ensure that you do not forget anything.

9   If the call is for your boss, explain this to the person and then transfer the call, making sure you first announce their name to your boss.

10 If you are cut off, as the caller it is your responsibility to call again.

■ DIY 8.1.4

1 Copy the telephone log sheet in Fig. 8.6 on to a piece of A4 paper. Use it to record all incoming and outgoing calls dealt with by you.
2 Include in this log sheet details of when you have had to leave messages on answering machines.

TELEPHONE LOG SHEET			
NAME		SYSTEM	
DATE	INCOMING TIME	OUTGOING TIME	DETAILS OF CALL

Fig 8.6 Telephone log sheet

▶ *What sources of information are available?*

You will inevitably use a BT *Phone Book* for your local area, together
with *Yellow Pages* and *The Thomson Local Directory*. Use these
books to find local telephone numbers, area codes, addresses and even
postcodes for business and private users.

Business Pages (similar to *Yellow Pages*) are used by business
suppliers and cover a wider area, but not retail outlets and services.

Your organisation should also have an Internal Directory giving details
of all personnel, departments and extension numbers. This should, in
addition, also give details of frequently used external numbers, eg
branch offices, so that staff do not use BT's Directory Enquiries, which
would incur charges.

The only free BT information service still available is the speaking
clock sponsored by Accurist. All other services are offered by private
companies, who make a charge for the service. These services are
usually advertised in newspapers and start with the prefix 0891. The
Freefone service does not provide information but does encourage
potential customers to ring free of charge either through the operator
or by using an 0800 number.

Remember that there are other companies, such as Mercury, that
supply telecommunications equipment and services in competition
with BT.

■ DIY 8.1.5

It is very important that when you receive information for another person it is
passed on as soon as possible. You may wish to pass the information on
verbally, perhaps in a small office, but in a larger office it is important that you
write everything down on the appropriate message slip so it is not forgotten.

Information in the form of a fax, telex or electronic mail (these are explained
later on) may also be received and must be forwarded to the correct person as
quickly as possible.

1 On a piece of A4 paper explain the routing procedure in use at your
   workplace or training centre.

2 Attach to this sheet a copy of the message slip used for telephone messages and, if there is one, a copy of the incoming record for fax, telex and/or electronic mail which should detail who received the message and who they passed it on to.

3 If your organisation does not have such a log, now is the time for you to design one.

▶ *What about international communications?*

Most international telephone calls can be made using IDD (International Direct Dialling), but if problems are encountered the International Operator can be contacted on 155 for assistance. The International Operator will not only help with international calls but can also give you a demonstration of the tones to expect to hear when calling internationally.

Remember that international telephone calls and fax messages are charged at a higher rate than domestic calls and, therefore, it is important that you choose carefully the time of day when you make your call or send your fax. You can use the *Phone Book*, International Time Zones page, to calculate the time difference between Britain and the country you wish to contact.

▶ *How do you maintain security?*

The first thing to remember is to use your discretion – if you are ever unsure, ask your supervisor. You will find that during your working duties you will have access to many types of information. It may just be part of a day's work to you but the information you deal with could be very sensitive and of use to other people or organisations. Be helpful, but never disclose information to others that may be considered confidential by your organisation.

Personnel and wages records, financial and medical reports, and information such as sales and profit reports, are examples of records that contain information that should not be given to callers. Think how you would feel if your name, address and personal details were given to 'someone' over the telephone. Would you like to think that other people were given information about your bank account or medical details?

▶ *What other telecommunications equipment is available?*

The telephone network can be used to communicate verbally (voice); to communicate data, using services such as Prestel and **modem** (modulator/demodulator) equipment to down-load data from one computer to another many miles away; and to communicate text using facsimile equipment and electronic mail software to transfer information from one computer screen to another using services such as Telecom Gold and Prestel Mailbox. All of these methods of telecommunications use the telephone network to communicate information.

Voicebank and Voicecom are computerised BT services that allow recorded messages to be left in a central voicebank. This can be accessed by the registered user keying in a personal identity number (PIN) to obtain their messages.

▶ *What is telex?*

For legal and security reasons many messages have to be in writing. Telex provides a fast, clear textual communication between national and international customers that is available to send and receive messages 24 hours a day. Proof of sending and receiving is made possible by the use of answerback codes which are printed at the top and bottom of all telex messages. The answerback code is usually an abbreviation of the company name.

Customers are issued with a Telex Directory which lists users in alphabetical order followed by the address and the user's answerback code. An Answerback Directory which lists answerback codes in alphabetical order followed by the name and address of the user is also useful. International directories are also available.

A telex terminal consists of a printer, keyboard and screen as shown in Fig. 8.7, or the terminal can be connected to an existing printer terminal so that its computer keyboard and screen may be used. Some telex machines allow messages to be keyed in, edited and proofread

214

Fig 8.7 A telex machine

before being sent, and will allow messages to be set to a timer so that they are sent to coincide with another country's working hours.

Telex is short for '*tel*egraphic *ex*change' and its main advantages are:

- a message in a foreign language is easier to translate than a telephone call
- it is faster than sending a letter
- messages can be received automatically
- a written confirmation/response can be supplied quickly
- all telex machines can communicate with each other
- there are millions of users worldwide
- the use of answerback codes confirm the telex has been received
- the telex is recognised as a legal document

The telex system works via special telegraph lines connected to the machine. Charges are calculated according to distance and length of time the connection is used.

```
      93-03-18  11:28


      67457+
      67457  BXNTER G
      1621  93-03-18  11:28

      TO: PAM SCOTT
      FM: LYNDA BOURNE

      PLS SEND ME 4 CPS OF ADMIN. NVQ
      LEVEL 1 ASAP.

      REGARDS

      LYNDA*
      67457  BXNTER G
      261367 PITMAN G
```

Fig 8.8 A telex message, showing the answerback code

To keep costs low, messages should be as brief as possible. Therefore, abbreviations are commonly used and unnecessary words left out, as shown in the example in Fig. 8.8. Abbreviations often used are:

ABS   Absent or office closed
CFM   Confirm
DER   Out of order
EEE   Error
MOM   Waiting
NCH   Customer's number has changed
NR   My call number is ... or indicates your call number
OCC   Engaged
OK   Agreed
R   Received
RAP   Will call back
RPT   Repeat
RQD   Required
STLG   Sterling
SVP   Please
W   Words
+   Message end
++   No further messages

216

▶ *What is Prestel?*

Prestel is a type of viewdata, because it can be viewed on screen, which links television screens or personal computers to large computers via BT lines. Information is updated every 24 hours and includes:

- company information
- directories
- market research
- business news/services
- share prices
- government statistics

- travel information
- weather information
- sport and entertainment
- banking and investment
- mailbox
- customer guide.

This service allows the user to actually make bookings using their keyboard, for example theatre tickets and air tickets. The user is charged according to how long they have used the line, in the same way as making a telephone call. Faults in the Prestel service result in it being unavailable, or sometimes you may find characters missing from words. In extreme cases you may find a TV screen full of gibberish!

▶ *What is a facsimile?*

Commonly known as 'fax' this machine, as illustrated in Fig. 8.9, will transmit an exact copy of a page from one place to another – much like a photocopier, but with the copy emerging from another fax machine at a different location. To send a fax you will need to know the fax number of the company you wish to receive the copy – the number can be found on the company's stationery or in BT's *Fax Book*. If you are a BT registered customer your fax number can be found by dialling 192 (this information is now detailed in the *Phone Book*).

The original sheet is fed into the machine which scans and then translates the information into a code that can be transmitted via the telephone network – some machines are able to print a confirmation slip once transmission is complete to confirm transmission time, number of pages and number dialled. Fax is particularly useful for sending pictures, graphics, written or printed material accurately and at great speed – average speed is 48 seconds per A4 page.

Fig 8.9 A fax machine

The cost of sending a fax is exactly the same as if you had made a telephone call to the same destination, except that to convey the same information verbally would take much longer and would therefore cost more. Extra costs are also incurred if a telephone call, for example an order, needs to be confirmed in writing – one fax would accurately satisfy both of these needs. The company receiving the fax incurs no charges other than the initial cost or rental of the fax itself plus the cost of the paper and toner required for the message. Some fax machines allow messages to be set to a timer so that they can be automatically transmitted during cheap rate times to save money.

Modern fax machines are able to diagnose faults. The machine displays a number which can be looked up in the user manual. The number identifies the problem with the machine, eg paper misfeed, insufficient paper, cover not closed, etc, and an alarm light will also light up. The user manual also tells the user how to put the problem right.

▶ What is electronic mail?

The terms 'electronic mail' 'Elmail' or 'Email' are used to describe the process of sending and receiving messages electronically either internally in an organisation or externally using telephone lines. With electronic mail, a central computer becomes the equivalent of a postal sorting office, sorting incoming messages into the correct mailbox ready for collection by the mailbox holder. Each holder is identified by their own mailbox number and can be given a unique password to enable them, and only them, to retrieve their messages.

Messages can be transmitted internally within an organisation, perhaps spread over different sites, by using specialised software linked to a central computer – transfer of messages is then free of charge. Messages transmitted externally would need to pass through a system such as Telecom Gold or Prestel Mailbox, which incur a registration fee together with a charge for each A4 page sent. The organisation would also have to provide a computer with built-in modem, or a separate modem, and for Prestel Mailbox, viewdata communications software.

When using Email the message is read from the screen, therefore paper is not required unless a printout of the message is needed. Some companies use Email for sending internal memos as it saves time in terms of delivery, saves paper and often postage if the company has computers in different areas networked together – this is called LAN

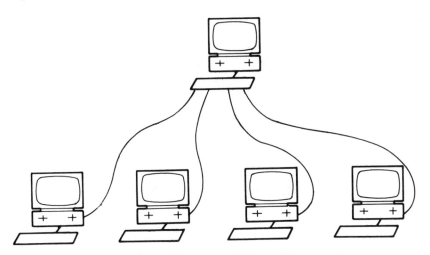

Fig 8.10 A networked computer system

or 'Local Area Network' (*see* Fig. 8.10). Users are notified of a waiting message either by a flashing light on their screen, often with a number to show how many messages are waiting, or a picture such as an envelope appearing on screen.

■ DIY 8.1.6

1 What telecommunications equipment is used in your organisation? Write a brief report giving details of each piece of equipment, what it is used for, and how to decide upon the best method to use taking into account urgency, cost and security.
2 Copy the log sheet in Fig. 8.11 which can be used to record details of when you have transmitted or received information electronically by using fax, telex, voicebank or electronic mail. Use a separate sheet for each. The information on your log sheet must be supported by evidence of material prepared and transmitted by you. Also include material that has been received and routed to others by you.

RECEIVE AND TRANSMIT INFORMATION ELECTRONICALLY				
NAME				
SYSTEM USED... LOCATION.........................				
DATE	TIME RECEIVED	TIME SENT	NO OF PAGES	DETAIL OF MESSAGE

Your supervisor should sign the bottom of each sheet

Fig 8.11

▶ *What about safety?*

Using electronic equipment should not be a dangerous activity, but safety rules still apply.

1 Do not trail wires across the floor or walkway.
2 Keep the earpiece and mouthpiece clean.
3 Do not eat or drink over equipment.
4 Keep equipment in an accessible place.
5 Do not sit on desk tops whilst using the equipment.
6 Use sufficient equipment for the number of people in the office.
7 If the equipment does not work check the electric cables are secure and the electricity supply is switched on, but do not attempt to carry out repairs yourself.

Completing Element 8.1

To prove competence in this element it is necessary for you to transmit and receive information electronically. You must show that you are able to choose the most suitable equipment for the task, prepare information accurately and transmit the material to the correct location, by the required deadline, using the correct operating instructions and organisational procedures. You must deal with outgoing and incoming messages, routed correctly, following the organisation's security and confidentiality procedures. Faults must be rectified or reported promptly. You must prove competence using voice, data and text transmission systems.

Claiming credit

Once you have completed your final assessment, you will need to write in your record book or folder how, when, where and what you have done to prove that you are competent.

The following is an example of how one trainee completed this claim:

In the training centre I made sure my fax messages were readable and when a fax was received that could not be read I telephoned the company and asked them to send another one. I only faxed the number of sheets shown on the Fax Top Sheet. I made sure there were no extra pages attached by mistake. I sent faxes to the number written on the top sheet. Sometimes I had to look numbers up in the Fax Directory. When faxes were received they were logged in and then delivered to the correct person immediately. A fax log book was filled in with details of all outgoing and incoming faxes. This was accurate and legible. If the fax had a misfeed or stopped for any reason, it would show a fault code number on the display. I would look the number up in the manual to find out what was wrong with the machine.

Please see work folder for evidence of faxes sent/received. I was also assessed using Email on the training centre's computers. If a message was waiting an envelope would show up on the screen. I have completed a log sheet detailing all messages sent/received together with examples.

I also used the Prestel system in the library to look up information when arranging travel details. I was able to obtain flight details, weather forecasts and currency exchange rates. I could have also booked flights using this system.

■ Element 8.2
RECEIVE AND SEND MAIL

Performance criteria

- Incoming mail is correctly processed and promptly directed to correct destination
- Organisational procedures for dealing with suspect items are correctly followed
- Outgoing mail is appropriately prepared for dispatch
- The most appropriate mailing system, in relation to cost, urgency and security, is selected
- Mail is dispatched within required deadlines

▶ *Receiving mail*

Mail arriving at an organisation may include many different documents. There may be letters, quotations, orders, invoices, enquiries, applications for jobs and advertising material sent by other organisations. It is very important to open and distribute the mail to each department without delay, so that office staff are able to make a start on their day's work as soon as they arrive in the office.

In a large organisation, it is usual practice for mail-room staff to start work before the other office workers in order to make sure that all the mail has been delivered to each department by the time the office workers are ready to begin their day. However, in a small office it may be the case that only one person is responsible for opening, sorting and delivering the mail.

Some organisations rent a private box or bag from the Post Office for an annual fee. This allows the organisation to collect mail or parcels from the Post Office every day, except Sunday. The organisation can collect mail from their box or bag early in the morning to ensure that it has been sorted and delivered to each department ready for action at the beginning of the day. If an organisation has no private box or bag at the Post Office's delivery office, mail will be delivered in the normal way.

▶ *How should incoming mail be sorted?*

Each organisation will have its own procedure for dealing with incoming mail depending on the size and type of business carried out. For example, a large mail-order company would employ experienced staff working to a strict timetable, who are able to use specialist equipment. A smaller company may only employ one person who deals with mail as one of a number of responsibilities and, therefore, follows a less rigid timetable.

In both cases remember that all mail is important, regardless of the size of the organisation. Mail which fails to reach its destination quickly and accurately may result in the loss of valuable business.

▶ *How do most organisations deal with incoming mail?*

The following steps are likely to be followed:

1 Sign for registered and recorded delivery items. (Details of these may have to be entered into a Special Mail Register, as illustrated in Fig. 8.12.)

■ DIY 8.2.1

Make your own copy of a page from a Special Mail Register as in Fig. 8.12. Enter the details of the following post received by you at 9.00 am today:

- Recorded delivery letter from Ms C Villiers
- Recorded delivery packet from Cuthbert & Co
- Registered letter from Dr D R Stott

SPECIAL MAIL REGISTER				
Date	Time	Sender	Method of Delivery	Received By

Fig 8.12 Special mail register

- Recorded delivery packet from Ranjit Singh
- Trakback parcel from Head Office, Glasgow
- Swiftair letter from Brussels office
- Confidential letter to Miss J Arther

2 Remove all mail that is marked 'Private' or 'Confidential' and put to one side.

3 Open envelopes, using your finger or a paper knife. Alternatively, a letter opening machine may be used, in which case the contents of the letter should be 'tapped' down to the bottom of the envelope so they are not cut with the blade.

Do not open registered, recorded delivery, personal or confidential mail. This mail is usually taken to the person or department to whom it is addressed for opening.

4 Remove the contents carefully from each envelope, checking that nothing has been left inside. Attach all enclosures to the back of the letter with either a paperclip or staple. Enclosures are indicated at the bottom of the correspondence by the letters 'Enc' or 'Encs'. If the enclosure is not there, write 'Not enclosed' on the letter.

You or another member of staff will have the responsibility of contacting the sender of the letter to inform him/her of the missing enclosure.

5 Date stamp all the mail – in the case of mail which is registered, recorded delivery, private or confidential, date stamp the unopened envelope. (Some electric date stamps print the time as well as the date.)

6 Some organisations require a record of all incoming mail to be kept, usually in a special file or book. Most organisations will require mail that contains remittances in the form of cash, postal orders, stamps or cheques to be recorded in a Remittances Book, as illustrated in Fig. 8.13. Each day details of remittances received are entered into the book. They are then totalled up and handed over to the Chief Cashier who will sign the book in the 'signed' column. This signature acts as your receipt and transfers the responsibility for the remittances over to the Chief Cashier.

■ **DIY 8.2.2**

Make your own copy of a page from a Remittances Book. Enter the following remittances that have been received by you today.

REMITTANCES BOOK				
Date	Sender	Type of Payment	Amount £	Signed

Fig 8.13 Remittances book

- Mr Stone sent a cheque for £89.47.
- Mrs S Chandra enclosed a postal order for £75.16.
- Mrs Sally Allbright enclosed £10.00 in cash.
- Stott & Co enclosed a cheque for £119.57.
- Mr Singh enclosed a postal order for £19.99.
- Messrs Chaplain & Co enclosed £1.50 in stamps.

When you have entered all remittances, total the amount column ready for you to hand over to the Chief Cashier for signing.

7 Date-stamp empty envelopes as they may be needed at some future time to give details of when the letter was posted or indicate a return address. Some organisations use these envelopes for their own internal mail.

8 Sort mail. This can be done directly into pigeon-holes or wire trays labelled with details of departments or individual members of staff, as shown in Fig. 8.14. Also sort internal mail into the correct pigeon-hole or tray. All mail will then be delivered or await collection.

If the mail is not addressed to a particular department or person, look for a subject heading which may indicate where it has to go, or read through the letter to see if the contents give any clues. If you are still unsure, put the letter to one side and deal with it later. It is important not to hold up the rest of the mail while dealing with a query.

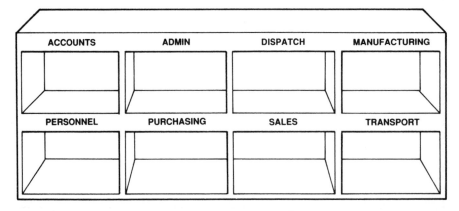

Fig 8.14 Pigeon-holes for mail

■ DIY 8.2.3

Copy the diagram in Fig. 8.14 of mail pigeon-holes.

Here is a list of mail received today. Each item has a number which should be written into what you feel is the correct department's pigeon-hole. If you have any uncertainties, place the number of the item below the pigeon-holes to indicate that you will sort this out later.

- Internal post for the van driver (8)
- Invoice for parts (9)
- Registered letter for Administration Assistant (10)
- Final demand for telephone bill (11)
- Internal post for Manufacturing Manager (12)
- Letter addressed to the Accountant (1)
- Leaflets regarding stationery supplies (2)
- Price list for office supplies (13)
- Job enquiry (14)
- Urgent letter addressed to Sales Manager (5)
- Request for a company price list (6)
- Wages query from Southampton Branch (7)
- Letter of resignation from Sales Manager (3)
- Internal post for transport clerk (4)
- Internal post for a Mrs Allsopp (15)

9 If a piece of correspondence requires the attention of more than one person or department, either take the required number of photocopies and send one to each department/person concerned, or attach a circulation or routing slip (Fig. 8.15) detailing the names of other people or departments who need to see it. Once the correspondence has been seen by the named person or a representative from the department, they will initial and date the slip and then pass the correspondence on to the next person. The last person on the list returns the slip and correspondence to the person who is named at the bottom of the slip by the specified date.

■ DIY 8.2.4

Make your own copy of a routing slip. In 2 weeks' time the electricity board wish to carry out major repairs outside your office. This will mean that there will be a

ROUTING SLIP		
Read or copy and pass on in order shown below:		
Name	Department	Initial/Date
Please return to:		
By:		

Fig 8.15 Routing slip

short cut-off in the electricity supply between 10 am and 12 noon. Your boss has asked a colleague to prepare a suitable notice and has asked you to prepare a routing slip, containing the names of all staff and trainees in the office or group. Your slip is to be attached to the notice and each member of the staff or group must initial and date the slip to confirm that they have read the notice.

You wish the original notice to be returned to you by Friday of next week.

Prepare the routing slips with the relevant information for your own office or group.

10 Once the bulk of the mail has been sorted, go back and deal with any mail that was put to one side.

▶ *What should you do with damaged or suspicious items?*

When you collect or receive the daily mail, check to ensure there are no damaged items. If any items are damaged in any way there may be a Post Office label to confirm this was done during sorting. If there is no label, point out the damage to the delivery person or contact the local customer care department. Your organisation may wish to claim compensation from the Post Office for the damage and can only do so if they have evidence that the item(s) were damaged before delivery or collection.

Always make sure you treat mail as instructed – if 'Handle with care', 'Do not bend' or 'Fragile' labels are used on the item, treat it accordingly. Also look for pictures on packages, such as a broken glass, which indicates fragile contents, or an arrow which is used to show the correct way 'up'. If you do not obey these instructions and damage the item, it is your fault and the organisation cannot claim compensation from the Post Office.

If you are ever suspicious about a piece of mail then do not open, prod, shake or squeeze it. Your suspicions may be aroused if the item has an unusual smell (some explosives smell of marzipan!), if it is of an unusual shape or size, or if it has strange writing, spelling or wrapping. In fact, anything that is 'out of the ordinary' should make you suspicious.

If you are suspicious of an item, the first thing you should always do is tell your supervisor. Your supervisor will then be able to contact the

Fig 8.16 Examples of labels for special handling

person or department to whom the item is addressed and ask if they are expecting such a package. If the package has a return address, this can be contacted to confirm the contents of the package. However, if there is no such address and your own staff are unaware of the delivery of such a package, then it is wise for all personnel to leave the office, lock the door and contact either security or the police.

Large organisations often use machinery that can scan mail, in the same way as luggage is scanned at airports. Mail and packages can be passed through a type of X-ray machine that produces an image of their contents on a screen. Staff are trained to recognise suspicious contents and to know the procedures to be taken if their suspicions are aroused.

Remember that 'suspicious' does not always mean a letter bomb. Individual staff may be 'under attack' for personal reasons or the organisation itself may be open to attack because of the nature of the work it carries out. Security procedures for mail should never be taken lightly – if you work in a government department dealing with sensitive information, or a fur coat manufacturers, or perhaps a cosmetics company that carries out testing on animals, you would have to take security very seriously!

▶ *What should you do if unable to deliver mail on time?*

There will always be times when things just do not go smoothly and you may find yourself unable to deliver the mail on time. If this happens, it is essential that you tell your supervisor what has happened immediately. It is only then that something can be done to help you out – if your supervisor is unaware of the problem, you will not be able to get help!

It is important for you to remember that your work colleagues will be organising their day according to priorities, some of which will be affected by what is in the daily mail. Therefore, one of your own priorities will be to ensure that your colleagues get their mail as early as possible.

If for any reason you are unable to do this, you should always look to see if any of the day's mail is marked 'URGENT'. If it is, make sure this is delivered immediately with an explanation that the rest of the mail will follow later. You should encourage colleagues to let you know if they are expecting an urgent delivery so that you can make sure it is delivered to them as soon as it arrives on your desk.

▶ *Dispatching mail*

If you are given the responsibility of dealing with the dispatch of mail, you must have a thorough knowledge of the Post Office mail service and its regulations. Mail services are also offered by other organisations such as Securicor, DHS, TNT and Group 4 – you will find other delivery companies detailed in *Yellow Pages*.

The organisation that you work for or train in will choose the delivery service that best suits its needs. Solicitors for instance use their own private methods for delivery of important documents between each other, but would use the Post Office for delivery of mail to their clients. A large organisation may use a private delivery service rather than the Post Office if they are able to negotiate a cheaper rate for bulk deliveries. Be aware that there are a number of different companies offering delivery services and that your organisation will be looking for the best service at the lowest price.

▶ *What is the Post Office?*

The Post Office Corporation is now made up of 3 separate businesses: Royal Mail, Parcelforce and Post Office Counters Ltd.

Royal Mail is responsible for the collection and delivery of nearly 60 million items a day to 24 million addresses nationwide. It provides a wide range of special services designed to cater for businesses and private mail users. Royal Mail uses a 2-tier system of service for postal delivery.

▶ *What is the 2-tier postal system?*

The Post Office offers a 2-tier system for the delivery of letters (parcel post is just a one-tier service). First class post costs more but arrives at its destination within about 24 hours. Second class post is cheaper but slower, although post should be delivered by the third working day. When preparing mail for dispatch it is important to consider costs – mail should be sorted and stamped according to its urgency. It is pointless sending mail by first-class if it is not urgently required, as this will only have the effect of increasing the company's postage costs.

Parcelforce provides a nationwide parcel delivery service. It offers a variety of services for business and private users, including Datapost.

Post Office Counters Ltd operates as an agent for many of the services offered by Royal Mail and Parcelforce through its network of 20 000 Post Offices across the country – over 1000 main post offices and over 19 000 owned and run by agents.

▶ *What Post Office services are available?*

The Post Office publishes a *Mail Guide* which gives details of all regulations, services and costs. The *Mail Guide* costs approximately £20. You may find a copy in the library or your place of work. It is updated by inserting replacement pages issued by the Post Office giving details of new services, conditions or prices. There are, however, many leaflets available from the Post Office that give you up-to-date information and prices on most of its services. Remember that if you are unsure of what service to use for a particular item, post office counter staff are there to help you and will give advice.

The Post Office offers many services in competition with private companies. Therefore, costs may vary considerably and will need to be taken into account when selecting the most appropriate service.

■ DIY 8.2.5

Call in to your local post office and collect as many leaflets as you can on postal services and rates. Leaflets that are particularly useful are: *UK Letter Rates, International Letter Rates, Wrapping up Well, Parcelforce Standard, Parcelforce International, Parcelforce Datapost.* Also collect an example of a Royal Mail Special Delivery label, Recorded Delivery label and a Certificate of Posting. Place all the leaflets, labels, etc in a safe place – as you will need to refer to them later.

Some of the more frequently used services are as follows:

Certificate of posting

This is the cheapest way of making sure that an inland ordinary letter or parcel or overseas ordinary letters have actually been posted. It gives the sender proof of posting and compensation can be claimed from the Post Office for loss or damage. The letter or parcel has to be handed in at a Post Office for the counter clerk to complete and stamp a receipt like that illustrated in Fig. 8.17. Delivery is made in the normal way and the item does not have to be signed for by the recipient. Compensation will not be paid if money or jewellery is sent in the ordinary post, even if covered by a certificate of posting.

Recorded delivery – first- and second-class mail

This service provides a certificate of posting and a signature from the recipient to confirm delivery. It can be used for important documents such as passports, examination certificates and legal documents. Limited compensation will be paid for loss or damage but this is only to cover for the inconvenience caused. Therefore, this service is not

Certificate of Posting

This is a receipt for ordinary letters. Keep it safely to produce in the event of a claim. The ordinary post should not be used for sending money or valuable items.

Royal Mail

Please write the name, address and postcode for each item you're sending in the column below (in ink).

number of items   Officer's initials   date stamp

name   address and postcode

please continue on the back (*if necessary*)   P326 Feb 92

Fig 8.17 Certificate of posting

suitable for money or jewellery. If you need a guarantee of delivery next day you should use **Guaranteed Delivery**.

The Post Office provides a blue adhesive label like that shown in Fig. 8.18 upon which you enter details of both your address and that of the recipient. The top portion of the label is peeled off and affixed to the top left-hand corner on the front of the letter (or close to the address on a packet). The middle portion of the label (which includes barcodes and sender's details) is affixed to the reverse of the letter or packet. The certificate is handed into the Post Office with the letter or packet and payment. The certificate is date stamped and initialled as your receipt and must be kept in a safe place as it will have to be produced in the event of a claim or to make an enquiry.

When the letter or packet is delivered a signature is collected from the recipient to confirm delivery. If you wish to confirm delivery yourself, telephone the number given on the back of the recorded delivery adhesive label and quote the 13 digit customer reference number on your barcoded receipt. The barcode allows tracking through the Royal Mail network so that progress and delivery can be checked. Recorded delivery charges are paid in addition to first- or second-class postage.

Registered post – first-class mail only

If you wish to send anything valuable in the post, such as cash or jewellery, you should use this service. The fee you pay will depend on the value of the item being sent. If the item is lost or damaged, compensation up to £500 will be paid according to the value of the item being sent. This service provides you with a certificate of posting and the signature of the recipient when the item is delivered. Letters and packets sent by registered post are handled with special security measures and kept separate from ordinary mail.

The Post Office provides a blue adhesive label like that shown in Fig. 8.19 which is completed in the same way as the Recorded delivery label.

The Registered Plus service can be used for valuable items which require extra security and compensation arrangements. On the back of the Registered Plus adhesive label you can choose compensation up to £1500 or £2200 by placing a cross in either of the 2 boxes. The cost of sending registered items increases according to the value of compensation required. The registered fee is paid in addition to the first-class postage.

234

Fig 8.18 Recorded delivery slip   **Fig 8.19 Registered post label**

Guaranteed delivery

This service is for first-class mail only and can be used for letters and parcels. Guaranteed Delivery guarantees next-day delivery by 12.30 pm to most UK destinations. Friday postings are guaranteed Monday delivery by 12.30 pm. The Post Office provides a blue adhesive label with barcodes that allows it to track the item through the postal network and check progress and delivery. The signature of the recipient is collected to confirm delivery of the item. If the item is not delivered by 12.30 pm, compensation can be claimed from the 'Double Money Back guarantee', providing a written claim with the certificate of posting is received by the Post Office within 14 days.

Parcelforce Datapost

This service provides delivery of urgent letters, packets and parcels by no later than 12.00 noon the next day. It guarantees overnight delivery within the United Kingdom and speedy delivery to many overseas countries. If an item is not delivered on time, compensation can be claimed. If Datapost is to be used regularly, a contract can be arranged. Arrangements can be made to have mail collected regularly or on demand.

FreePost

This service allows people to send mail to a company free of charge. The Post Office issues the company with a licence to operate a FreePost service, and the word 'FREEPOST' can then be included in the address. The service requires no special stationery, unless first-class service is required, and allows customers sending orders to a company, for example, to do this without having to pay postage. FreePost is often used to encourage people to reply to advertisements – you may have seen it used in magazines or on television.

▶ *What international services are available?*

The service you choose depends on how quickly your international mail needs to get to its destination.

Airmail

This service provides a speedy and cost-effective method of delivery. Delivery time is usually 3–4 days to cities in Europe, and 4–7 days for destinations elsewhere. Whatever you are sending by airmail, you should always use an airmail label like that shown in Fig. 8.20 or write 'PAR AVION – BY AIRMAIL' in the top left-hand corner of your envelope.

Fig 8.20 Airmail label

Fig 8.21 Swiftair label

Swiftair

This is a priority service for urgent documents and goods (*see* Fig. 8.21). All items sent by Swiftair receive special treatment which speeds sorting and onward dispatch to provide a faster service than airmail. A certificate of posting can also be obtained, although a particular delivery time cannot be guaranteed. The charge for Swiftair is paid in addition to the normal airmail postage.

Surface mail

This service is more economical than airmail but slower. Delivery time is usually between 3 and 5 weeks. Letters cannot be sent by surface mail to European destinations.

■ DIY 8.2.6

Your supervisor has asked you to recommend the most suitable postal service for the following items. Choose from the services already explained above which you think would be the best.

1   A letter containing £1000 in cash
2   A letter to a company complaining that they have lost your first letter
3   A watch worth £600
4   A returned examination certificate
5   An important contract that has to be in Berlin by tomorrow
6   A letter to Dublin inviting an applicant to attend a job interview in 2 days' time
7   A non-urgent letter to America
8   Routine business mail to overseas customers

9 Television programme inviting viewers to send in their answers to a competition

10 A pools company inviting people to become agents

▶ *How can you help the Post Office?*

First, always make sure you put the right postage on all items. Post Office charges are calculated on the service required, the urgency of delivery, the destination and weight of an item. Up-to-date charges can be found in the Post Office *Mail Guide* and leaflets, both national and international, which should be used at all times to ensure correct postage is paid. If too little has been paid, the person receiving the item will be asked by the Post Office to pay double the missing amount!

Always use standard size envelopes. The Post Office uses machinery that handles and sorts mail automatically and asks its customers to use envelope sizes that are 'post office preferred' – known as POP. You should use envelopes no smaller than 90 mm × 140 mm, and no larger than 120 mm × 235 mm. Envelopes should be oblong in shape, made of paper weighing at least 63 gsm (grams per square metre) and no thicker than 6 mm, including their contents. The most commonly used envelopes are DL (110 mm × 220 mm), C6 (114 mm × 162 mm), C5 (162 mm × 229 mm) and C4 (229 mm × 324 mm).

▶ *How do you fold documents to fit into their envelopes?*

The answer to this question is 'as few times as possible'. Letters and documents should be folded using the instructions in Fig. 8.22. Never try to guess where a fold should be – always measure the letter against the envelope to make sure you are folding in the right place. A letter that has been folded and unfolded a number of times before fitting in to the envelope will look scruffy and create a bad impression of the organisation.

Regardless of the service used, it is vitally important to address all mail legibly and always to use the postcode. Labels for envelopes should be typed or produced on a word processor. If you have to write envelopes, make sure your writing is 'readable'. Always write the town in CAPITALS, and put the postcode on a separate line. If you cannot fit

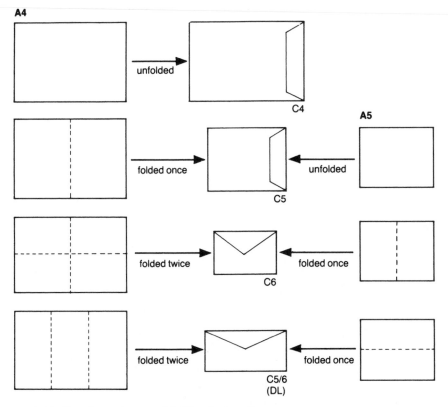

Fig 8.22 Envelope sizes and folding instructions

the postcode on a separate line, leave about 5 character spaces after the town and put it there.

In order to help the Post Office sort mail quickly and efficiently postcodes are used to identify the exact location of the addressee. Post Office sorting staff are able to key in the postcode using electronic keyboarding equipment that marks the envelope with a series of dots. Automated sorting equipment can read these dots and will divert the mail to the correct location according to the area indicated by the postcode.

Therefore, if you use the correct postal address and full postcode on all items, you will help to ensure quick and accurate delivery. If you are not sure of a full address or postcode, ask your local Postal Customer Care Unit (you can find the number in the *Phone Book* and in the *Mail Guide*).

```
Mr J L Protheroe
Mobley & Co Ltd
1 Somerly Close
COVENTRY
CL3 2UA
```

Fig 8.23

▶ *What items must not be sent through the post?*

Dangerous items and substances should not be sent through the post nationally or internationally. The *Mail Guide* provides a list of items and substances such as aerosols, lighters, asbestos, enamels, varnishes, explosives and prohibited drugs which should never be sent by post. Live creatures such as bees, leeches and worms can be sent provided they are sent first-class in adequate packing, but creatures such as poisonous spiders cannot be sent!

▶ *How should an envelope be addressed?*

Most organisations use a blocked style for addresses on envelopes (Fig. 8.23). The address may be typed directly on to the envelope or adhesive labels can be used which can be peeled from their backing and placed in the correct position on the envelope.

The address should be placed half-way down the envelope and a third of the way in from the left-hand side. Remember to leave enough space for the envelope to be franked across the top and, if stamps are used, the Post Office will need to cancel these out with an ink impression. If you have placed the address too high, the top half of the address may become unreadable if it is franked across!

If the letter is confidential, private or has a 'For the attention of' line, this should be placed one clear line space above the address in capitals, as shown in Fig. 8.24.

```
FOR THE ATTENTION OF MR J L PROTHEROE

Mobley & Co Ltd
1 Somerly Close
COVENTRY
CL3 2UA
```

Fig 8.24

Note that on both examples the town has been typed in capitals and the postcode placed on a line of its own. If any special instructions are included (for example, Confidential or Private), these should always be typed in capitals and/or underlined.

Special instructions such as 'Do not bend' or a postal label such as Recorded Delivery, Registered Delivery, Airmail, etc, should be placed on the top left-hand corner of the envelope – remember the stamp is placed on the right-hand corner.

Some organisations require staff to mark envelopes with a pencilled '1' or '2' in the top right-hand corner of the envelope to indicate to mail-room staff whether first- or second-class postage is required. However, if the envelope is to be delivered by hand and requires no postage, it is usual to type or write 'BY HAND' in the top right-hand corner of the envelope in place of the stamp.

■ DIY 8.2.7

Prepare envelopes or paper cut to DL, C5 or C6 size for each of the following mail items. Special instructions have been shown in brackets after each address. You must ensure that these instructions are placed on the envelope in the correct position. The Swiftair, Registered and Recorded envelopes will each require the correct Post Office adhesive label to be prepared with the relevant peel-off portions affixed to the envelopes.

1 Smith & Webb Co Ltd
12 Solent House
BRIGHTON
BR95 9BB
(for the attention of J Smith)

2 Mssrs Brown & Co
48 Dorchester Way
SOUTHAMPTON
SO11 9GH
(Confidential)

3 Miss Anja Eickshler
Malzstr 90 PSF 361
0-2000 Berlin
GERMANY
(Swiftair)

4 Internal Mail
Progress Department
(By hand)

5 Mr & Mrs D White
39 Allsop Road
COVENTRY
CV27 6AS
(Registered)

6 Mr H Beachamp
19 Moordown
WARRINGTON
CH9 8HH
(Recorded)

▶ *How should mail be prepared?*

All items for mailing should be securely sealed in appropriate sized envelopes, packets or parcels. Mail should be legibly addressed and the correct postal rates should be calculated and applied. Post Office sorting requirements should also be followed. You will find that each organisation has its own procedure for preparing outgoing mail; it is important for you to ensure that you know this procedure so that mistakes are not made.

If an organisation is large enough to have its own mail room there will be a system of regular collection of mail from every department during the day. Trays marked 'outgoing mail' are usually placed in each department so that mail can be collected and prepared during periods of the day when the mail room is not so busy. The mail room will probably advise staff of a final collection time, after which no mail will be accepted for that day. This will avoid a last-minute rush and ensure that Post Office collection times can be met.

In the case of bulky envelopes, these will have to be weighed and the correct postage calculated. The job of putting the contents into their envelopes may be down to individual members of staff who typed/keyed in or wrote them, or it may be done by staff in the mail room itself.

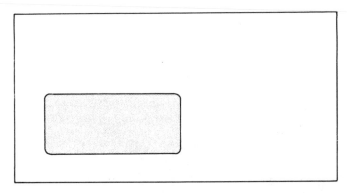

Fig 8.25 A window envelope

The procedure for outgoing mail should be as follows:

1 Check the bottom of the letter for 'Enc'. If the enclosure is not there, put the letter to one side while you prepare the other mail.

2 Check that the letter has been signed.

3 Check that the inside address is the same as the address on the envelope.

4 If the letter is marked 'Confidential' or 'Private', make sure the envelope is too. Also check that 'For the Attention of ...' information has also been included on the envelope.

5 Fold the letter so that it is creased as few times as possible.

If window envelopes are used like that shown in Fig. 8.25, check that the address on the letter can be read through the window. Some organisations mark their headed paper with a small box into which the address should be typed and/or mark the edges of the paper to show where the letter should be folded. This ensures the address is in the correct place to be seen through the window in the envelope.

6 If the letter is bulky or addressed to a country overseas, it may need extra postage. The correct postage can be calculated by weighing the item on a set of scales (Fig. 8.26) and then looking the weight up in the correct *Post Office Rates* leaflet or *Mail Guide*.

7 Affix correct stamps and place letter in to one of the following three categories:

243

Fig 8.26 Electronic scales for weighing post

- First class
- Second class
- Registered/Recorded Delivery – taken to Post Office as a receipt has to be obtained.

All first-class items should be placed in a red post office bag and second-class in a green post office bag. The mail is now ready to be collected by or delivered to the Post Office. Remember that there will be a cut-off time in the afternoon, usually around 1700 hours, after which the Post Office will not accept post for that day.

■ DIY 8.2.8

Prepare for dispatch the envelopes completed in DIY 8.2.4. Write in pencil in the top right-hand corner of each envelope the correct postage required or, if possible, use a franking machine to frank each envelope ready for dispatch. Match the item number given in DIY 8.2.4 for each envelope to tell you the service required.

1 2nd class
2 1st class

3 Swiftair
4 By hand
5 Registered (1st class)
6 Recorded (2nd class)

Remember that charges for Registered and Recorded Delivery services are added to the normal postage.Swiftair charges are added to the airmail postage.

On a separate piece of paper work out how much it would cost to send the following items using:

1 Airmail
2 Swiftair
3 Surface mail

- Letter weighing 210 g to Amsterdam
- Packet weighing 550 g to Pakistan
- Printed papers weighing 170 g to New Zealand
- Letter weighing 99 g to Greenland

Did you remember that letters cannot be sent by surface mail to European destinations?

8 Once the mail is prepared, go back to any items that were put to one side. You will have to inform the person responsible for the correspondence the reason why it has missed the post. Remember that it is not your fault if he/she has forgotten to sign the letter or perhaps left out the enclosure. However, do try to inform them of the problem as soon as you can so that it can be put right, if possible, in enough time to catch the afternoon's outgoing mail.

9 If stamps have been used for the mail, complete the Postage Book. This book gives a detailed record of all letters, packages and parcels posted, as in Fig. 8.27. It also keeps a check on how many postage stamps have been used. Remember that stamps cost money and are not for private use. Therefore, a receipt (in other words some form of postage record) is completed to identify how the stamps have been used. The Postage Book and the stamps themselves should always be kept safe and secure, usually under lock and key to prevent dishonest use.

POSTAGE BOOK			
Stamps Bought	Name and Town of Addressee	Stamps Used	Special Services
£20.00	2.7.9–	£ p	
	J Jones – Derby	48	
	S Ferry – Cardiff	97	Reg Mail
	Messrs Pike & Co – Hull	7.40	Parcel
	Smith & Son – London	54	Rec Del
	TOTAL	£9.39	
	Balance c/f	£10.61	
		£20.00	

Fig 8.27 Postage book

■ DIY 8.2.9

Copy a page from a postage book like that shown in Fig. 8.27. Stamps bought today – £45.00. Enter details of the mail you prepared for dispatch in DIY 8.2.8. Remember to include details of special services used. Add up the total of all stamps used. Deduct this from the £45.00 you started with. The amount left will be carried forward to the next day.

▶ *What is a franking machine?*

This machine prints on an envelope, postcard or adhesive label (used for parcels) in coloured ink the value of a stamp, as well as the date and place of posting (Fig. 8.28). The Post Office licence number and an advertising slogan can also be included if required. It saves time when preparing mail, makes a record of all postage used and is easier to keep secure than postage stamps.

Franking machines can be bought or hired from manufacturers such as Pitney Bowes and Roneo (Fig. 8.29), but a Post Office licence is also required. There are 2 meters on the machine – one that shows how many postage units have been used to date (ascending register), a

Fig 8.28 Franking mark

second that shows how many postage units are left in the machine (descending register). When the descending register is low, this means that more postage units need to be bought from the Post Office.

It is important not to let the descending register run too low – this may result in postage units running out and mail missing the Post Office deadline. Some machines allow a small part to be lifted off and taken to the local Post Office, who use a special key to open the machine and add units once payment has been made.

Modern, computerised franking machines are linked to a Post Office computer and have credits added simply by making a telephone call. The Post Office computer automatically prints an invoice and sends it to the franking machine user. Modern machines can use a credit card

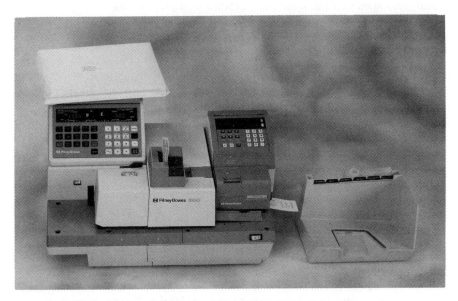

Fig 8.29 An electronic franking machine with built-in electronic scales

247

system which allows credits to be added to the machine by simply inserting a plastic card which is bought from the Post Office.

Franking machines can be locked to prevent dishonest use. The machine has to be set with the day's date each morning before use and the ink roller regularly re-inked. If a franking is incorrect, it should be put to one side and used, if possible, later in the day. Otherwise, the franked item can be taken to the Post Office, which will give a refund, less 5 per cent. If a franking machine is taken to the Post Office for credits to be added, a record card is completed showing units used and units purchased.

When franking mail, the counter on the machine can be set to the amount of postage required, so that all items can be prepared easily without the need for the correct value of postage stamps. Franked mail can pass through the Post Office much faster as the franking on each item does not require cancelling by the Post Office in the same way as postage stamps.

However, franked mail does have to be posted in a special way – either handed in over the counter of a Post Office, tied in separate first- and second-class bundles facing the same way, or posted in a letterbox in a special envelope marked 'franked mail'. Some organisations use red post office bags for first-class mail and green bags for second-class mail, and special mail items are placed in a yellow bag.

▶ What about security?

Firstly, remember that stamps are worth money and should be locked away until needed. Petty cash is normally used to buy stamps and should also be kept in a special tin box out of sight to prevent temptation. Incoming remittances in the form of cheques, postal orders, cash or stamps are also valuable, so make sure that you enter each remittance received into the remittances book and get the book signed.

The franking machine should also be kept locked and out of the way until it is required. It should only be used for business and not personal use. If a mistake is made, never throw the envelope or label away, but try to use it later or get a refund from the Post Office. Do not be afraid to admit that you have made a mistake. Your supervisor would prefer to get a refund, less 5 per cent, than find out you have been throwing your mistakes in the bin!

▪ DIY 8.2.10

It is important that you understand the different services on offer by the Post Office, so that you can choose the most effective but most economical for the job. However, it is wise to remember that in city areas private companies can be used to express deliver letters and parcels at competitive prices. Nationally there are many large operators who will deliver packages and parcels overnight throughout the UK and abroad. Look in the local *Yellow Pages* and make a list of private companies. Contact one of these companies and ask for a price list or details of their charges. Compare your findings with the prices charged by the Post Office and make recommendations as to which company you think offers the best service for the type of mail despatched by your workplace or training centre.

Completing Element 8.2

To complete this element on receiving and sending mail you must correctly process and distribute mail. Suspicious items must be dealt with according to established procedures. Outgoing mail must be prepared for dispatch, with correct postal rates applied. You must prove that you are able to select the most appropriate mailing system in relation to cost, urgency and security. In-house and external mail must be dealt with in accordance with security and confidentiality procedures.

Claiming credit

Once you have completed your final assessment, you will need to write in your record book or folder how, when, where and what you have done to prove that you are competent.

The following is an example of how one trainee completed this claim:

While in my workplace I received all mail. If any damaged or suspicious mail was delivered I pointed this out to my supervisor immediately. I checked all enclosures were present and stapled them to the document. If the enclosure was missing I told the person to whom the document was addressed and offered to telephone the sender to inform them of the missing enclosure. I made sure that any cash or valuables were delivered to the Chief Cashier as soon as they had been entered in the remittances book. I used departmental pigeon-

holes to sort mail into departments and this was collected by the staff as early as possible. If they could not collect the mail I delivered it to them.

All mail was addressed according to Post Office requirements and scales were used to weigh heavy items. The Postal Rates leaflet was used to calculate postage. I used Registered (for valuables), Recorded (for important documents), Airmail (for general international) and Swiftair (for urgent international) postal services. On occasions where an urgent delivery was requested I used a company called TNT. Franked mail was placed in green or red bags ready for collection at 3.00 pm. Registered or recorded items were taken to the Post Office.

UNIT 9
Maintain and issue stock items

■ Element 9.1
ORDER, MONITOR AND MAINTAIN STOCK

Performance criteria

- Sufficient stocks are maintained to meet current and anticipated demands
- Ordering of stock is in accordance with organisational procedures
- Stock is handled and securely stored in conformity with organisational requirements
- Stock check and inventory reconciliation are as instructed and any discrepancies promptly reported to the appropriate person
- Incoming deliveries are checked against order and any discrepancies promptly reported to the appropriate person
- Records are up to date, legible and accurate

Have you ever heard the terms 'stocktake', 'out of stock' or 'summer/winter stock'? The term 'stock' has the same general meaning, whether in a large industrial organisation or a small office. In the *Pocket Oxford Dictionary* it is described as 'Store of goods, etc, ready for sale, distribution, or use, supply of anything'.

In your college or workplace you will find different kinds of stock. This stock is usually kept together in a special place called a storeroom, stockroom, or 'the stores'. The stock is kept here to protect it and to make sure it is ready to be taken out when required. You must always remember that stock is worth money; it is of value to the organisation and you must treat it with great care.

▶ *What types of stock are there?*

The stock held by any organisation will generally fall into one of five categories:

1 Raw materials

This type of stock is held ready for use in the manufacture of goods. Sufficient stock of raw materials and components must be held for a regular supply to the production department. Can you imagine what would happen if the production department was brought to a halt because there were not enough raw materials in stock to make the goods? Examples of raw materials would be cocoa in a chocolate factory or cotton and other textiles in a clothing manufacturer's factory.

2 Consumables

These are supplies that are necessary for the smooth running of the organisation, but which are used up in the day-to-day running of the business and do not make a profit in themselves. Consumables may be used up quickly so there must always be a reserve in stock. Examples of consumables in an office would be stationery, such as envelopes, rulers and notebooks.

3 Finished goods

These are the goods that have been manufactured by the organisation and are held in stock awaiting orders from customers. The organisation will want to sell this stock as quickly as possible to make a profit, in order to buy more raw materials and make more finished goods. The organisation will always keep in stock popular lines which sell quickly, so that delivery can be made upon the receipt of an order – this is called delivery 'ex-stock'. Examples of finished goods are cars, bicycles, computers, furniture and carpets.

4 Goods purchased for resale

Retail shops and wholesale warehouses purchase a variety of stock which they display and hope to sell at a higher price than they paid the manufacturer, to make a profit. These outlets usually offer a wide range of stock from which customers can choose as and when they require it. Examples of resale stock would be clothing, food and drink, and electrical equipment.

5 Spare parts

These are required so that they are readily available in the event of the breakdown of the factory machinery, vehicles, plant, etc. Examples of spare parts would be engines, gear boxes, and smaller items such as nuts and bolts, and fan belts.

∎ DIY 9.1.1

List five types of stock that you deal with in your organisation or centre. Next to the items write down which types of stock they are, eg raw materials, consumables, etc.

▶ *How might stock be ordered?*

The stock used in your organisation will be purchased from suppliers (retail shops, wholesalers or manufacturers). The organisation will send out an initial **enquiry**, perhaps to three or four suppliers, in order to find out which supplier can offer the best deal. In return the suppliers will send a **quotation** detailing the goods required and the price and terms that they are prepared to offer. The supplier may also take this opportunity to send price lists, catalogues and free samples, or arrange for a sales representative to call.

The purchasing department will decide upon the supplier to use and will send out an **order**. When the supplier receives this order, an **acknowledgement** will be sent back to the organisation's purchasing department to confirm that the supplier has received the order. Once the order is ready to be delivered, the supplier will send an **advice note** by post, containing the delivery details for the goods.

A **delivery note**, containing the same details as the advice note, will be sent with the goods. It is the responsibility of the person receiving these goods to ensure that the goods correspond with the goods detailed in the delivery note. Any discrepancies must be written down on the delivery note and confirmed by the signature of the persons delivering and receiving the goods.

An **invoice** will be produced by the supplier for each delivery of goods sent to the organisation. This will give full details of the goods supplied, together with a breakdown of costs, including any discounts (money off) and VAT. At the end of each month the supplier will send the organisation a **statement** which details the amount payable for all the invoices for that month, less any refunds for goods returned or damaged. The organisation then arranges for a **cheque** to be sent to the supplier in settlement of the account.

This process will be used when an organisation is first looking for a supplier of a particular range of goods. Once contact has been made and a suitable supplier found, it is usual for the organisation to place regular orders with the supplier. However, in the case of an emergency supply being required at short notice, most suppliers will take an order over the telephone. This should, however, be supported by giving them an order number, and an authorised order form should be sent by post or fax as soon as possible.

In the case of smaller organisations you may find yourself being sent in person to collect goods which are urgently required.

▶ *Checking*

It is usual practice to check deliveries against the initial order, to ensure that the correct goods and quantities are being delivered. The delivery note (complete with corrections if there are any) will then be compared against the invoice sent to your organisation to make sure the correct amount has been charged.

If at any stage a mistake is identified, this must be reported to a supervisor immediately. It may be that incorrect goods have been delivered, which will need to be returned, or that your organisation has been charged for goods that it has not received. In both cases it may be your responsibility to find these errors and mark them on the delivery note before signing it. Remember that the delivery company uses the delivery note as a receipt for goods delivered and will, therefore, work out your organisation's final invoice based on these details.

■ DIY 9.1.2

In order to help you remember the procedure necessary for ordering stock, copy the flowchart given in Fig. 9.1 on to a piece of paper and fill in the gaps.

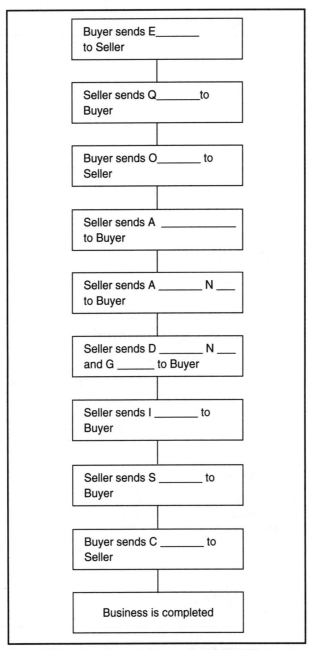

Fig 9.1 Flowchart for ordering stock (DIY 9.1.2)

PEMBROOKE MARKETING SERVICES LTD

115–119 Cavendish Square, Bridport, BR4 9PQ

Order Number: 123890   Date: 12.9.– –

Please supply the items listed below:

Quantity	Description	Cat. No.	Unit Price £	Total Price £
12	HB12 Pencils	16354		10.69
4	Markers (red)	11987	0.60	2.40
4	Markers (green)	11988	0.60	2.40
4	Markers (yellow)	11989	0.60	2.40
10	Reams A4 Bond (white)	20675	4.15	41.50
2	Reams A4 Bank (yellow)	20667	4.10	8.20
			TOTAL	67.59

Authorised by

A. Nother

PEMBROOKE MARKETING SERVICES LTD

115–119 Cavendish Square, Bridport, BR4 9PQ

Order Number: 123892   Date: 15.10.– –

Please supply the items listed below:

Quantity	Description	Cat. No.	Unit Price £	Total Price £
12	HB14 Pencils	19875		10.69
2	Staplers	35627	5.95	11.90
5	Sticky tape	36728	0.98	4.90
24	Correction fluid	09758	1.54	39.96
7	Staple removers	67301	1.37	9.59
			TOTAL	77.04

Authorised by

A. Nother

Fig 9.2 Order forms for DIY 9.1.3

■ DIY 9.1.3

Compare the order forms opposite on page 256 (Fig.9.2) with their delivery notes (Fig. 9.3a below and Fig. 9.3b on page 258). Make a list of the errors you find in the delivery notes, writing the correct details next to each error.

The Stationery Company Limited

97 Fontmell Street
Bridport, Dorset

Date: 20 September 199—

Order No: 123890   Delivery Note No: 1675
Delivery Address: Pembrooke Marketing Services, 115–119 Cavendish
                      Square Bridport

Quantity	Description of goods	Catalogue number	Total £
12	Pencils	16355	10.69
4	Markers (red)	11987	2.40
14	Markers (green)	11988	12.40
4	Markers (blue)	11990	2.40
10	Reams A4 Bank white	20665	41.50
2	Reams A4 Bank yellow	20667	8.20

Please mark errors or damaged goods before signing.

....

Do not pay until you have received our official invoice and statement.

Fig 9.3a Delivery note for DIY 9.1.3

Often organisations use stationery packs which contain all the relevant documents for one order. Each document is either made from NCR (no carbon required) paper, or will have carbon paper placed between each sheet. When the order details are typed or written on to the top sheet they are automatically copied on to the other sheets – delivery note, stores requisition, accounts advice, invoice, and so on.

This saves time, as the documents do not have to be prepared separately. Sections of information that are not needed on certain forms can be blanked out (for example, it is usual practice not to have price details on the delivery note).

The Stationery Company Limited

97 Fontmell Street
Bridport, Dorset

Date: 27 September 199—

Order No: 123892   Delivery Note No: 1897

Delivery Address: Pembrooke Marketing Services, 115–119 Cavendish
                            Square, Bridport

Quantity	Description of goods	Catalogue number	Total £
10	Pencils	19875	10.69
2	Staple packs	35677	1.50
5	Adhesive tape	36728	4.90
20	Correction fluid (yellow)	09757	39.96
7	Staplers	35627	41.65

Please mark errors or damaged goods before signing.

....

Do not pay until you have received our official invoice and statement.

Fig 9.3b Delivery note for DIY 9.1.3

▶ *Why do organisations hold stock?*

It is essential to have a reserve supply of all the goods and materials required for your organisation to operate efficiently. Delays in the supply of such stock will cause hold-ups in production and possible loss of profits if an order cannot be delivered on time.

Another point to remember is that it is cheaper to order goods in 'bulk' and put the excess into stock so that advantage can be taken of discounts and lower prices. However, care must be taken not to over-order. Remember that stock is worth money to an organisation and a storeroom full of stock that is not used for a long time is tying up money that could be used elsewhere.

▶ *What quantity of stock is usually held?*

This will vary according to the type of organisation, size of organisation, and how much business is carried out. There are also five other very important considerations.

1 Money

You are already aware that stock is worth money and that it would be unwise for an organisation to have too much money tied up in stock. It is also wise to remember that some stock may be perishable and have a limited shelf-life. Stock may become dated and therefore unsaleable, or it may age with time and become unusable. Examples are fashionable clothing, fruit and vegetables, and even paper, which may become yellow in time.

2 Time

It may be difficult, or indeed impossible, to obtain stock immediately and valuable orders may be lost to other organisations who are able to deliver the goods on the date required. You will find that, to prevent this situation arising, most organisations will carry a sufficient amount of stock to ensure that when orders are received they can be fulfilled immediately.

3 Space

The storage of stock is expensive. It uses valuable space in areas which must be maintained, heated, protected and secured. Staff are employed to take charge of stock and insurance must be paid to provide cover in the event of damage. The organisation will anticipate the maximum amount of each item of stock that should be kept at one time to prevent profits being spent purely on storage costs.

4 Sales

The organisation will anticipate the actual quantity of stores, spares, raw materials, etc, it will need to keep itself operational. While it is important not to carry too much stock, it is more important to ensure that there is enough stock available to prevent production being halted and money lost.

5 Usage

It is very important to have a regular supply of the stock that is used most often. In an office you might find yourself needing typewriter cartridges, lift-off tapes, paper and envelopes on a regular basis. A clothes manufacturer would need material, sewing cotton and zips/buttons readily at hand in order to keep production going.

Therefore, it is usual to find that regular orders are placed for high-usage items so that they do not run out.

■ DIY 9.1.4

To show that you understand stock control, answer the following questions. Try to write as much as you can.

1 Why is it important to order the right amount of stock?
2 What rules should be followed when storing stock?
3 What is stock rotation?
4 How should heavy stock be lifted and stored?
5 How should hazardous stock, such as correction fluids and cleaning materials, be handled and stored?

Refer to Unit 2 on health and safety when answering questions 4 and 5.

▶ *How are stock levels checked?*

Stock levels are checked at regular intervals by a process called **stocktaking** or **reconciliation**. This means that every item of stock in the organisation is counted to calculate how much money is tied up in the value of the stock. This stocktaking produces a document called an **inventory**. It is the stocktaker's job to check that the balances of stock shown on the record cards are the same as the amount of stock actually in the stockroom, and that every issue of stock has a requisition form to support it – if it does not, then this means that the stock has been taken without authority.

It is possible to keep an up-to-date record of stock levels by using a computer, which is what is done by the barcode reading tills you see in supermarkets. The computer will deduct from the total stock level every time some item of stock is taken out, and add to the stock level every time stock is replaced. This is a very good method of keeping a check of the stock, but one disadvantage is that the figures it gives you are those that it has calculated to be correct. It cannot take into account theft, pilfering, damage, loss, etc, unless these details are keyed into it.

Therefore, you will find that manual stocktaking still has to take place at least once a year so that the actual value of stock can be entered into the organisation's annual accounts sheet. It is during this stock-take that damaged stock, or perhaps stock which has become obsolete (out of date) and is no longer required, can be 'written off' and its value deducted from the organisation's assets. Some organisations will have a sale to reduce the amount of 'written off' stock which they hold.

You should now be aware of the type of stock you are likely to find in any organisation. You also know that consumable items, such as stationery, are used in the administration of the business. Whether you work in a large or small organisation, it is of great importance that stock is stored correctly, especially hazardous stock. A regular check should be made to find out current stock levels and to indicate any loss or damage.

▶ What legislation is there relating to the receipt of goods?

When you or your organisation buys goods or services, you are called a 'consumer'. Did you know that there are a number of 'consumer laws' to protect you? Possible dangers that may be encountered are:

- misleading advertisements
- dangerous goods
- incorrect description of goods
- incorrect weight or size
- goods not suitable for their purpose
- goods paid for but not delivered
- poor quality, making goods unusable
- incorrect price information giving idea of a bargain
- businesses getting together to keep prices high
- credit terms not showing exactly how much you pay
- persuasive or pressurised buying that you later regret.

There are a variety of organisations set up to give advice and provide consumer protection. These include the British Standards Institute (BSI), the Consumers' Association and the Citizens' Advice Bureau. However, as a consumer you are also protected by law – this protection is in the form of a number of 'consumer laws'.

Sale of Goods Act 1979

This Act sets out the conditions under which goods can be bought and sold. The goods must:

- be legally owned by the seller
- suit the purpose for which they are sold
- fit their description
- correspond with samples
- be capable of use for the purpose intended.

The buyer has the right to return the goods and have their money refunded, or to claim compensation, depending on the particular breach of law involved.

If someone tried to sell you 'Big Ben', or wellington boots which let in the water, or A3 paper instead of A4, then they would be in breach of this law and you could take legal action.

Weights and Measures Act 1963 to 1979

These Acts make it an offence to give a short (too little) weight or measure, even by accident. Local authorities employ trading standards officers to enforce these Acts, and as part of their work they regularly visit shops and other premises to check the accuracy of scales and other measuring devices used. As a consumer you would be protected when buying goods such as potatoes, petrol or a pint of beer in a pub.

Trade Descriptions Acts 1968 and 1972

It is an offence to describe goods or services for sale in a false or misleading way. This applies to verbal as well as written descriptions, and suppliers must ensure that advertisements do not contain wrong information about goods for sale.

As a consumer you must be told the origin of the goods, ie where they were made, together with the original price of an item which is now being offered at sale price.

Unsolicited Goods and Services Act 1971

This Act protects you if you are sent goods that you did not order. If you inform the supplier that you do not wish to keep the goods, it is the supplier's responsibility to collect these goods from you within 30 days or the goods become your property. Alternatively, you need do nothing other than to wait for six months, after which time the goods will also become your property.

Fair Trading Act 1973

This Act set up the Office of Fair Trading under the Director-General of Fair Trading. It has very wide responsibilities concerning unfair trading practices which affect consumers. It is the responsibility of the Office of Fair Trading to ensure that trade is carried out according to the law.

STOCK INVENTORY RECORD SHEET				
STOCK		QUANTITY		
Description	Unit	Date	Date	Date

Fig 9.4 Stock inventory record card

■ DIY 9.1.5

It will be necessary for you to show your understanding of an inventory. You will need to check stock in an organisation that keeps stock record cards when receiving and issuing stock. Prepare a simple stock inventory sheet using the same layout as in Fig. 9.4. Carry out a stock check of a small stationery cupboard on 3 separate days. Compare your final set of figures with the stock record cards held on each item. Why might the figures be different? What would you do if the figures did not agree?

Completing Element 9.1

To complete this element on ordering, monitoring and maintaining stock you will need to put all the DIY tasks in your folder and carry out a final assessment. Competence must be proven in dealing with the ordering of stock from internal and external sources. The items ordered must include office consumables, small items of office equipment (eg staplers, hole punch) and other materials. You must also demonstrate that you can carry out instructions provided by the organisation to ensure you follow relevant legal requirements and codes of practice.

Claiming credit

Once you have completed your final assessment you will need to write in your record book or folder how, when, where and what you have done to prove that you are competent.

The following is an example of how one trainee completed this claim:

During my work placement at Crazy Jacks I was responsible for the stationery. I counted and checked the stock in the office stationery cupboard during the first week and made out up-to-date stock cards for all the items. There were 22 items altogether. When people wanted anything they completed a requisition form and I issued the stock as requested. I then kept my cards up to date by deducting the amount issued. After the second week I counted all the items in the cupboard and checked them against the record cards. Some of the figures did not agree and when I spoke to the supervisor I found out that some of the people staying later in the evening took what they needed without filling in a requisition form. I made a note of the differences on the cards and made sure the figures were correct. At the end of my placement I carried out another count of the stock. This time the figures agreed and I had requisition forms for all the items issued.

During my second week it was necessary to order some more items from the central stores. I completed an internal requisition form and got it signed by my supervisor. The stock arrived after 3 days and I updated the cards and stored the stock safely away in the cupboard. I also labelled the shelves so that the items were stored correctly, the heavy items I put at the bottom, eg boxes of paper. We ran out of fax paper and I needed to go to a local supplier to get an emergency supply. This was paid for by petty cash and not ordered through the normal central stores. Requests for special purchases were normally carried out by the central stores. To make sure I understood this procedure I was allowed to work in the central store for 2 days. We placed several orders and I received goods. When the goods came into the stores I checked them against the original order. Unfortunately I was not there long enough to see any of my orders come back in for checking.

■ Element 9.2
ISSUE STOCK ITEMS ON REQUEST

Performance criteria

- Issue of stock is in accordance with organisational procedures
- Requests are responded to promptly and accurately
- Stock is handled and securely stored in compliance with organisational requirements
- Records are up to date, legible and accurate
- Damage to stock is promptly and accurately reported to the appropriate person

▶ *Why is it necessary to keep control of stock?*

Small organisations may use a 'visual' system of stock control – in other words, stock is ordered when a need is seen. Larger organisations, especially those involved in manufacturing, use a 'bin' system where all components are given a bin number which identifies the component's position in the storeroom. However, most organisations will use 'stock cards' as a system of keeping an up-to-date record of the stock in hand.

A **stock card** (*see* Fig. 9.5) will show details of each item used by the organisation (**1**). Each time stock is delivered by a supplier this will be *added on* to the record (**2**), and each time stock is issued to a

265

STATIONERY STOCK CARD

Item <u>A4 Bond Paper</u> ①   Maximum level <u>50</u> ⑤   Bin No <u>100</u>

Minimum level <u>10</u> ⑥

Unit <u>Ream</u>   Reorder level <u>20</u> ⑦

Date	Receipts ②			Issues ③			Balance
	Qty	Inv no	Supplier	Qty	Req no	Dept	in stock ④
199–							26
Jan 1							26
3				6	141	Accounts	20
4	30	A133	J Smith & Co				50
10				3	159	Personnel	47

Fig 9.5 A stock card

department in response to a **stock requisition form**, this is *deducted* from the record (**3**), thus showing exactly how much is in stock at any one time (**4**).

We have already discussed how important it is for an organisation not to have too much stock or too little stock. To prevent either of these situations arising a stock record card is used to indicate the *maximum* (**5**) and *minimum* (**6**) level for each item of stock required by the organisation.

The stock record card also indicates the *reorder level* (**7**), which shows the stock level (quantity of stock) at which an order needs to be requested so that delivery is made before the remaining stock runs out. It is at this point that a **purchase requisition** is sent to the purchasing department (the buying department) to instruct the buyer to order the stock.

A stock record card will be kept for every item of stock and will therefore provide an up-to-date record of issues and requisitions, reorder levels, and the maximum and minimum amounts of stock required for any one particular organisation, department or office. The reorder level will take into account how long it takes for orders to be delivered together with the 'usage' level for that particular item.

You would expect to order regularly those items that have a high usage level because these are used more frequently. For example, A4 bond typing paper would be used daily in an office and you would need to keep up a regular supply. Whereas staplers, although used daily, are long lasting and their usage level would be very low, so that you would find you very seldom reorder these.

■ DIY 9.2.1

Look at the example of a stock record card in Fig. 9.6. Notice that the columns give details of date, quantity received from supplier, invoice number, name of supplier, quantity issued to the individual departments, number of the requisition form, name of the department and the total balance left in stock. Colour coding can also be used to help you to identify a particular type of stock. For example, all stationery records may be on green cards, and manufacturing on yellow cards.

Anything coming into the organisation will be shown under the heading **Receipts**, and anything going out of the stockroom will be shown under the heading **Issues**. You may have already noticed that in this example the maximum stock level is shown as 800 reams, the minimum as 250 reams and the reorder level as 350 reams. A ream of paper is 500 sheets.

As you can see, this stock record card is incomplete, because the figures have not been added to or deducted from the total. Please copy the card on to a piece of paper and fill in the missing details.

It is important that your calculations are correct. If they are not, you may find yourself in trouble for ordering stock that is not required or even worse, not ordering stock that is required. Imagine how you would feel if someone found that the organisation had run out of A4 typing paper but had 20 staplers in stock!

STATIONERY STOCK CARD

Item <u>Bond A4 Paper white</u> Maximum level <u>800</u>   Bin No <u>102</u>

Minimum level <u>250</u>

Unit <u>Reams (500 sheets)</u> Reorder level <u>350</u>

Date	Receipts			Issues			Balance
	Qty No	Invoice	Supplier	Qty No	Req no	Department	in stock
July							500
1				75	S202	Sales	
				10	A500	Accounts	
4				30	P302	Purchasing	
				150	R1010	Repro	
8	350	ML10321	Moore Ltd	150	G543	General	
10				50	P493	Office	
				100	S206	Personnel	
12						Sales	
18							
18							
20							
22							
23							

Fig 9.6 Incomplete stock record for DIY 9.2.1

■ DIY 9.2.2

The stock record card shown in Fig. 9.7 has been completed incorrectly. It is important to any organisation that mistakes are not made. Please check the card and copy the outline on to a piece of paper. Then rewrite the card and make the necessary corrections.

STATIONERY STOCK CARD

Item <u>Bond A4 Paper white</u> Maximum level <u>800</u>   Bin No _____

Minimum level <u>250</u>   102

Unit <u>Reams (500 sheets)</u> Reorder level <u>350</u>

Date	Receipts			Issues			Balance
	Qty No	Invoice	Supplier	Qty No	Req no	Department	in stock
Aug							500
1				25	S212	Sales	475
				30	A520	Accounts	440
6				40	P332	Purchasing	380
				75	R1410	Repro	305
9	250	ML10321	Moore Ltd				605
12				155	G553	General	550
14				60	P523	Office	495
15				40	S256	Personnel Sales	450

Fig 9.7 Incorrect stock record card for DIY 9.2.2

▶ *How is the stock ordered within an organisation?*

You should now be familiar with the sequence of events leading up to the delivery of goods to an organisation, and how such a delivery is recorded on the stock record card. However, as a member of an organisation, you will need to be aware of the procedures required in order to request supplies for your own working area.

Most organisations use **stock requisition forms** which are completed by the person needing the stock. These forms are usually countersigned by the supervisor and then passed over to the stock controller, who will arrange for the items to be taken from the stockroom.

If the stock controller identifies that stock is low and needs to be reordered from the supplier, then a **purchase requisition** would be sent to the purchasing, or buying, department to inform them that the reorder stock level had been reached and that new stock should be ordered immediately. It is the responsibility of the purchasing department to ensure that the stock is ordered, and also that the correct quality has been ordered at the best possible price.

Remember that every time stock is issued to a department it should be *deducted* from the stock record card, and every time stock is delivered by a supplier this should be *added* to the record card. The stocktaker is employed to check the figures of stock received against stock issued to departments or sold to purchasers throughout the organisation, in order to calculate the total value of stock in hand and discover any mistakes.

You will find that the stock you are most likely to be called upon to order frequently in an office will be stationery. Stationery is classified as a consumable item of stock and is used in the administration of the organisation. It may be kept in the general office, with a member of the office staff being responsible for it.

Items of stationery could include paper, envelopes, typewriter ribbons and lift-off tapes, paperclips, pencils, glue, pens, and so on. The value of this type of stock is very high and great care must be taken to control its use and ensure that staff are not requesting it for personal use, or storing unnecessary quantities.

■ DIY 9.2.3

You need to order some items for your section. Copy and complete the requisition shown in Fig. 9.8 for the following items: A4 paper white 2 reams, 4 correction fluids (white, green, yellow and blue – one of each), 1 box of DL size envelopes, 1 stapler, 2 packets of staples, 1 stapler remover, 2 blue pens, 1 red and 1 green. The next requisition number for your section is 443. Remember to date and sign the form.

▶ *How is stock stored?*

You should now be aware that stock is a valuable asset to the organisation and must be kept in perfect condition. The type of storage required will depend upon the kind of stock and the size of the organisation. Large organisations will have a stockroom or department

```
┌─────────────────────────────────────────────────────────┐
│              STATIONERY REQUISITION                       │
│                                                           │
│                    No.....................................│
│                                                           │
│                    Date...................................│
├──────────────┬──────────────────────────────────────────┤
│  Quantity    │  Description                              │
├──────────────┼──────────────────────────────────────────┤
│              │                                           │
│              │                                           │
│              │                                           │
│              │                                           │
│              │                                           │
│              │                                           │
├──────────────┴──────────────────────────────────────────┤
│  Signed.............................  Storekeeper's initials │
│  Department .........................                     │
│  Authorised.........................  ....................│
└─────────────────────────────────────────────────────────┘
```

Fig 9.8 Stationery requisition form for DIY 9.2.3

with staff employed to take charge of the stock, whereas a small organisation may have a stock cupboard with only one person in charge of the keys. What you must remember is that, however large or small the organisation, it is essential that the stock is stored correctly.

■ DIY 9.2.4

Make a list of 20 items of stock which includes consumables and equipment that would be kept in a general office. You are in charge of the stock and have a large walk-in cupboard in which to store everything. Opposite the 20 items listed write where you would store the item. Your selection may be made from the top, middle or bottom shelves, or space on the floor.

Every item of stock must be stored neatly and be easily accessible when required. Shelves should be labelled so that it is easy to find what is needed, and the stockroom or cupboard should always be kept locked. It is important that the stockroom or cupboard is kept dry at all

271

times to prevent paper-based stock from becoming damp and going mouldy. Large or heavy items should be kept low down and, when new stock arrives, it should be placed at the back or at the bottom of the existing supply so that older stock is used first.

It is important that you treat hazardous stock with care. Any liquids that are dangerous or inflammable, for example thinners, glue or duplicating fluid, must be kept in a separate area, and staff must never smoke in this area or in the stockroom itself.

■ DIY 9.2.5

Answer the following questions to show that you understand stock control systems.

1 What record systems are needed to control stock?
2 What would you need from a member of staff before issuing stock to them?
3 What precautions would you take for storing toner, adhesives and cleaning agents?
4 What would you do with damaged stock and who would you report it to? Which records would need amending?
5 What is a reorder level?
6 What would you do if someone asked you for toner for the photocopier and there was none in stock?

Completing Element 9.2

To complete this element on issuing stock items on request you will need to put all the DIY tasks in your folder and carry out a final assessment. Competence must be proven dealing with office consumables, small items of office equipment and other materials.

Claiming credit

Once you have completed your final assessment, you will need to write in your record book or folder how, when, where and what you have done to prove that you are competent.

The following is an example of how one trainee completed this claim:

During my work placement at Crazy Jacks I was responsible for the stock in our section. As detailed in Element 9.1 I counted stock and made out the necessary stock record cards. The section did not have any formal system before. I issued stock on every day but understand that if I worked in a larger office it may be necessary to issue stock once a week or at regular times. It was not necessary for me to lift any really heavy items – the heaviest were the boxes of A4 paper which contained 5 reams. I made sure that I bent my knees and kept my back as straight as possible. The only stock that was slightly damaged was some old paper that had become dirty. I cut this in half and it was used for telephone messages and rough calculations by the staff.

I have samples of the stock cards used in my evidence folder and my supervisor has written a confirmation letter of the work I carried out.

UNIT 10
Process documents relating to goods and services

■ Element 10.1
ORDER GOODS AND SERVICES

Performance criteria

- Instructions are understood before ordering goods and services
- Ordering of goods and services is in accordance with authorised procedures
- Documentation for ordering goods is completed in accordance with specified procedures
- Competitive prices have been obtained prior to placing order, where applicable

All businesses are involved in buying and selling. Numerous documents are used for this process, each serving 2 purposes:

- to give information to the other party
- to enable the business to keep its own records.

Various documents will be used by different companies involved in buying and selling transactions. It is normal practice for these organisations to allocate document reference numbers in order to assist identification and clarify payments. Sales and geographical references can be used to identify each customer and each individual order placed. Corresponding documents carry the same number so that all parties know what order or delivery is being dealt with. If a company were to receive 2 invoices for the same delivery, it would be easy to identify this because each invoice would carry details of the same order number.

Larger organisations will allocate official order numbers to orders, which may have to be signed by an authorised member of staff. Printed

274

order forms may carry a warning stating that if the order does not carry an official order number and is not authorised, the delivery of goods will not be accepted.

Documents that you are likely to come across are:

- Order
- Acknowledgement
- Advice note
- Delivery note
- Consignment note
- Pro-forma invoice
- Invoice
- Statement of account
- Credit note
- Debit note.

A business will send out an initial **enquiry**, perhaps to 3 or 4 suppliers, in order to find out which supplier can offer the best deal. In return the suppliers will send a **quotation, estimate, catalogue** or **price list** detailing the price and terms they are prepared to offer. The supplier may also take this opportunity to send free samples or arrange for a sales representative to call.

The Purchasing Department will decide upon the supplier to use and will send out an **order**. When the supplier receives this order it will send an **acknowledgement** back to the organisation's Purchasing Department to confirm that it has received the order. Once the order is ready for despatch the supplier will send an **advice note** by post, containing the delivery details.

A **delivery note**, containing the same details as the advice note, will be sent with the goods. It is the responsibility of the person receiving them to ensure that the goods delivered correspond with those detailed in the delivery note. Any discrepancies must be detailed on the note and confirmed by the person delivering the goods.

The supplier will produce an **invoice** for each delivery of goods, which will give full details of the goods supplied together with a breakdown of costs, including any discounts, transport charges and VAT. At the end of each month the supplier will send the organisation a **statement of account** which details the amount payable for all the invoices for that month, less any refunds for goods returned or

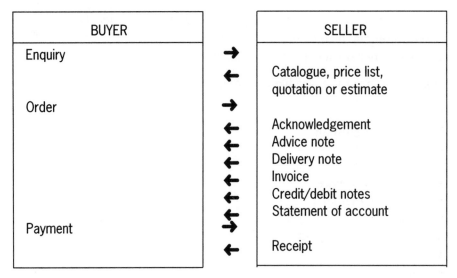

Fig 10.1 Document flow between buyer and seller

damaged (detailed on the **credit note**), plus any charges for additional goods or underpayments (detailed on the **debit note**).

The business may pay separately for each invoice received (this will depend on how often the business uses the supplier and how many deliveries are made in one month). When the invoice or statement of account has been checked arrangements are made for payment to be sent to the supplier in settlement of the account.

In general terms, the usual flow of some of these documents is as shown in Fig. 10.1.

There will always be occasions in a busy company where office goods such as stationery and small items of office equipment need to be checked and reordered to maintain a usable level. The office cannot afford to run out of items used on a daily basis or have essential equipment out of order as this will have the effect of slowing down the operation. Services, such as maintenance of office equipment, servicing contracts and organising staff cover with an agency, also have to be arranged so that the office can 'tick over' efficiently.

▶ How are goods and services ordered in an organisation?

As a member of an organisation you will need to be aware of the procedures required in order to request supplies for your own working area. Most organisations use **requisition forms** (*see* Fig. 10.2), which are completed by the person making the request for goods, usually countersigned by the supervisor and then passed to the Stock Controller, who will arrange for the items to be taken from the stockroom.

If the Stock Controller identifies low stock that needs to be reordered, a **purchase requisition** would be sent to the Purchasing Department to inform them the minimum stock level had been reached and new stock should be ordered immediately. It is the responsibility of the Purchasing Department to ensure the stock is not only ordered, but that they have ordered the correct quality at the best possible price.

In order to do this the Purchasing Department may order from a regular supplier or may choose to send out a number of letters of enquiry to various suppliers to find who will offer the best deal. When large orders are required it is usual practice to put the order out to tender. The Purchasing Department will contact a number of suppliers giving details of the goods or services required and invite each supplier to tender a quotation (a newspaper advertisement may also be used). The cheapest tender offering the required quality of goods or service is usually the one that is accepted by the Purchasing Department.

■ DIY 10.1.1

Does your organisation or training centre use requisition forms and purchase requisition forms? Find an example of each type of form and place it in your evidence folder with a brief explanation of how each form is used. If you do not use such forms, write a report on how goods and services are requisitioned internally by members of staff.

The Purchasing Department takes on the responsibility for buying goods and services on behalf of the company. It is their job to get the required quality, quantity and price from suppliers offering goods and services. The Purchasing Department may use catalogues and price

	(company name and address)			
ORDER NUMBER: SUPPLIER:			DATE:	
Please supply the items listed below:				
QTY	DESCRIPTION	CAT. NO.	UNIT PRICE	TOTAL PRICE
	Authorised by		TOTAL	—— ——

Fig 10.2 Requisition form

lists supplied by companies; prices and terms offered by each company will be compared and the best deal identified.

▶ *What services may need to be arranged?*

Services offered by companies will also be compared in terms of price and quality. Office machinery will need to be serviced and maintained regularly if it is to operate efficiently. Service contracts may be set up by the Purchasing Department with a company who, for a fee, will provide a maintenance service for a period (usually one year). If the service given is of the required standard, the contract will be renewed for another period.

During busy periods or staff holidays there may be a need for extra members of staff to cover those who are absent. Your organisation may be large enough to have a contract with a staff agency who will send extra staff upon receipt of a telephone call. It may, however, be the case that you will have to contact a number of agencies to enquire what their rates are and if they have suitable staff available.

■ DIY 10.1.2

Type a list of all the suppliers used by your company, giving details of the type of goods supplied and the telephone number for each supplier. If such a list already exists ask if you can photocopy it (or part of it if it is too large). Select 4 suppliers from your list and write a letter to each requesting that they send a quotation for three pieces of equipment. You can choose these yourself but should remember to include the part or reference number for each in your request. Your letters must give precise details of the goods required and ask for terms and discounts available. You also need to know how long they take to deliver. Ask your supervisor for permission to send the letters, but if this is not possible you should place the letters in your work folder as evidence.

▶ *What about emergency orders?*

It is vital that the Purchasing Department is notified of a stock shortage as soon as possible. This will give staff time to send out enquiry letters and look for the best deal in adequate delivery time. If an emergency occurs due to an oversight this may not allow time to find the best supplier and a more expensive price may have to be paid for immediate delivery.

It is usual practice for a supplier to accept and start to process an order upon receipt of a telephone call. However, a written confirmation and order number would usually be expected before the goods are

QUOTATION

BRIGHT SPARK LTD   NO. 7879
ELECTRICAL SUPPLIES   YOUR REF: 241
SOUTHERN ROAD   DATE: 5.9.93
WORTHING SUSSEX

TO: Bales Paint Supplies, 144 Knight Lane, Kinstone

CODE NO.	DESCRIPTION	UNITS	PRICE PER UNIT	QUANTITY DISCOUNT
24647	40w Light bulbs	1 x 10	8.70	10% on 5 packs and over
56986	60w Light bulbs	1 x 10	8.99	10% on 5 packs and over
672984	100w Light bulbs	1 x 10	9.20	15% on 6 packs and over

PRICE EXCLUSIVE OF VAT

TERMS: 2%, 30 days
DELIVERY: 14 days
Carriage paid

For and on behalf of
BRIGHT SPARK LTD

A.N.Other

Sales Manager

Fig 10.3 A quotation

dispatched. In an emergency the order could be telephoned to the supplier with the written confirmation arriving later by fax or telex.

■ DIY 10.1.3

You work for Bales Paint Supplies and have received the quotation from Bright Spark Ltd shown in Fig. 10.3. Copy the order form shown in Fig. 10.4 and make out the following orders. Your supervisor must allocate an official order number and authorise the orders to verify that they are correct.

1 Order dated: 1.6.94
    4 pkts of 40W light bulbs

```
┌─────────────────────────────────────────────────────────────────┐
│                    BALES PAINT SUPPLIES                           │
│              144 Knight Lane, Kinstone, KJ32 7BB                  │
│                                                                   │
│                           ORDER                                   │
│                                                                   │
│   Order Number:                        Date:                      │
│   Supplier:                                                       │
│   Address:                                                        │
│                                                                   │
│                                                                   │
│   Please supply the items listed below:                          │
├──────┬─────────────────────┬────────────┬─────────┬──────────────┤
│ QTY  │ DESCRIPTION         │ CODE NO.   │ UNIT    │ TOTAL        │
│      │                     │            │ PRICE   │ PRICE        │
├──────┼─────────────────────┼────────────┼─────────┼──────────────┤
│      │                     │            │         │              │
│      │                     │            │         │              │
│      │                     │            │         │              │
│      │                     │            │         │              │
│      │                     │            │         │              │
│      │ Authorised by       │            │         │              │
│      │                     │            │         │              │
│      │                     │            │         │              │
│      │ .................   │            │         │              │
│      │ (Goods deliveries will          │         │              │
│      │ only be accepted if │           │         │              │
│      │ accompanied by an   │            │         │              │
│      │ order number) ......│            │ TOTAL:  │              │
└──────┴─────────────────────┴────────────┴─────────┴──────────────┘
```

Fig 10.4 Order form

    4 pkts of 60W light bulbs
    5 pkts of 100W light bulbs

2 Order dated: 1.7.94
    5 pkts of 40W light bulbs
    7 pkts of 100W light bulbs

3 Order dated 1.8.94

7 pkts of 60W light bulbs
10 pkts of 100W light bulbs

4 Order dated 1.9.94
10 pkts of 40W light bulbs
10 pkts of 60W light bulbs
10 pkts of 100W light bulbs

Remember to add 17.5 per cent VAT to each order. The VAT must be calculated on the total amount less the 2 per cent discount. (Refer to page 285 for information on VAT.)

▶ *What is a pro-forma invoice?*

If goods are ordered on approval, allowing inspection of them before payment, they may be sent with a pro-forma invoice. This shows what the charges would be if the buyer decides to keep the goods or order them as usual. If a seller decides that goods must be paid for in advance a pro-forma invoice can be sent before the goods to request payment in advance of the goods being delivered (*see* Fig. 10.5).

▶ *What departments are involved in buying and selling?*

Large organisations employ specialist staff who provide a central service for ordering supplies – usually called the Purchasing Department. It is the responsibility of this department to ensure that the organisation gets the 'best deal' when buying supplies – this is achieved by collecting all departmental orders, combining them and thus gaining discounts through bulk buying. The Purchasing Department uses letters of enquiry to identify suppliers offering the best discounts. It may also offer regular contracts to suppliers to attract better discounts.

A purchase requisition is used if you request an item that is not held in stock. The Stock Controller may have to obtain quotations prior to ordering the item and therefore needs ample time to do this before the item is required. It is important that you think ahead and anticipate demand for supplies or special items so the Purchasing Department staff have enough time to find the most appropriate supplier. However, in the event of an emergency you may have to rely upon a supplier

The Stationery Shop
19 Station Street
WALSALL   WL9 9JH
Telephone 0230 92928 Fax 0230 92950
Telex 27192 Station S

PRO-FORMA INVOICE

Date:

To:

_____

Please receive   parcel(s) containing:

No commercial value.

Not for resale.

Value for customs purposes only: £

Country of origin:

Reason for export:

I certify that this no charge invoice is correct to the best of my knowledge.

Signed _____

The Stationery Shop Registered Office: 19 Station Street Walsall WL9 9JH Registered number E50225 England

Fig 10.5 A pro-forma invoice

who, although not offering the best deal, will accept an emergency order over the telephone or fax and will deliver immediately.

The work of the Sales Department can be divided into different areas such as overseas sales, home sales, advertising and marketing. All these functions deal with selling the goods/services offered by the company. Staff in this department are responsible for sending out price lists and catalogues and preparing invoices for customers. Customer complaints and after-sales service are also dealt with by this department. The Sales Department may also be responsible for calculating transport charges that need to be added to customers' invoices. The following pricing terms are used to indicate transport charges:

- **Carriage paid** means the price includes all transport costs.
- **Loco** is the factory price and does not include transport costs (often used for motor cars).
- **Free on Rail (FOR)** means the seller pays all costs up to a named railway station.
- **Carriage forward** means the cost of delivery is not included in the price.
- **Cash With Order (CWO)** means payment must accompany the order.
- **Cash On Delivery (COD)** means payment must be made to whoever delivers the goods.

The Accounts Department is probably the most important in the company. Its job is to see that all invoices sent to the company by its suppliers are paid promptly and, similarly, that all invoices are sent out promptly to the customers of the company, and that they too are paid on time. Staff in this department are responsible for ensuring that all invoices are checked against orders and delivery notes to ensure the company is not paying for something it has not received. Once an invoice has been checked against the order and/or delivery note it can be passed for payment – this is usually indicated by a person's signature across the invoice or a rubber stamp authorisation.

▶ How is value added tax calculated?

When in receipt of an invoice, note that VAT is often entered in a separate column. When invoices are being processed you will have to identify purchases that include VAT, calculate how much VAT is included in the price, and then check that this is correct before the invoice is paid. The VAT total should always be rounded down.

If you are presented with an amount which includes VAT, divide the total by 117.5 and then multiply by 17.5. This will tell you how much of the total price is VAT (you can also multiply by 7 and divide by 47 to arrive at the same answer!). If you are given a figure that requires VAT to be added, divide the figure by 100 and then multiply by 17.5, and this will tell you how much should be added on.

The VAT column is particularly important if the company is registered for VAT, as this registration enables the company to claim back all VAT paid on goods and services. It is therefore essential that accurate records are kept not only for the benefit of the company, but also because they are required by law.

The rate of VAT is currently set at 17.5 per cent, but remember that some goods (such as some foods, children's clothes, shoes, newspapers and books) are exempt. In effect, the government uses registered businesses to collect VAT from the consumer on its behalf. These businesses have to pay on the VAT collected every quarter, but are allowed to deduct all the VAT they have paid out.

Some businesses do not have to add VAT on to the price of their goods or services, because they are unregistered or exempt. Unregistered businesses will not obtain a refund of the VAT they have themselves paid on goods and services bought by them.

1 Small businesses do not have to become VAT registered provided their annual turnover is less than £45,000. Once it has exceeded this amount they have no option but must become registered and keep relevant, up-to-date VAT records that can be checked by HM Customs and Excise at will.

2 Some businesses, such as banks and insurance companies, do not charge VAT on their services, but can reclaim VAT paid out, if they are zero-rated.

Zero-rated businesses do not have to add VAT to the selling price of goods (strictly, they do add VAT, but at zero per cent!), but can obtain a refund of all VAT paid on the purchase of goods or services. A zero-rated business, such as a publisher or a business selling food, is thus in a better position than an exempted business, which cannot reclaim VAT paid out.

The only business that is allowed, by law, to charge you VAT is one that is registered to do so. You will be able to check whether a business is registered by asking for its VAT registration number, although this should be detailed on the invoice and any other business documents used by the business.

▶ *What other calculations are there?*

Businesses often use various methods to attract custom. Two methods are:

1 **Trade discount**. This is usually given by the seller to buyers who order in large quantities. A discount percentage is given on orders over a certain amount and, therefore, encourages bulk orders.
2 **Cash discount**. This is given by the seller to the buyer to encourage quick payment. The discount is usually shown as 'Terms: 2 per cent one month', meaning that if payment is made within one month the buyer can deduct 2 per cent from the total price.

■ DIY 10.1.4

It may be your responsibility to obtain competitive quotations from selected suppliers. It is important therefore that you are able to calculate how and when VAT is charged and how trade and cash discounts operate. You must be able to recognise the quotation that is offering the best deal; this is not always the one with the cheapest prices! The prices offered by different companies will differ greatly when taking cash and trade discounts into account.

For example:

If a quotation for £50 was received showing a trade discount of 10 per cent and a cash discount of 5 per cent one month, you would deduct £7.25 from the invoice and pay only £42.75, provided the payment was made within one month. The formula used for this is:

$£50 \div 100 \times 10 = £5.00$ (trade discount)
$£50 - £5.00 = £45.00$
$£45.00 \div 100 \times 5 = £2.25$ (cash discount)
$£45.00 - £2.25 = £42.75$

VAT is added to the amount after any trade discount and/or cash discount has been deducted.

Your company wishes to order £100 worth of stationery and has received a number of quotations from different suppliers. Work out the best deal for your company from the following quotation details (show all your calculations):

Supplier A: 5% trade discount
10% cash discount, 1 month
17.5% VAT

Supplier B: 7.5% trade discount
5% cash discount, 8 weeks
17.5% VAT

Supplier C: 10% trade discount
7.5% cash discount, 6 weeks
17.5% VAT

▶ How do you check progression of orders?

This will depend upon your organisation's procedures. It may be that a simple telephone call is required to chase up a delivery, or it may be the case that an official letter must be sent. Generally speaking, the delivery of ordered goods will take place as soon as the supplier is able to dispatch them. The time it takes for delivery is usually stated on the quotation, and if this period of time is exceeded than the order can be cancelled.

However, it may be that the supplier is awaiting payment for previous deliveries before dispatching further orders. In this case your Accounts Department will need to be contacted to find out if payment has been made. It is of no use telephoning or writing to a company to progress an order if the hold-up is because of a problem with your own company. Large companies often employ 'purchase order expeditors' or 'progress chasers' whose job it is to check the progression of orders.

It is normal practice for companies to identify and use reliable suppliers who provide goods and services of the right quality at the right price. When a company uses a regular supplier for certain goods or services a relationship is built up between them. In this way all that is needed is a telephone call to a named person to sort out any

287

problems with delivery. Providing each company treats the other with respect in terms of quality and price, delivery and payment, then a long-term, established relationship is likely to form between them.

There are, however, certain circumstances and organisations that will employ specialist 'buyers' whose job it is to find the best deal for every item being ordered. Letters of enquiry are often used to request prices from a number of suppliers so that the buyer can compare them against each other for the best. Large orders or service contracts are often put out to 'tender' which is a type of advertisement inviting suppliers to send their best quote for the supplies or services required. In this situation all the replies are opened at the same time and the supplier offering the best deal is given the contract.

Whilst it is important always to find the best deal for the company, in certain cases this may not be possible. If your organisation has taken out a contract with a supplier then this contract must be honoured and only the named company or service used. It is usual practice for an organisation to state a set period of time when taking out such a contract so that when the contract expires, the organisation can look around for a better deal elsewhere. Service contracts often include a set number of visits by a service engineer per year, and photocopier contracts often state that the organisation will be charged for a set number of copies per year, even if these are not taken. Once a contract has been signed it must be honoured, and even if you feel that you could get a better deal elsewhere it could cost a lot of money to get out of an existing contract.

■ DIY 10.1.5

How does your organisation ensure that it gets the best deal? And how would it go about checking the progress of an order that is needed urgently? Remember that chasing an order may entail contacting different staff or departments in your own organisation to check progress before the order has even reached the supplier. Write a brief report on how your organisation deals with both of these situations.

Completing Element 10.1

To complete this element on ordering goods and services you will need to put all the DIY tasks in your folder, and carry out a final assessment. This must prove that you are able to ask questions to clarify the requirements for goods and services and that you are able to confirm your understanding of those requirements before orders are placed. You should show that you are able to identify suppliers of goods and services and that you can obtain competitive quotations from selected suppliers. Goods and services must be ordered according to organisational procedures and you must be able to check the progress of orders. Organisational and suppliers' procedures must be followed at all times and reference made to contractual agreements.

Claiming credit

Once you have completed your final assessment, you will need to write in your record book or folder how, when, where and what you have done to prove that you are competent.

The following is an example of how one trainee completed this claim:

At Coopers & Co I spent 4 weeks in the purchasing department where I had to dispatch letters to suppliers requesting quotations for goods and services. When the quotations were received these were passed on to the Chief Buyer who decided which supplier to use for the goods. She then passed the quotation details and the order requisition back to me and I made out the orders following the company procedure (see evidence folder). When I was unsure of requirements I checked these with my supervisor before placing an order. I was asked to make enquiries to 6 different companies to find out if they could offer a better deal than a supplier with whom we had a contract. I found out that one of the companies offered much better trade and cash discounts and wrote a memo to the Chief Buyer informing her of this (see folder). When sending out an order I had to enter this into an order book which gave me an official order number. In the book I wrote details of the order and my supervisor initialled it. The order was passed to the Chief Buyer for signature before it was sent out.

■ Element 10.2
PROCESS CLAIMS FOR PAYMENT

Performance criteria

- Claims are verified in accordance with organisational procedures
- Computations are checked for accuracy and validity

- Discrepancies are investigated and resolved within own authority or referred to an appropriate authority
- Referral of verified claims to appropriate others is in accordance with organisational procedures
- Records are accurate, complete and legible

When goods or services have been delivered or provided and are satisfactory the supplier will expect payment to be made on the due date. Likewise, when members of staff submit claim forms for travel expenses, etc, these should also be paid as soon as possible. However, before any payments can be made the claims for payment must first be checked and authorised only if they are correct.

▶ *What might your duties include?*

Checking invoices

Before paying any supplier you should make sure that the invoice has been checked and authorised. The department receiving the goods should check the invoice against the delivery note and, if it is correct, sign the invoice as 'Passed for Payment'. If the invoice is not authorised it should not be paid. You should always check the calculations are correct, including the VAT (see page 285 for further details on VAT) and that trade and cash discounts have been deducted correctly.

■ DIY 10.2.1

You have received the invoices shown in Figs. 10.6 to 10.9. Use a calculator to check the calculations, and note any errors. Round all of your figures down. Write a memo to your supervisor Doug Lewis telling him about the problems.

Remember that when checking the invoice shown in Fig. 10.9 you should deduct the trade and maximum cash discount before calculating and adding on the VAT.

If your company places regular orders with the supplier it will probably wait until the statement is received at the end of the month before

	W G HUGHES & SONS Stationery Suppliers 132 Avenue West SHEFFIELD SH2 3MM **INVOICE** No 2424	
12	Boxes of pencils HB	£9.45
5	Reams of Bond paper @ £1.85 per ream	£9.25
5	Boxes of window envelopes @ £2.50 per box	£12.00
	TOTAL AMOUNT DUE	£34.25
	Less 10% Trade Discount	£3.42
		£30.83
	Add VAT @ 17.5%	£5.39
	TOTAL DUE	£36.42
Terms:	Payment should be made in 30 days from 30 June	

Fig 10.6

	W G HUGHES & SONS Stationery Suppliers 132 Avenue West SHEFFIELD SH2 3MM **INVOICE** No 2425	
24	Carbon typewriter ribbons	£30.00
12	Correction tapes	£3.00
	TOTAL AMOUNT DUE	£33.00
	Less 10% Trade Discount	£3.30
		£29.70
	Add VAT @ 17.5%	£5.20
	TOTAL DUE	£44.90
Terms:	Payment should be made in 30 days from 28 June	

Fig 10.7

	W G HUGHES & SONS Stationery Suppliers 132 Avenue West SHEFFIELD SH2 3MM **INVOICE** No 2426	
6	Typist chairs, adjustable back. Red @ £12 each	£72.00
2	Coat stands – pine £50 each	£100.00
	TOTAL AMOUNT DUE	£172.00
	Less 15% Trade Discount	£17.20
		£154.80
	Add VAT @ 17.5%	£27.09
	TOTAL DUE	£181.89
Terms:	Payment should be made in 30 days from 28 June	

Fig 10.8

	W G HUGHES & SONS Stationery Suppliers 132 Avenue West SHEFFIELD SH2 3MM **INVOICE** No 2427	
12	Lever arch files @ £3.50 each	£42.00
40	Ring binders (20 red, 20 blue) @ £1.89 each	£75.60
	TOTAL AMOUNT DUE	£117.60
	Less 10% Trade Discount	£11.76
		£105.84
	Add VAT @ 17.5%	£18.06
	TOTAL DUE	£123.90
Terms:	Payment should be made in 30 days – 2.5% cash discount	

Fig 10.9

payment is made. The statement will detail all the invoices sent during the month as well as any debit or credit notes. The invoices, credit and debit notes should be checked against the statement before checking the calculations and paying the amount due. If there is any error, it should be noted, checked with your supervisor, the relevant department and the supplier.

▶ When would you use a credit or debit note?

The use of **credit notes** and **debit notes** allow adjustments to be made without having to create another invoice. If you discovered you had been overcharged, or were invoiced for an item you had not received, you would request a credit note to make up the difference. If you had been undercharged or accepted items not listed on your invoice, then a debit note would be forwarded. The amount under- or overpaid will be rectified on the next statement of account.

The business transaction documents that pass between buyers and sellers often detail terms specially agreed between the 2 parties. Therefore, it is important that these documents are not discussed or shown to unauthorised personnel. Think how useful it would be to a supplier to know what discounts the local competition offers its customers. A quick look at an invoice can also give an indication of the profit being made by the business if it is reselling the goods bought – another piece of information that should be kept to authorised personnel only.

■ DIY 10.2.2

These invoices have been received and have been 'Passed for payment'.

Invoice No 2390	£26.90
Invoice No 2409	£53.87
Invoice No 2503	£232.94
Invoice No 2555	£88.56
Invoice No 2646	£49.24
Invoice No 2745	£66.99

Credit and debit notes have been received for the following amounts.

Debit note for Invoice No 2390	£12.60
Debit note for Invoice No 2409	£10.20
Credit note for Invoice No 2646	£50.30
Credit note for Invoice No 2745	£20.00

Check the above documents against the statement received shown in Fig. 10.10.

Identify any errors and calculate the total due.

W G HUGHES & SONS
Stationery Suppliers
132 Avenue West
SHEFFIELD
SH2 3MM

STATEMENT

4/5	Invoice 2390	26.90
6/5	Debit Note	12.50
8/5	Invoice 2409	53.87
10/5	Debit Note	10.20
11/5	Invoice 2503	223.94
14/5	Invoice 2555	88.55
18/5	Invoice 2646	49.24
20/5	Credit Note	50.00
25/5	Invoice 2745	66.99
27/5	Credit Note	20.00

TOTAL AMOUNT PAYABLE	

Fig 10.10

▶ *What systems might be used to check documents?*

Manual systems involve the use of files to keep all business transaction documents. Box files and lever arch files are often used to keep documents such as invoices and delivery notes in order. It is likely that a separate file will be kept for each supplier with invoices kept either in date order or numerically by their invoice number.

When an invoice or statement of account is received it is checked against the original order form to make sure the correct goods have been delivered before payment is made. Some organisations will also check the invoice against the delivery note, although the invoice is often used instead of a delivery note.

Computerised accounts systems, such as Pegasus and Sage, can be used to store all information detailed on buying and selling documentation. Information regarding sales can be keyed into the computer and stored indefinitely, invoices and other documents can be printed out and invoices received by the company checked against the original order information held on the computer. A computerised accounts system can automatically calculate VAT, discounts and transport charges.

▶ *What is a tax point?*

In most cases the date of the invoice will be the same as the tax point. This is the date on which the goods transfer hands and VAT is payable. The seller and the buyer of the goods will have to enter details of VAT charged and paid on to their records for that particular date. This date is very important as VAT is paid to HM Customs and Excise department every 3 months (quarterly) so it is important for a business to know in what quarter to place the VAT paid or collected. If, for example, a company were to receive their goods in separate deliveries the tax point date would be different to the invoice date, as the VAT would only be charged once the total amount of goods had been delivered.

<table>
<tr><td colspan="3" align="center">**BALES PAINT SUPPLIES**
144 Knight Lane
Kinstone KJ32 7BB</td></tr>
</table>

Pickford Chemicals Salisbury Way Bury	**ORDER NUMBER** C/6785/245 DATE 27 January 93

Please supply the following:

ITEM	CODE	QUANTITY
White Spirit	WD99/B	8 x 4 litres
Methylated Spirit	MS56/A	9 x 4 litres
Caustic Soda	CS/02/C	5 boxes

DELIVER TO: above address   AUTHORISED BY: A.N.Other

NOTE: Goods deliveries will only be accepted if accompanied by an official order number.

Fig 10.11

■ DIY 10.2.3

Check the orders shown in Fig. 10.11 to 10.13, placed by the Purchasing Department of Bales Paint Supplies, against their respective invoices shown in Fig. 10.14 to 10.16 (on the following pages). List any errors you find and report these in a memo to the Accounts Supervisor, Mrs Gill Grant. When checking the invoices make sure you deduct both trade and cash discount from the price before calculating the VAT. Round down all figures.

▶ *What do the letters E&OE mean?*

This means **Errors and Omissions Excepted**, so if delivered items are left off the invoice or pricing errors are made, the seller can add/deduct that amount later. A note can be issued once the error is found and contains details of the error and the amount overpaid or underpaid by the purchaser. This term also covers the supplier if the person responsible for preparing invoices makes an error – imagine if they put £1000 instead of £10000!

BALES PAINT SUPPLIES
144 Knight Lane
Kinstone KJ32 7BB

Patterson's Stationery
The Long Yard
Ilkeston

ORDER NUMBER
F/2639/23

DATE
29 January 93

Please supply the following:

ITEM	CODE	QUANTITY
A4 Copier Paper (white)	45/A/9	10 reams
A4 Bank Paper (yellow)	23/67/8	4 reams
Staplers	15/87/A	6
Staple removers	25/784/1	10
Comb Binding machine	123/87	1
Lever Arch Files	12/5/89	2 x 10
Box Files	72/6/90	2 x 10

DELIVER TO: above address   AUTHORISED BY: A.N.Other

NOTE: Goods deliveries will only be accepted if accompanied by an official order number.

Fig 10.12

▶ *What is the purpose of a delivery note?*

A delivery note, containing the same details as the advice note, will be sent with the goods. It is the responsibility of the person receiving the goods to ensure that the goods actually delivered correspond with those detailed on the delivery note. If there are any discrepancies, these must be detailed on the note so that the supplier is aware of the error. It is then up to the supplier to issue a credit or debit note. If the person receiving the delivery does not have time to check it immediately then he/she should write across the delivery that the goods have been accepted but not checked. If an error is found when the delivery is finally checked, the company will have to notify the supplier either by telephone or in writing. Obviously, in this case the supplier will rely upon the goodwill and honesty of the company.

BALES PAINT SUPPLIES
144 Knight Lane
Kinstone KJ32 7BB

Ace Computer Supplies
Catchpole Gardens
London SE9

ORDER NUMBER
C/7648/54

DATE
31 January 93

Please supply the following:

ITEM	CODE	QUANTITY
Concept 35 computer chair	24-m-2309	3
Laser Toner Cartridges	34-n-3425	6
Double Density Diskettes	38-p-4879	3 x 10
Diskette Library Case	56-o-3099	2
Economy PC Stand	11-r-5888	5

DELIVER TO: above address   AUTHORISED BY: A.N.Other

NOTE: Goods deliveries will only be accepted if accompanied by an official order number.

Fig 10.13

Remember that companies do not necessarily have their own delivery or transport department and may rely upon an outside carrier company to deliver goods on their behalf. If this is the case, a consignment note is usually used in place of the delivery note. The driver of the vehicle has to obtain a signature for the delivery of the goods as this acts as the delivery company's receipt. The delivery note will be checked back against the original order and this in turn will then be checked against the invoice for the goods. Any errors can be put right by issuing a debit or credit note and adjusting the end of month statement of account. The delivery note will also detail any charges made for delivery; these charges are subject to VAT.

Pickford Chemicals
Salisbury Way
Bury BY14 8BB

VAT NO: 675/75876/32   **INVOICE**

Invoice No: 27/56/90/A   Date/Tax Point
Goods delivered to: Bales Paint Supplies   20.2.93
144 Knight Lane
Kinstone KJ32 7BB

Order No: C/6785/245

QTY	DETAILS	UNIT PRICE	TOTAL PRICE	VAT	TOTAL
5	CAUSTIC SODA	0.98	4.90	0.85	5.75
8	METHYLATED				
	SPIRIT	4.00	32.00	5.60	37.60
9	WHITE SPIRIT	4.20	33.60	5.88	39.48
TERMS: 30 days net monthly NOTE: 1 x Methylated Spirit to follow			70.50	12.33	82.83

Fig 10.14

▶ *Checking expenses claims*

Apart from checking invoices and statements, you may also have to
check travel and expense claims. This is to make sure that employees
do not claim more than they are entitled to. Expenses and travel
payments may be paid to the employees by cheque or it may be added
to their wage or salary (through bank giro credit). When a member of
staff travels on behalf of the company there are usually rules about
how much they are allowed to claim – check with your supervisor what
the current regulations are.

The following are examples of travel expenses that may be allowed:

- public transport fares or equivalent amounts
- fixed amount per mile travelled in own transport
- additional amount paid per passenger taken.

As far as other expenses are concerned, employees could be allowed to
claim for:

PATTERSON'S STATIONERY SUPPLIES
THE LONG YARD, ILKESTON, IK3 9DD
VAT REG NO: 333/555/22

INVOICE

OUR REF: pg/aw/897   DATE/TAX POINT: 9.2.93
YOUR REF: F/2639/23

TO: Bales Paint Supplies
       144 Knight Lane
       Kinstone

QTY	DESCRIPTION	UNIT PRICE	TOTAL PRICE	VAT	AMOUNT TO PAY
10	A4 Copier Paper White	£2.99 ream	29.90	5.12	35.02
4	A4 Bank Paper (Yellow)	£2.55 ream	10.20	1.75	11.95
6	Staplers	£4.75	28.50	4.88	33.38
10	Staple Removers	£1.15	11.50	1.97	13.47
2 x 10	Box Files	£10.70	21.40	3.67	25.07
2 x 10	Lever Arch Files	£8.50	17.00	2.91	19.91
					238.80

TERMS: 2% One Month
E&OE   TOTAL PAYABLE £238.80

Fig 10.15

- bed and breakfast or hotel costs
- meals away from home (sometimes a set amount is paid, called subsistence, for all meals and incidentals)
- telephone calls.

Ace Computer Supplies
Catchpole Gardens
London SE9   VAT. No. 423/75894/11

Invoice No: 55.2.78.93 Order No: C/7658/54   Date and Tax
                                                              Point: 30.2.93

Qty	Description	Code	Price	Total
3	Comp. chairs	24-m-2309	57.69	173.04
6	Cartridges	34-n-3425	45.90	275.40
3 x 10	Diskettes	38-p-4879	8.90	26.70
3	PC stand	11-r-5888	27.50	82.50
2	Diskette Cases	56-o-3099	5.99	11.98
TOTAL PRICE EXCLUDING VAT				569.62
VAT @ 17.5%			89.71	659.33

Goods delivered to:	Terms:	Note: 2 x PC
Bales Paint Supplies	5% – 28 days	Stands to follow
144 Knight Lane	10% – 14 days	next week under
Kinstone	E&OE	separate invoice

Fig 10.16

■ DIY 10.2.4

Using the following figures work out the expense claims for the following staff.
Travel: 40p per mile up to 50 miles, 20p per mile thereafter.
Subsistence: £4 if absent for 6 hours or more.

- Mr Spencer Shaw – travelled 75 miles, away from the office for 4 hours.
- Mrs Stephanie Barrett – travelled 35 miles, away from the office for 3 hours.
- Mr Gary Relton – travelled 118 miles, away from the office for 8 hours.
- Mr Ben Wright – travelled 66 miles, away from the office for 6 hours.

Check the claims that the following staff have made:
- Katie Small – travelled 45 miles, away from the office for 4 hours – amount claimed £18.00.
- Eva Dacosta – travelled 79 miles, away from the office for 5.5 hours – amount claimed £25.80.
- Sharon Frampton – travelled 25 miles, away from the office for 2 hours – amount claimed £9.50.
- Kelly Farrell – travelled 85 miles, away from the office for 7 hours – amount claimed £31.90.

It is the usual practice for an employee to complete a form and sign it, certifying that the expenses claimed are accurate. The form is then passed to an authorised supervisor and department manager for authorisation. An unauthorised claim should not be passed for payment.

Expenses claims are used by employees to claim back money spent on the organisation's behalf or during the course of carrying out their business. Expenses claim forms have to be checked, problems or queries sorted out and the forms finally passed for payment. The employee will be expected to support their claim form with receipts, orders or advice notes; calculations will also have to be checked. The expenses claim will have to be authorised as valid and will need an expenses code before payment can be made.

The type of expenses claimed will depend upon the size and type of business. A company with a large sales team will expect to pay expenses for accommodation, meals, telephone charges, travel tickets and taxis. An employee can also claim for items such as entertaining clients, tips and petrol.

■ DIY 10.2.5

Look at the expenses claim form shown in Fig. 10.17 for a typical 3-day sales trip. Copy out the form and work out the total claim amount. Using the expenses code table in Fig. 10.18 complete the code column with the correct code against each expense.

The receipts supplied with the expenses claim form will have to be checked against the entries on the form. The hotel bill will give a breakdown of what was spent and will look something like Fig. 10.19.

The expense claim form has been completed with details of meals that include drinks at the bar. Money spent over the bar does not count as subsistence (necessary meals) and some organisations would expect Mr Jones to pay this amount himself as a personal expense. However, some organisations will allow their employees to spend money, usually up to a certain limit, on personal items. This is treated as a gesture of goodwill to compensate the employee for having to spend time away from home.

302

CARTER CARE LTD – EXPENSES CLAIM FORM				
NAME	DATE	DATE FROM	DATE TO	LOCATION
D Jones	6.12.94	2.12.94	4.12.94	Bath
DATE	DETAILS		EXPENSE	CODE
2.12	Train ticket – RETURN		89.90	
	Taxi		3.20	
	Dinner		24.78	
	Telephone		5.90	
	Lunch (on train)		6.89	
3.12	Newspaper		1.20	
	Taxi		4.60	
	Theatre × 2		52.00	
	Dinner × 2		59.00	
	(Sales Manager – Northern plc)			
	Newspaper		0.86	
4.12	Taxi		2.30	
	Lunch (on train)		5.99	
	Hotel (B&B)		76.00	
Signed			Total amount of claim.................	
Authorised..				

Fig 10.17

Expense	Code
Telephone	Tel
Accommodation	Acc
Entertaining	Ent
Tips	Tips
Petrol	Pet
Taxi	Taxi
Travel tickets	Trav
Food	Fd
Newspapers	Nwsp
Personal items	Pl
Bar	Bar

Fig 10.18

	THE COUNTY HOTEL	
	GRAND PARADE	
	BATH	

DATE OF DEPARTURE: 4.12.93   VAT REG NO: 34526 67548

Name of Guest: Mr D Jones   Room No: 201

Method of Payment: Credit card

Date	Detail	Cost
2.12	Accommodation	76.00
	Meals	15.89
	Bar	8.89
	Telephone	5.90
3.12	Newspaper	1.20
	Meals	48.50
	Bar	10.50
4.12	Newspaper	0.86
	TOTAL	167.74

Fig 10.19

Every organisation will have its own rules and allowances for personal items. The Inland Revenue, however, do not, and would see spending money at the bar as a perk of the job which should be taxed. This means that when an expenses claim form is submitted the items that do not attract tax, such as accommodation and travel, are paid back in full. Items, such as drinks at the bar, will be taxed in the same way as a salary.

It is important for you to understand your own organisation's policy for payment of expenses. Small amounts are probably paid from petty cash, although these still need a receipt to be provided. Expenses that are taxable and non-taxable depend upon whether they are deemed to be necessary as part of the job – your local tax office will be able to give you up-to-date information on this.

■ DIY 10.2.6

For this DIY you are asked to write a brief summary of how expenses are paid back to employees in your workplace or training centre. How do you check that the mileage on a travel claim is correct? Do you use a mileage chart? Find a mileage chart if your office does not already have one, and calculate the distance between each of the following towns and cities.

1 Aberdeen – Carlisle
2 Bristol – Glasgow
3 Holyhead – Leicester
4 Manchester – London
5 Reading – Coventry
6 Inverness – Nottingham
7 Cardiff – Plymouth
8 York – Aberystwyth
9 Birmingham – Southampton
10 Sheffield – Exeter

Completing Element 10.2

To complete this element on processing claims for payment you will need to put all DIY tasks in your folder, and carry out a final assessment. This must show that you are able to check calculations in order to verify claims. Discrepancies must be investigated and resolved within your own authority or referred to your supervisor if necessary. Records must be kept accurate, complete, legible and verified claims passed on to the appropriate person according to your organisation's procedures. Invoices must be checked against delivery notes and orders; expenses claims against mileage charts and receipts. Discounts and charges must also be checked.

Claiming credit

Once you have completed your final assessment, you will need to write in your record book or folder how, when, where and what you have done to prove that you are competent.

The following is an example of how one trainee completed this claim:

My work placement required me to spend one day per week in the accounts office. I checked all expenses claims forms by cross-referencing receipts, checking calculations and confirming mileage claimed against a mileage chart. Invoices were checked against the order (this had to have an official order number and signature) and delivery note. If I identified any discrepancies I reported these to the supervisor immediately. If the claim or invoice for payment was correct it was entered into a payments book before being passed for payment. This book was kept neat, tidy and correct at all times (see evidence). I have also included in my evidence folder examples of order forms, delivery notes, claims and items that have had discrepancies noted on them.

Organise travel and accommodation arrangements

■ Element 11.1
ARRANGE TRAVEL FOR PERSONS

Performance criteria

- Instructions for travel requirements are understood
- Travel arrangements conform to specified instructions and organisational procedures
- A clear and accurate schedule, containing all arrangements made, is provided to the appropriate person
- Travel documents are complete and accurate
- Security and confidentiality procedures conform to organisational requirements
- Arrangements are made within agreed deadlines

As businesses expand, their contacts and customers tend to come from a wider area. One consequence of this is that the company's staff will have to travel further and more frequently to discuss business. It may be a part of your job to organise all the arrangements necessary for business travel, whether it be a day visit locally, a three-day visit in Europe or a several weeks' visit internationally. A company representative should always arrive at their destination feeling their best, able to discuss matters and take part in meetings to the benefit of the company, even if they have had a long, tiring and perhaps difficult journey.

Large companies, whose staff travel frequently, may have a travel department that would make all the necessary arrangements for the staff, in consultation with a travel agent. In this case you would still need to be able to give them full details of what is required to ensure the most suitable arrangements are made for the individual travelling. If you are making the arrangements direct with a travel agent, make sure that the one selected has a good reputation and it is registered with ABTA (Association of British Travel Agents).

Most companies will have an agreed policy regarding travel which will state the class of accommodation and travel that members of staff are entitled to, the mileage rate paid to those using their own cars, and the method of travel permitted. Companies would request that employees take into consideration the most economic and efficient type of travel for the circumstances. When you are responsible for organising travel and accommodation you need to take into account not only the most suitable method of travel and accommodation but also the number of people travelling, the rank of those concerned, the aims of the visit and the destination.

Whatever arrangements are made it is useful to gather all the relevant information and documents together in a travel file, and all the information for the traveller in a travel pack. The travel file will enable you to compile travel plans and monitor the progress of the bookings. It will also allow you to brief staff travelling with information regarding their travel plan.

▶ *What should you take into consideration when arranging methods of travel?*

Car

For most local journeys it is practical for employees to drive, either their own car or a company car if it is available. Employees using their own cars should check that their insurance covers them for such journeys. A company will usually pay employees a fixed rate per mile for journeys made on business. This rate should take into account petrol used (distance and cubic capacity (cc) of the car) and wear and tear on the vehicle. The rate agreed by companies seems to vary enormously – currently between 10p and 40p per mile. Some companies also have a limit on how much can be claimed per month, or have a decreasing scale, for example 30p for each mile up to 300,

20p for each mile between 301 and 500, 10p for each mile between 501 and 700.

Companies with a number of cars available for employees' use will probably have an account at a local garage, which will service the cars regularly, sort out mechanical problems and allow employees to obtain petrol. Some of the cars may be allocated to specific personnel: for example, directors usually have cars as a 'perk' of the job, as do sales representatives to enable them to visit customers. Companies that offer a maintenance and repair service are likely to have a fleet of vehicles, usually vans, for use by the engineers and technicians.

If an employee does not have their own car or access to a company car, it may be necessary to hire. Car hire rates vary considerably and it is worth checking several companies before deciding which to use. You should take into account the distance to be travelled and the frequency of visits, as it may be that the hire company would be prepared to negotiate special rates if you use their cars on a regular basis. If the cost of hiring cars is regularly increasing, it may be worth investigating options available, eg purchasing or leasing. Leasing vehicles is becoming extremely popular. The leasing company allocates vehicles to the business in exchange for a regular payment over a fixed period (for example 1–3 years), at the end of which the business has the option of purchasing the vehicle or leasing a new one for another fixed period.

■ DIY 11.1.1

Using your local telephone directory look up the following:

1 A local car hire company that has uniformed drivers
2 A local car hire that specialises in transfer to the nearest airport
3 A local mini cab company
4 A car rental company which is nationwide
5 A car rental company that offers international travel

When planning a journey by car, you will need to look at the routes available. The AA and RAC Handbooks, published annually, provide maps as well as information on the cities and main towns, hotel accommodation and garage services available. Computerised route planners are also available and these will produce a printed map, plus the mileage, so that a choice can be made taking into consideration the quickest and shortest routes. The cost of the journey can also be included in the printout if the mileage rate is entered.

Whichever planner is used, it will not advise you of any major roadworks or diversions in operation so it would still be worth checking with AA, RAC or local travel help lines (sometimes on local radio). During the holiday periods traffic builds up at particular spots and the motorways and major roads can become congested. Time should be allowed for such delays.

Train

British Rail operates accounts for companies whose staff use the rail system frequently. A warrant card can be issued to the person travelling, and on presentation to the booking office the cost of the ticket will be charged to the company account. Tickets can also be prebooked by telephone and charged to the account. If a company does not hold an account and staff travel by train only occasionally, individuals may purchase their own tickets and be reimbursed by the company at a later stage when they submit their travel claim form.

When booking rail tickets you may also book a particular seat. Many people prefer to sit facing the direction of travel and this should be stipulated. (The terms 'face to engine' and 'back to engine' are used by the rail booking clerks.) First and second class, smoking and non-smoking carriages are also bookable on most of the InterCity trains. You should make yourself familiar with the requirements of the person you are making the booking for before contacting the booking office. You will need to inform those travelling of the departure and arrival times and they may also wish to know whether a buffet car will be available on the train or not. Additional services such as sleeper trains and motorail (transporting cars) are also available on some trains. It will be necessary for you to check the timetables, in the *ABC Rail Guide* (published monthly), which lists the services available in addition to the times of arrival and departure. Double check with the booking clerk when reserving your tickets that the information printed in your timetable is still current.

The advantages of rail travel are that it is quicker than road on direct routes, the person travelling is able to rest and review documents if they wish, and on longer journeys the cost will be cheaper than a car mileage claim.

The disadvantage is that it is often necessary to change one or more times during the journey and connecting trains may not be available immediately, which will result in a 'waiting period' at stations. If connections are good this may not be such a problem, but bear in mind the transfer time required, especially if it is necessary to change stations. This would be most likely to occur in London, where several main line stations serve different parts of the country.

It is unlikely that you will need to book trains abroad but, if the occasion arose, liaison with a travel agent is recommended. *Cook's International Timetable*, published monthly, gives details of the principal rail services of Europe, Africa, America, Asia and Australasia.

■ DIY 11.1.2

Using an *ABC Rail Guide*, local timetable or local booking office complete the following:

1 Find out how to get to Birmingham on Wednesday at the earliest possible time.
2 Plan a route from your local station to Darlington. Do not forget to list the times of any changes.
3 Find out which trains you would need to get to travel from Cambridge to Portsmouth.
4 Using *Cook's International Timetable* find out the times of trains that travel from Paris to Dijon. How long will the journey take?
5 How can you tell from your timetable whether there is a buffet service on a train or not?

Sea

There are many companies that operate routes from the UK by sea, and the services offered are increasing as the demand for access to Europe, in particular, increases. Sea travel is limited to the routes available, and it is unlikely that your manager would travel by sea, unless air travel was feared, or they wished to take a car abroad. To avoid inconvenience it is wise to make a booking on car ferries, especially during the peak holiday periods. Cabin accommodation may also be booked on some ferries, and this would be essential for executives travelling overnight, who wish to arrive fresh to carry out their business. Service timetables and brochures are available from operators at seaports, from travel agents, or the *ABC Shipping Guide* which is available on a monthly basis.

Air

For long distances and international travel, time can be saved by flying. Internal flights (shuttle services) are available frequently and it is reasonable to expect an executive based in London to fly to Glasgow to attend a meeting and fly back the same day. There are nearly 60 airports in the UK, although not all have shuttle services. There is no need to book these flights and 'booking in' time at the airport is reduced to the minimum required for security reasons. Special company accounts can be opened for those using these services frequently. However, the availability of internal flights is still limited and this restricts the alternatives open when planning a journey. Transfer time from the airport to the meeting venue must also be taken into consideration.

■ DIY 11.1.3

Write down the name, address, telephone number and fax number of your local airport. List 5 of the destinations that are accessible from the airport. What would be the quickest method of travel for your boss to get to London's City Airport from your local town?

Internationally, there are many airline operators – some who specialise in travel to specific parts of the world. Increased competition between the operators has resulted in special conditions and prices being offered to attract business customers. Most airlines offer economy, executive and first class travel on long-distance flights, although all Concorde's seats are first class. Companies generally make use of the executive and first class options to ensure that their staff arrive as relaxed and alert as possible to carry out business. In these two classes there is more room round the seats for increased leg comfort and to enable travellers to carry out work undisturbed – some flights offer fully reclining chairs or bunk beds for sleeping. To assist the travellers on the ground there are separate booking-in arrangements and usually a separate waiting lounge – all designed to speed up the travelling process and make the journey as comfortable as possible. When it is necessary to change flights to reach a destination, time should be allowed. Quite often, as with rail stations, it will be necessary to change airports, although it is customary for the travel operators to offer a transfer service, either by minibus, car, helicopter or plane – such a service operates regularly between Gatwick and Heathrow.

Although there are many advantages to air travel, there are some considerations that should be taken into account which may affect the travel plan of a business person. There is a restriction on how much luggage may be carried without incurring a charge, although most business travellers do not take much. The weather often creates problems and once plane departure times are delayed there is a knock-on effect which can result in planes being delayed for some time. Bookings need to be made well in advance, especially to popular destinations. Waiting lists operate for some flights, but this would not be appropriate for someone who had to attend a meeting at a specific time.

Do not forget that when the destination has been reached it will be necessary for your manager to reach the meeting venue. Advice will need to be given as to whether a taxi, company car, hire car or a representative will be available for transfer.

The *ABC World Airways Guide* and *ABC Guide to International Travel* contain information and timetables for airlines. However, unless you are working within a specialised travel department, most air travel would be booked through a travel agent or direct with the airline operators who would supply you with all the information required. Before booking you should familiarise yourself with the requirements of your manager as to whether they wish to sit near the window, prefer smoking or non-smoking, and which class of travel is required.

■ DIY 11.1.4

Using a British road map, list the roads and towns that your boss would need to travel through when driving on the following journies.

1 From Dingwall to Dumfries. Calculate the approximate mileage between these 2 towns.

2 From Cardiff to Hull. Calculate the approximate mileage between these 2 towns. Which of these roads are motorways and which are major ('A') roads?

Arranging the travel and accommodation is only part of what is required when organising a business trip. Depending on the destination, you may need to arrange vaccinations, and on most journeys insurance will be required.

▶ *What about health requirements?*

Many places abroad need confirmation of vaccinations or inoculations before allowing personnel into the country, especially against malaria, typhoid, polio, cholera and yellow fever. An embassy, a doctor or travel agent will inform you of the requirements of the countries to be visited. Health certificates may be required and should be obtained from a doctor along with any special health requirements such as insulin for diabetics or tablets for heart patients. Spare spectacles should be taken, in case of accident or loss. In some hot countries it would be as well to take some insect repellant cream, antiseptic cream and 'gyppy tummy' medicine in addition to the normal medicinal aids such as indigestion and headache tablets. A suitable pack should be put together and stored where it is easily accessible.

▶ *Would you need to arrange passports?*

Not necessarily, but you should check with the person travelling that their passport is still valid. British passports are valid for 10 years and can be renewed by completing a form, available at main post offices, and sending it to one of the passport offices. It can take 4 to12 weeks for a new passport to be issued, and the Passport Office recommends that applications are made as quickly as possible. Two 2.5 × 2 inch photographs are required, along with birth and marriage certificates. Passports valid for one year are available direct from main post offices but are not valid worldwide. A list of countries accepting these passports is printed on the form. It would be useful to keep the passport number in your file in case it is stolen or lost during the visit.

Although you may not need to arrange for a passport you may have to organise entry/exit permits or visas.

▶ What about visas and permits?

Some countries require additional documentation before allowing people access. The list of countries requiring permits and visas is constantly changing, and you should check with the appropriate embassy, or a travel agent, whether or not one is required. If one is, apply as quickly as possible as some embassies take a long time to process them. Some embassies will also wish the person travelling to attend in person to support the application. Exit permits may also be required and it is important to check this before travelling.

■ DIY 11.1.5

Find out whether you would need a visa when travelling to the following countries:

France	Oman	Australia	America
Mexico	Zaire	Japan	Qatar

▶ Are there any other documents that might need arranging?

Your manager will require some money and Eurocheques or traveller's cheques. Both can be ordered from a bank or travel agent. It should only take a few days to arrange, but it would be worthwhile advising the bank once you know how much is required. Your manager should also carry a charge card (such as American Express) or credit card (such as Access or Visa) as these are acceptable in almost all countries and will assist in case of cash problems. Always check that the cards are valid and will not expire during the visit; also ensure they are acceptable in the countries being visited.

If your company has a large finance department these arrangements may be part of their responsibilities. Your manager may be travelling to

315

carry out business and there may be some financial transactions requiring credit transfers, bills of exchange, letters of credit or exchange of currency. Small amounts of currency can be ordered from your bank or from the travel agency. If large amounts are required they can be purchased on a futures market, which will ensure a fixed exchange rate for large sums of money. Information on currency restrictions can be obtained from the national bank of the country concerned or from your travel agent, who will advise you of the best method of transfer.

■ DIY 11.1.6

1 Find out from a bank, newspaper or computer information source the current exchange rates for buying currency for the following countries:

Spain   Portugal   Iceland   Canada   India

Using a calculator, calculate how much currency you would obtain for £500.

2 Find out what Eurocheques are, how they can be purchased and where they can be used.

▶ *What is an itinerary?*

The itinerary is the travel plan, which includes the dates, times, addresses, telephone numbers and contacts, mode of travel and any other useful information. Most people prefer the itinerary to be typed on postcards, as they fit neatly into pockets or bags and are readily available. If the trip is a particularly long one, several cards may be required and these can be divided into separate weeks or separate locations. A complete itinerary should also be available which can be kept in the travel pack. Copies of the itinerary should also be prepared for yourself, the travel file, the main office, your manager's superior and deputy, his or her home, and the contact (if there is one) in the country to be visited. An example of an itinerary is shown in Fig. 11.1.

```
               I T I N E R A R Y
     for Simone Mitchell's visit to Rome
                24-26 May
Monday 24 May
0900 hrs  Taxi from home to Gatwick airport
1030 hrs  Arrive Gatwick, terminal 2
1200 hrs  Depart flight BA235
1500 hrs  Arrive Rome (1 hour ahead)
          Taxi to Hotel Bellaway, 35 rue Chartwais
          (Tel 39.69.25.53)
1900 hrs  Dinner with M. Cravet at Picolo (Tel
          39.65.35.85)

Tuesday 25 May
0915 hrs  Car to collect to take you to meeting
0930 hrs  Meeting with Mme Dupount at Lasta Vista,
          r.Chantro (sales documents required)
1300 hrs  Lunch with Mme Dupount at Lasta Vista
1500 hrs  Car to collect to return to hotel for
          meeting
1600 hrs  Meeting in hotel with Mr Williams and
          Mrs Crosby from our Rome branch (board
          papers required)
1930 hrs  Dinner with Rome branch board of
          managers at La Botte (Tel 39.65.36.36)

Wednesday 26 May
0930 hrs  Car to collect to take you to production
          plant
1000 hrs  Tour of plant with Mr Williams (file -
          new specification - required, meeting
          brief included)
1300 hrs  Lunch with new customers (list in file)
          at La Palmera (tel 39.63.62.64 meeting
          room reserved)
1600 hrs  Car to hotel, collect luggage etc (car
          will wait), transfer to airport
1800 hrs  Booking-in time for flight BA522
1915 hrs  Depart Rome
2015 hrs  Arrive Gatwick (one hour behind), taxi
          to home
```

Fig 11.1 An example of an itinerary

■ DIY 11.1.7

Your boss Dorit Becker requires an itinerary. The information you have is that she is travelling from Coventry to Southampton by car on Monday, leaving Coventry at 0700. The journey will take about 4 hours, and she is due to catch the ferry to Cherbourg from Southampton which leaves at 1200. She will not be taking the car to France, but leaving it in the ferry car park. The ferry arrives in Cherbourg at 1800, and she is staying at the Hotel Sur la Mer in Cherbourg for one night. The telephone number is 010 220 83759. On Tuesday she will be visiting the Cherbourg Chamber of Commerce and returning to Southampton on the midnight ferry the same day (you have booked a cabin for her) which arrives in Southampton at 0600. Dorit will then collect her car and travel back to Coventry.

Completing Element 11.1

To complete this element on arranging travel for persons you will need to put all the DIY tasks in your folder and carry out a final assessment. Competence must be proven in dealing with travel by road, rail, sea and air for individuals and groups of people. You will need to complete accurate itineraries and provide the relevant documents for travel within the agreed deadlines set by your supervisor.

Claiming credit

Once you have completed your final assessment, you will need to write in your record book or folder how, when, where and what you have done to prove that you are competent.

The following is an example of how one trainee completed this claim:

When working for my tutor, Mrs Woods, I arranged several trips for her. We discussed the requirements for travel and decided on the best method. I then planned the best route (by car) for the visits locally and nationally. I also contacted other centres which Mrs Woods was visiting to make arrangements for her car parking and to agree an itinerary. During the holidays Mrs Woods visited France and I carried out the necessary booking arrangements for her and her party on the ferry and worked out the best route for her to travel to Vannes. This journey was for 4 people and I prepared an itinerary. All the necessary documents were sent by Brittany Ferries 3 weeks before departure, I checked them before passing on to Mrs Woods.

I also arranged a trip to Brussels for 30 GNVQ students. This included air and coach travel, visit to the EU buildings and a day at Eurodisney. The full itinerary and travel arrangements were made by me and 2 other NVQ students in liaison with the GNVQ tutor. All the documents were checked when received before passing to the tutor.

I have also arranged my own travel arrangements, locally, nationally and for holidays abroad, as listed in my evidence folder.

■ **Element 11.2**
BOOK ACCOMMODATION FOR A SPECIFIED PURPOSE

Performance criteria

- Instructions for accommodation arrangements are understood
- Accommodation arrangements meet specified instructions
- A clear and accurate confirmation of all arrangements made is provided to the appropriate person
- Security and confidentiality procedures conform to organisational requirements
- Arrangements are completed within agreed deadlines

In addition to arranging travel it may be necessary for you to book accommodation for your boss or for others in your organisation. The accommodation may be necessary for a meeting, conference, seminar, or training programme, or may simply be hotel accommodation for staff staying away on business. The type of accommodation you book will depend on who it is for, how long they are staying, and how many are involved.

1 Who is it for? If the accommodation is for your Managing Director it is likely that they will want a good class of accommodation. If, however, it is for one of your sales representatives, they are likely to want something which is convenient and comfortable rather than something which is high class. Your organisation will probably have a list of accommodation that they use on a regular basis, or have agreed terms with. You will need to check with your supervisor to find out what the regulations are relating to booking residential accommodation for staff.

2 How long are they staying? If someone is staying for one night only then the class of accommodation may not be so important. However, if they are staying several weeks it is important that the accommodation is comfortable and a reasonable price. Many types of accommodation have special rates for people staying over 3/5 days. It will be necessary for you to find a reasonable place at a competitive price.

3 When booking parties of people into accommodation it will be necessary to give the organisers as much notice as possible. Many places have special discounted prices during off season to attract customers – this sometimes makes it difficult to find accommodation for groups of people. You must also take into account the different needs of the people in your group – do you have any that require wheelchair access, special dietary needs? Will office support services be required, eg photocopying, faxing, typing/word processing, projectors, etc?

There are many different types of accommodation available in this country and abroad. You will need to find out from your supervisor the type of accommodation usually booked for different people within the company.

Accommodation available in most cities and towns includes:

1 Hotels. Some companies have special accounts and agreed costs with a group of hotels. If this is the case, the only concern will be which hotel is closest for your purposes. If a hotel has to be selected, AA and RAC Handbooks, together with the *Hotels and Restaurants in Great Britain* guide published by the British Tourist Authority are all good references. A star grading system is used and details of the facilities available are given in all these publications. Information is also given regarding market days, and the hotel's proximity to the centre of town. A telephone number and fax number (if available) will be given and further details can be ascertained by contacting the hotel direct before arranging a booking. Bookings are normally made verbally and later confirmed in writing, either by letter or fax. A confirmation of booking should be sent by the hotel to you and this should be placed in the travel pack.

■ DIY 11.2.1

Using a suitable reference book, find a 3 star hotel in Lincoln. List the facilities the hotel has as well as the full name, address, telephone number and fax (if there is one).

2 **Motels**. Motel accommodation is increasing in Britain. They have facilities for overnight accommodation or longer term if preferred. They are located on the main routes round the country as well as the centres of towns and cities. They do not usually have the luxury or style of a top-class hotel but are comfortable and have shower/toilet facilities in most of the rooms. The dining facilities depend on the size of the motel, but the majority will offer a variety of menus for breakfast, lunch and dinner.

■ DIY 11.2.2

There are several chains of motel accommodation available in this country, especially located on motorways and major roads. Find out the name of one, and the location of the nearest accommodation to your town.

3 **Residential centres**. These are centres built specifically to meet the demands of conferences and meetings. They may be converted from country houses or similar properties, are usually located in the countryside, and cater solely for executive levels. Due to their specialism they offer properly equipped meeting rooms in addition to excellent accommodation and food. There are usually facilities for entertainment and relaxation, which may include a sports centre, swimming pool, golf course or even a cinema. It is not usual for these centres to accept bookings not associated with the functions being held. Therefore booking such a centre would have to be confirmed at the initial stage of any plan as most of them have bookings at least a year in advance. Information regarding such venues can be obtained from professional conference or conference placement agencies.

4 **Bed and breakfast lodgings**. These can be found in most towns, but especially in the coastal areas. This type of accommodation is very popular with tourists, but is also used by sales representatives.

321

The accommodation may be purpose-built but many are family homes; rooms are standard and may have washing facilities or a small ensuite bathroom. The food served is normally home cooked. Lists of bed and breakfast accommodation can be obtained from the tourist information office for the area.

■ DIY 11.2.3

Using your local directory find the name, address and telephone number of 2 bed and breakfast lodgings in your local area or nearest town.

It is necessary to keep all travel and accommodation bookings confidential and secure. In the office you should keep a special file for each booking made and ensure that it is kept in a secure cabinet, especially when the office is unstaffed. Always keep copies of letters and faxes sent to book or confirm arrangements made. It is also a good idea to keep notes of telephone conversations carried out regarding the booking of accommodation and place them on file. This will ensure that anyone needing to look at the up-to-date position regarding the arrangements will have all the necessary information in the file. When booking accommodation you will need to inform the necessary people of the names of those staying, any special requirements, time of arrival and departure, and who will be paying and how. You should also provide a contact name and number for any queries.

■ DIY 11.2.4

Write a letter to the hotel you found in DIY 11.2.1, reserving a room for 3 nights (Mon–Wed, first week of next month). It is required by Mr J Watson who is your sales manager. He is carrying out some visits in Lincoln to try and get some new customers. He is vegetarian and would like to eat at the hotel in the evenings. The bill for the accommodation should be sent to you, rather than Mr Watson paying for it, and you can then arrange for a cheque from the accounts department. Ensure that you give the hotel the necessary information and nothing additional.

If you need to book accommodation overseas it is important to take into consideration the time zones. If people are travelling from other countries they will need a certain amount of time to rest and prepare for work. It is most likely that you will book this type of accommodation through a travel agent.

■ DIY 11.2.5

Find out the local time in the following places if it is 9.00 am in London.

New York   Calcutta   Sidney   Maputo   Costa Rica

▶ *What types of accommodation should I book for a meeting or conference?*

You will need to choose accommodation which is accessible to everyone attending. This will mean that you need to take into consideration the access by road, rail and possibly air. Once you have decided on which part of the country the venue is going to be you can start to look for suitable accommodation. You will need to know how many delegates are expected, or at least an estimate of numbers. You will also need to take into consideration speakers and any support staff needed in attendance. Once the numbers are known, the layout of seating will need to be decided. There are several ways in which a room can be laid out for a conference or meeting.

Classroom style – all seats face to the front with tables or desks for delegates to spread their papers.

Boardroom style – one large table with delegates seated around and suitable for meetings involving discussion amongst all attending. A maximum of about 25–30 people can be accommodated this way.

U-shaped – tables are placed in a U shape, useful for training sessions or where a speaker wishes to approach individuals.

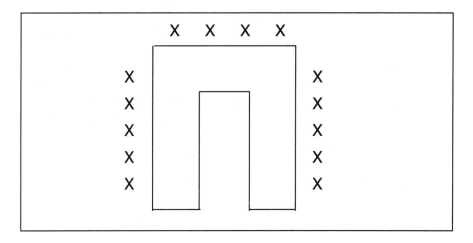

Theatre style – where all delegates face front, usually without tables or desks. This type of layout is commonly used in lecture theatres where the seats are tiered – similar to cinemas. Sometimes the chairs may have folding side tables for delegates to lean on to take notes. This layout is commonly used for large numbers of people listening to speakers at the front and where group work for the delegates is not involved.

If the meeting or conference involves the delegates working in small groups on workshop activities, syndicate rooms may be required in addition to the main room. These rooms will need to be big enough for the numbers involved and may require facilities such as a flip board, desks, etc.

Once you know the requirements of your organisation you will be able to start researching the accommodation available.

▶ *How should I carry out this research?*

It will be necessary for you to contact suitable venues by telephone, assuming you do not have suitable accommodation within your organisation. Most major hotels have conference facilities but they vary enormously – a pack of information is usually supplied if requested. There are a few publications available listing conference facilities, such as the *Conference Blue Book* and *Meeting Places*. It is unlikely that you will need to refer to such publications for your purposes. There are also conference agencies who keep computer lists of venues and facilities available around the country. These can be contacted for information, although some charge for the information supplied.

Once you have found a suitable venue it will be necessary to confirm the booking and arrangements required by fax or letter.

▶ *What types of venue are available?*

Hotels – many hotels have conference facilities. The main room may be a disused restaurant or ball room, and syndicate rooms may be converted bedrooms. Care should be taken when booking such venues as some may not be suitable for the purposes of your organisation. The costs involved are usually reasonable and some are able to cater for a wide variety of supporting materials and choice of food.

■ DIY 11.2.6

Find a local hotel which has conference facilities suitable for 30 people. Write a letter to the hotel confirming that you require accommodation for 30 delegates to stay one night (25th of next month), a meeting room with 4 syndicate rooms to be available from 0930–1600 on the 26th. Catering facilities required will be an evening meal on the 25th, and breakfast and buffet lunch on the 26th (combination of vegetarian and non-vegetarian food). Tea and coffee with biscuits will be required in the meeting room at 10.30 and 3.00. Delegates will be leaving at about 4.30. In the meeting room you will require an overhead projector and screen and the syndicate rooms will need flipcharts and pens.

Universities and colleges – most of the higher and further education institutions have excellent facilities which are available to external organisations during the educational holiday periods. However, the residential accommodation may not be available or easily accessible outside of the centre. However, for a day conference these institutions should not be forgotten.

Conference centres – many towns now have central conference facilities available to organisations. Some are owned and run by the local councils, others are privately owned. These centres are able to deal with large numbers of delegates (some up to 5000) and the facilities available are usually excellent. Accommodation may be available or special arrangements may exist between the conference centre and local hotels.

If possible it is always best to visit and inspect the facilities available before making a confirmation of your booking. If you are visiting more than one use a checklist so that you can compare the information gathered before making a final decision. Brochures and promotional material do not always reflect the true image of the facilities available.

■ DIY 11.2.7

Prepare a typed or word processed checklist that could be used when visiting potential conference/meeting venues. Include in your list number and size of rooms available, access to the venue (nearest roads, rail station, airport), access within the venue, eg stairs/lifts, seating facilities (as listed earlier), other facilities such as projector, slide, screen, microphone and sound system, fees charged for accommodation, use of equipment and facilities, heating and lighting, air conditioning, car parking space available, catering facilities, etc. Add to this list any other relevant items you can think of.

Completing Element 11.2

To complete this element on booking accommodation for a specific purpose you will need to put all the DIY tasks in your folder and carry out a final assessment. Competence must be proven in dealing with residential and non-residential accommodation for events and overnight stays. Arrangements should include individuals and groups.

Claiming credit

Once you have completed your final assessment, you will need to write in your record book or folder how, when, where and what you have done to prove that you are competent.

The following is an example of how one trainee completed this claim:

During my work at Patterson & Co (May–June) I assisted the director's secretary in arranging accommodation. This included overnight accommodation at hotels for the 3 directors who were attending a meeting in Scotland, and a local hotel for a training session for staff (30 people). I had to telephone 5 different hotels locally to find a suitable one that had accommodation available at the time we needed. The training session needed a meeting room and 4 smaller rooms for group work with flipcharts. I drafted the letters to the accommodation organisers and this was checked by Di Cripps, the secretary, before they were posted to ensure that I included all necessary information. I have also completed a venue checklist for the hotels contacted so that a suitable one could be selected. Di and I visited the hotel to make sure the facilities were suitable before making the booking.

UNIT 12
Contribute to the arrangement of events

■ Element 12.1
ASSIST IN ARRANGEMENTS FOR THE PROVISION OF SUPPORTING FACILITIES AND MATERIALS AT EVENTS

Performance criteria

- The quantity, type and quality of supporting materials is as directed
- Equipment and materials are located to suit purpose of events within agreed deadlines
- Instructions for the safeguarding of equipment and materials are followed
- Facilities for persons with special needs are confirmed

There are many different facilities and materials that may be required at a meeting or conference. It will depend on the size of the event and who is attending as to what you will need to arrange or organise.

In most businesses meetings are held on a regular basis. The type of meeting will depend on the matters to be discussed. There are 2 types of meeting: informal and formal.

▶ *What is the procedure for informal meetings?*

This type of meeting is generally held in order to make decisions, reach agreements and decide future action. They are usually relaxed as the participants are normally known to one another and the meeting may be called at short notice. When arranging an informal meeting you would probably telephone each of the people invited to find out when they are available; once a date and time had been agreed you would send a memo to remind them of the date, time and venue for the meeting.

The procedure will depend on the nature of the meeting. For example, staff meetings will probably have an agenda (a list of items to be discussed) and a chair (the person leading the meeting). Notes will probably be taken and later distributed. On the other hand, a parent-teacher's meeting may be far less documented – they could meet just to discuss some ideas for the coming year.

▶ What types of groups are likely to have informal meetings?

Working parties are formed to address a certain matter. Once the solution or alternatives have been resolved, the committee is dissolved. The findings of a working party are reported to the parent committee. Recommendations can be made but only limited action can be taken without the approval of the parent committee.

Groups of staff, such as sales representatives, will meet on a regular basis. Managers of a business will also meet regularly as this is essential for good communication. The degree of formality varies, but the decisions made usually have considerable influence.

■ DIY 12.1.1

You have arranged a convenient date (12th of next month) for 3 of the sales staff to hold a meeting. The time of the meeting will be 10.30 and it will be in Room 24. Write a memo to the staff concerned confirming the date, time and venue of the meeting. Write a memo to the restaurant manageress to request coffee and biscuits to be available for this meeting (do not forget to include all the necessary information).

▶ What is the procedure for formal meetings?

This type of meeting is controlled by regulations. A business which has limited liability (a limited company or plc) will be required to set out its meeting procedures in its Articles of Association – the document that sets up the company. Clubs will have a constitution; local authorities, standing orders. If the meeting is not run in accordance with the regulations the decisions made may be invalid.

```
Notice is hereby given that a meeting of the
Development Committee will be held on 8
December, at 2.00 pm in the Conference Room.

Please let me know if you will not be able to
attend.
     Name of Chairperson
     Date
```

Fig 12.1 Notice of meeting

All the people invited to attend must receive a written notice of the date of the meeting. The notice would state the date, time and place of the meeting and the type of meeting to be held. The length of notice required will depend on the type of meeting and the regulations. It is essential that the person arranging the meeting ensures that sufficient planning and bookings are carried out before the notice is sent out to the members.

▶ *How should a notice of meeting be prepared?*

A notice may be typed as part of the agenda, or as a separate letter or memorandum. As the notice contains only the details of the time, date, place and type of meeting it is sometimes combined with the agenda.

The wording is not formally set. An example is shown in Fig. 12.1.

▶ *What is an agenda?*

The agenda is a list of items to be discussed at the meeting, and there is a traditional order. It should contain the purpose of the meeting and give the members an opportunity to bring with them any documents they may need and enable them to prepare themselves for effective discussion on the points arising. An example is given in Fig. 12.2.

AGENDA

1 Apologies for absence
(The Chair (sometimes called the Chairperson) will read out the names of those people that were invited but are unable to attend.)

2 Approval of the minutes of the previous meeting
(Copies of the last minutes would have been circulated to all members. Approval is necessary to ensure that all agree with the record. If approval is given, the Chair will sign the master copy on each page, which will then be filed in the minute book. If changes are required this will be noted and approved.)

3 Matters arising from the minutes
(Quite often, members will be required to take action, for example find out costs of new equipment. These items will be discussed before any new business.)

4 Correspondence
(Any letters, circulars, memos etc received will be brought to the attention of the members.)

5 Reports
(From officers such as the Treasurer or from sub-committees.)

6 New business
(Items that members have requested be placed on the agenda for discussion or decision.)

7 Any other business *(sometimes abbreviated to AOB)*
(Urgent items that need to be discussed. Generally these have arisen after the agenda was circulated and cannot wait until the next meeting.)

8 Date of next meeting
(A date is agreed by those present, the same time next month, quarter or year.)

Fig 12.2 Example of an agenda

A special agenda may be typed for the Chair as in Fig. 12.3. The information would be typed only on the left-hand side of the page, to allow notes to be written during the meeting on the right-hand side. It may also have prompts and reminders for the Chair included under the listed items.

CHAIR'S AGENDA   Notes

1 Apologies for absence

Apologies have been received from Ms Williams, Mr Stevens & Miss Beeney.

2 Approval of last minutes

No suggested alterations have been received.

3 Matters arising

Minute numbers 24, 26, 31 and 45 need to be followed up.

    (etc)

Fig 12.3 Example of the Chair's agenda

■ DIY 12.1.2

You have been asked to draw up a combined notice of meeting and agenda for the staff in the general office. The meeting is the second meeting looking at quality standards and the Chair wishes to cover the following points: review of standards set at last meeting, problems with measurement indicators, new standards for the month. Do not forget to include on the agenda the usual opening and closing items – see the example of agenda in Fig. 12.2. The meeting will be held in the manager's office, Room 214, at 4.30 on Wednesday next week.

▶ *What are minutes?*

The minutes should be a true record of all that occurred at a meeting. They should contain the details of the type, date, time and place of meeting; names of those present (the Chair's name goes first followed by a deputy, if there is one, and the Secretary; after that the names are in alphabetical order); and a summary of the business discussed, in agenda order. An example is shown in Fig. 12.4.

```
THE OSMUND CHURCH RESTORATION COMMITTEE

Minutes of the meeting held in the Church annexe
on 24 July 1993 at 7.00 pm.

Present:  Miss Janice Scott (Chair)
          Mrs Pam Blakemore (Secretary)
          Mr Lewis Floyd
          Mr John Gillespie
          Mrs Anje Sepanje

They should be written in the third person and
past tense, as in this example:

Mrs Blakemore reported that the hall would be
decorated by Saturday lunchtime. It was agreed
that all furniture would be replaced by Sunday
afternoon.
```

Fig 12.4 Example of the minutes of a meeting

▶ *What types of formal meeting are there?*

The most common type of meeting is the Annual General Meeting (AGM), sometimes called an ordinary general meeting. It is held once a year for all members, whether club members or shareholders.

A statutory meeting would mean that the group has to hold a meeting by law. It would be included in the regulations drawn up when the group began.

Board meetings are held on a regular basis. Members will be those elected to the board by the general members (eg staff, club members, shareholders) or those required by the regulations to be there, usually because they hold a particular position in the company, such as the company secretary.

An extraordinary meeting would be called to discuss something which has arisen and is urgent, one that the group considers cannot wait until the next ordinary meeting. It may also be held to discuss one particular problem that would otherwise take up the whole of the time devoted to an ordinary meeting. This ensures the topic has time for full debate.

▶ *What are committees and why are they set up?*

A sub-committee belongs to a main group and may be set up as a standing committee or an advisory committee.

A standing committee is one which is permanently set up to deal with a specific issue, such as accommodation, repair and redecoration. *Ad hoc* (Latin for 'to this') committees would be set up to deal with a specific problem (a committee to see 'to this') and once the problem is resolved the committee would be disbanded.

An advisory committee may be set up by the main/parent committee to look at a specialist area and advise on matters of policy. This type of committee can make recommendations but does not have authority in its own right.

▶ *What positions are held by the members of a committee?*

As mentioned earlier, the **Chair** would be the person responsible for running the meeting. The Chair is appointed by the members of the committee and must ensure that the meeting follows the agenda, and the correct procedure and order are followed. Anyone wishing to speak at the meeting must address their comments to the Chair and not to the meeting in general. The Chair will summarise the points made at the end of discussion and take decisions on points of order. If a vote is necessary the Chair will receive the votes and declare them.

The meeting is always closed by the Chair and can be adjourned if it is considered necessary. A good Chair will make sure that the meeting does not drift away from the matter in hand and that the speakers are kept to relevant matters.

The **Secretary** is the 'legal' representative, whose responsibility it is to ensure that the signed copy of the minutes is kept in a minute book. They should not be confused with a personal secretary who may deal with the office administration in general. The committee secretary should be totally familiar with the regulations and be on hand to assist the Chair in matters of procedure. They are usually responsible for the documentation of the meeting, drafting the notice and agenda, preparing the room, taking the minutes (although a minute secretary may also attend the meeting), listing who attends, and ensuring that the necessary action is taken on the agreed points. Quite often many of these tasks will be delegated to a personal assistant or personal secretary.

There may be other officers such as treasurer, social secretary, publicity manager, etc, although this will depend on the type of committee and its purpose.

▶ *What needs to be done before a meeting?*

First of all a suitable place needs to be found to hold the meeting. This may be on the company premises or an external venue may have to be found. Many hotels and centres now offer meeting and conference facilities. Before you are able to book a venue you will need to know how many people are likely to attend and from where they are travelling. It is essential that the venue be central to those attending, and that rail and road connections are good. If you were arranging a meeting for members coming from other countries you would also have to take into consideration the location of airports and seaports.

■ **DIY 12.1.3**

Write out a set of instructions for a new junior who is going to be responsible for looking after the filing of meeting documents. List the type of documents that are involved and how they are filed. Where possible this should be based on the filing system used in your organisation or ask your trainer how meeting documents are filed in the training organisation.

Once the date, time and venue are agreed the agenda would be drawn up. A notice of meeting and copies of the agenda would be sent to all those invited to attend along with any documents to be discussed at the meeting. When members receive the agenda, those with prior commitments are likely to write or telephone to give their apologies. Make a note of these and pass them on to the committee secretary.

Check the agenda and make a list of the equipment required. This could include an overhead projector (OHP), which may require transparencies (OHTs), slide projector, flipchart, video, microphones – it is a good idea to check with the meeting secretary what equipment is likely to be needed.

Usually the personal secretary will be responsible for organising the room. If the venue is external this will be done by the conference department at the centre used, but you will still need to check prior to the meeting that everything is in order. Apart from the room layout, check that the equipment supplied is working: projector bulbs have a habit of breaking when constantly moved from room to room. Also make sure that the cables reach the plug sockets and are placed so that no one will trip over them. Rubber mats are usually available to cover trailing wires on such occasions.

The tables used should be large enough to enable all members to sit round. If small tables are used then they may be placed in a 'U' shape. The Chair would normally sit at the head of the table, although some Chairs now prefer to sit at the side of a large table to make their presence less formal. The secretary and minute secretary would be close to the Chair. Each member should be supplied with pen/pencil and paper, and place names should be made ready for all those attending.

Special pens will be required if an OHP or flipchart is to be used; at least one of each colour available should be to hand. Sufficient stationery should be ordered well in advance of the date and fresh water and glasses should be placed within easy reach of all members. If you are using an external centre, these should all be provided and it is likely they will supply mineral water in addition to orange squash.

However, it is not necessary to have such a selection for meetings held internally. A check will need to be made with the committee secretary to see what refreshments are required – although traditionally coffee is supplied in the morning and tea in the afternoon, tastes are now changing and most members would expect both to be available. If the refreshments are to be supplied by an outside agency or your refectory they will need to be ordered. If you are intending to provide them yourself, supplies will need checking.

If the meeting will last all day, lunch will have to be provided. You should agree with the committee secretary the type of lunch (formal or buffet) and whether there are any members with special dietary requirements. Ashtrays will also be required, unless the Chair has a policy of 'no smoking' at meetings. If members are unfamiliar with your premises ensure that prominent notices indicate where the toilets and cloakrooms are located.

Finally, a list of members attending should be sent to your receptionist and/or security officer so that they are fully aware of who is expected. Some of the members may have requested parking spaces, if you have them available, or cars/taxis to collect them from the station. All these details should be agreed and notified to the relevant people. Some meetings may last several days, in which case accommodation will also need to be booked.

It is quite likely that, on the day of the meeting, one or more of the members will forget their meeting documents. An efficient secretary will always have at least one spare set available and have access to a photocopier if more are required.

■ DIY 12.1.4

There are many documents and different types of equipment that may be needed at a meeting. Make a checklist of all the documents and equipment that you can think of, type it and keep it on file ready to use when helping to arrange the next event for your organisation.

▶ *What special security measures should you take when dealing with meetings and meeting documents?*

Meeting documents should be kept securely in a locked cabinet and should not be accessed by anyone who does not have the authority to look at the contents. Circulation of the documents is usually restricted to the members of the committee only, and at no time should the documents be left unattended on desk tops, a photocopier, typewriter or on the screen of the word processor. You should arrange for the documents to be sent to those attending the meeting well in advance (at least a week), especially if there are detailed papers to read before the meeting. Many companies insist that meeting documents are numbered and each committee member has an allocated number. Thus only the exact number of required copies are made and these are circulated according to a strict list. For instance:

Chairman   1
Secretary   2
Sales Manager   3
Purchasing Manager   4
etc

Extra copies of minutes may be made to take to the next meeting, in case someone forgets their own, but once the meeting has finished these should be shredded. Any outdated documents should also be destroyed by either shredding or incinerating. The only copy kept permanently would be the master set, usually by the Chair or secretary and stored in a fireproof cabinet. Each page of the minutes would be numbered, so that missing pages can be easily identified.

If the documents are on computer disks or microfiche, these should be stored safely under lock and key and the documents on computer disk saved using passwords or keywords.

In large companies industrial espionage (spying) is quite common as secret information can be traded for large sums of money. For instance, the news of a take-over or of financial problems in a company may be useful information for a competitor.

▶ *What arrangements would be needed for conferences and seminars?*

The booking of accommodation and suitable venues is covered in Unit 11.2. The documentation involved with conferences and seminars is usually in the form of a delegate pack. This pack will usually include a copy of the agenda or the programme, the address and details of the venue including a map, registration details, supporting papers or reading documentation (this may include summaries of the speeches made, or copies of the transparencies used), details of workshop activities (if any), a list of the delegates attending and the organisations they represent (but not full addresses), a list of speakers, paper for note taking, pen and name badge. All of this is contained in a document case or wallet, and some organisations will also include promotional material, menus, local entertainment and hotel facilities. Some delegate packs also include an Attendance Certificate for delegates to complete as evidence of their attending the event. This certificate will include the date and venue of the event, the name of the conference or meeting, space for the delegate's name, the organiser's name and space for the organiser's signature. The delegate packs may be distributed by post prior to the event or at the event. If they are given out at the event, the venue address and registration details must be posted.

▪ DIY 12.1.5

Design an Attendance Certificate to be included in a delegate pack for people attending a conference on 'Ways of Protecting the Environment'. The conference will be held at your local conference centre on 12 November (next year) and is being hosted by the 'Friends of the Globe in Action'. If possible use graphics to make the certificate look authentic.

Completing Element 12.1

To complete this element on assisting in the arrangements for the provision of supporting facilities and materials at events you will need to put all the DIY tasks in your folder and carry out a final assessment. Competence must be proven in dealing with locations internal and external to the organisation, include organisation stock and hire arrangements. In addition material should include prepared documentation, consumable stationery and event items.

Claiming credit

Once you have completed your final assessment, you will need to write in your record book or folder how, when, where and what you have done to prove that you are competent.

The following is an example of how one trainee completed this claim:

During my college course and work placement at Coopers & Co I have assisted in arranging meetings, conferences and training events. Part of my duties have been to help type and word process the documents to be used at the events, sending the documentation to those attending, arranging for name badges and setting up the room with OHP, paper, pens and water. I have written letters and memos to confirm the materials required in the meeting rooms and physically checked that all was in place before the meeting started. I made sure that the documents were stored safely and securely before sending them out in suitable envelopes which were sealed. The envelopes were addressed direct to the participants. In my evidence folder I have copies of checklists used by me to ensure that everything was covered, samples of letters, memos and meeting documentation (non-confidential only) and a schedule of the events I have helped to organise. Further documentation on all these events can be seen in my workplace if required.

■ Element 12.2
ASSIST IN ARRANGEMENTS FOR THE ATTENDANCE OF PERSONS AT EVENTS

Performance criteria

- Persons invited to attend the event are as directed
- Accurate and complete event directions and supporting documentation are provided to persons attending, appropriate to their role and need
- Arrangements, when required, for the transportation of persons are appropriate and within budgetary allocation
- The reception and routing of persons at events provides adequate support and direction
- Attendance records are in accordance with organisational requirements

Once the venue and topic of the event have been decided it will be necessary to arrange for the attendance of the delegates. It may be that the event is being advertised nationally in magazines, mail shots, newspapers, etc, in which case applications can be expected from all over the country. Once a person has contacted your organisation saying that they wish to attend your event, they will need to supply details of their name, organisation and address, telephone number, fax number (if any), names of any other people attending, and special requirements, eg access, dietary, etc. It is best to design a registration form to gather this information. This can then be sent to anyone enquiring. When applicants return the form it is also usual to enclose a cheque to cover any payment necessary.

■ DIY 12.2.1

Design a registration form for delegates wishing to attend a conference at the International Centre on 20 December. Do not forget to include a name and address for the applicants to return their form. The cost for attendance at the conference is £35 per delegate, and cheques should be made payable to your organisation.

Once all the registrations have been received it will be possible to set up a database of information or a datafile ready for sending a mail shot of further information to the delegates. This will enable you to send personalised letters to the delegates when further information is available.

▶ *What further information might you send to the delegates?*

The first letter to the delegates will probably include an acknowledgement of their registration, a receipt for their payment and confirmation of any arrangements that they have requested, eg accommodation. Enclosed with this letter may be a programme for the event, and details of the venue, including a map and joining instructions.

■ DIY 12.2.2

Draw a map which would be suitable for sending to delegates attending a meeting at your place of work or training. The map should be easily read and suitable for people coming by train or car from anywhere in the country.

▶ *What transport arrangements might you need to make?*

Most of the time people attending events will make their own arrangements for travel to and from the venue. However, you may be required to book car space at your organisation, or arrange for people to be collected from the local railway station or airport. If the venue you have selected is some way from local transport the venue organisers may have a special minibus that can be used to transport people to and fro. Alternatively taxis may have to be used in which case you should try to find out the requirements of those attending before the day finishes. This will avoid those wanting taxis having to wait unnecessarily and a rush to get to telephones at the end of the seminar or meeting. You should make it clear whether your organisation is paying for transport or whether the delegates are expected to pay themselves. If the organisation is paying it should be authorised by your supervisor or boss and be within any budget allowed for transportation. A fixed amount should be agreed at the time the function is being organised.

You may have visitors attending with special needs, for example in a wheelchair or on crutches, or they may be unable to see. Such visitors may require assistance in accessing the building, especially if there are any narrow corridors or doorways.

▶ *What action should you take on the day of the event?*

You should make sure that there is plenty of room for people to register and sufficient staff to receive them. There is nothing worse than having travelled some distance to have to wait in a queue to sign in. Tea, coffee and biscuits should be available for those arriving for registration – usually at least half an hour before the day is due to begin. Clear signs should show the way to the meeting room as well as the ladies' and gentlemen's toilets. If cloakrooms are available these should be signposted as well. Do not forget that if you have any people that are attending who are unable to see, they will need special instructions on the layout and may need escorting to the different facilities.

■ DIY 12.2.3

Design an attendance record that could be used for any event. Ensure there is space to fill in the date, the venue of the function, the name of the function and the name of the person organising it. You will need to indicate whether you want your visitors to sign or print their name (or both) and whether they should list the organisation they are representing.

Completing Element 12.2

To complete this element on assisting in arrangements for the attendance of persons at events you will need to put all the DIY tasks in your folder and carry out a final assessment. Competence must be proven in dealing with events which are internal and external to your organisation and involve notification, transportation and registration of people taking part in the event and the event administrators.

Claiming credit

Once you have completed your final assessment, you will need to write in your record book or folder how, when, where and what you have done to prove that you are competent.

The following is an example of how one trainee completed this claim:

During my work at Dixon & Sons I have assisted in arranging for people to attend meetings and conferences. I entered records on to a database making sure the entries were 100 per cent accurate and typed a letter. I then mailmerged the datafile entries with the letter and printed the necessary copies. Once the letters were ready I attached the meeting papers and a map of the venue (a local hotel) to the letter and posted them. It was necessary to book car spaces for 5 of the visitors attending. I made sure that the notices to the cloakrooms were in a good position and typed out an attendance list. The list was given to reception and they checked the names of the visitors as they arrived. I collected the visitors from reception and took them to the meeting room. I have also assisted with meetings internal to the company and although they were much smaller, similar arrangements were made, including an attendance list, notices and receiving of the visitors. Copies of the attendance lists are in my portfolio (although the names of the organisations have been left out as they are confidential).

■ Element 12.3
ASSIST IN THE ARRANGEMENTS FOR THE PROVISION OF CATERING SERVICES AT EVENTS

Performance criteria

- Arrangements for catering services are as directed
- The needs of persons attending are identified and catered for
- Costs of catering services are within budgetary allocation
- Arrangements for catering services are made within agreed deadlines
- The arrangements for catering services are in accordance with organisational requirements
- Precautions taken with the provision of catering services provide adequate safeguarding of persons and property at events

When arranging events internally or externally it will be necessary to organise refreshments or catering to suit the event. If it is a short meeting for internal staff held within the organisation, it may only require coffee and tea – possibly some biscuits. External visitors may be supplied with a choice of cakes and biscuits. Meetings that are longer and go over the lunch period may require a lunch to be organised. If the people involved are internal staff it may not be necessary to arrange lunch – the meeting may be halted for lunch and staff would gather again at an agreed time. However, if external visitors are involved it would be unusual for them to be sent out to find lunch for themselves, it would probably be provided by the host organisation. It is becoming quite popular to arrange working breakfasts – this would be a meeting called before the normal day starts (usually anywhere between 7.30 and 9.00). An executive breakfast may be a full traditional English breakfast or just coffee and croissants.

When arranging lunch, or any other meal, it will be necessary to find out certain information before you can proceed. This information will then be passed to the restaurant manager or manageress, or the catering section of your organisation. Quite often there is a special form to be completed which prompts the necessary information. This will probably include the following.

Name of person requesting the lunch – this will be the name of your boss. Only some of the staff will be authorised to order lunches for visitors and staff. You should check with your supervisor if you are unsure before ordering a lunch for someone. Sometimes junior staff may be given permission to order lunches by the manager or director. This will be allowed due to the visitors involved or the topic of the meeting, ie it is important enough to permit a lunch. As well as the name, the person's title, department and telephone extension would probably be included.

Name of person ordering the lunch – this will be your name or the name of the person that should be contacted if there are any queries. Your boss will not want to deal with every single query arising from the arrangement of catering services. The title, department and telephone extension should also be included to deal with any queries arising.

Date, time and location – the date and time are important, but so too is the room or location where the lunch is to be served. It will be necessary for the catering staff to access the room prior to the time of the lunch in order to prepare the room and lay out the necessary crockery and cutlery. If the room in which the lunch is going to be served is also the meeting room, the catering staff may lay out the basic requirements the evening before or early before the meeting starts. This will save them interrupting the meeting.

Number of people involved – this will be the total number of people wanting lunch and refreshments. This may include special requirements such as people attending with dietary requirements, eg vegetarian, vegan, low fat, etc.

Type of lunch required – the catering staff will want to know whether the lunch is going to be buffet (which could be finger buffet or full service buffet), hot or cold, or full lunch with 2 or 3 courses. The type of lunch ordered will depend on who is attending and how much time can be spent on lunch. Quite often internal staff will have a working lunch, which means that they will eat but continue working and discussing issues. There will only be a short 'comfort' break (to stretch the legs, get a breath of fresh air and go to the cloakroom). A finger buffet lunch will take about 30–45 minutes, so that by the time people have also taken a comfort break the total time taken out of the meeting will not be less than an hour. A formal lunch, however, is likely to take at least one and a half hours and much longer if the venue is external to the organisation. Many people do not like to have a full lunch during the day as it makes them tired, less dynamic and slower in making decisions and therefore less effective.

The cost of lunch must also be considered as you must make sure that whatever is ordered is within the allowed budget. Obviously a formal sit-down, 3 course lunch will cost far more than a finger buffet. It is also likely that the catering department have different 'grades' of finger buffet. A cheaper one will have perhaps sandwiches (ham, cheese, salad), quiche, sausage rolls, crisps, etc, while a more expensive buffet lunch may have prawn, beef, cream cheese and avocado sandwiches, ie more expensive contents and the accompanying dishes would be more unusual and contain more expensive ingredients.

■ DIY 12.3.1

Find out whether your organisation has a catering service and if they have a selection of menus available for staff wishing to order lunches for visitors. Find out what the cost range is for lunches provided by the catering staff.

Drinks required – you will need to cater not only for tea and coffee to be served after the meal, but cold drinks during the lunch. This may be orange, blackcurrent or lime juice, spring water or wine (red and white). It will depend on your budget and your boss's requirements – wine is not always included as it can make people tired and less receptive.

Cost – the total cost of the lunch will need to be approved and the money obtained from somewhere. Many organisations have a budget code for entertainment and catering. This budget is usually controlled by one of the managers, who will approve the arrangements before anything is booked or agreed with the catering staff. The approval may need the manager's signature on the form in addition to the budget code and the 'grade' of refreshment being ordered. It is essential that any order is within the budgetary allowance approved by the manager.

■ DIY 12.3.2

Design a form that will give you all the necessary information you require to book a lunch within your organisation. If your organisation already has a form check this against your form and list any differences.

▶ *How do you order the required services once you have the information?*

There will almost certainly be an agreed deadline for ordering catering requirements. Some internal catering staff require notice of a week or more for lunches; tea and coffee for meetings may be 2/3 days. Whatever the time restriction is it is essential that you are aware of it, get all the information and complete all the necessary documentation in time. It would be very embarrassing for your boss's visitors not to have their refreshments because you did not complete a form on time!

▶ *What if the catering is provided from outside the organisation?*

You will still need to gather the same information to order goods and services from an outside agent. This may be an agent that delivers to your organisation or it may be a restaurant that your boss and the others involved visit. There are many catering services that now deliver, from the small company (which may only be one or two people) that delivers sandwiches in a basket to the large organisation that can provide a full banquet.

■ DIY 12.3.3

Look in your local telephone directory and find the name, address and telephone number of a caterer who:

1 specialises in finger and fork buffets
2 advertises special menus for vegetarians
3 states that they can provide special business lunches
4 is the nearest to your organisation
5 has 24 hour delivery service.

347

When using external catering agents for the first time you should check that they meet the requirements of the environmental health regulations relating to the transportation of hot and cold foods. These change regularly and you would need to contact your local environmental health officer to find out the latest requirements. Whenever possible obtain sample menus from the caterers – with prices – and discuss these with your boss before deciding on a particular caterer. Some firms are happy to discuss their menus with you and even provide samples of foods prepared. When placing future orders you should check that the prices you have are still current.

▶ *What further action should you take?*

A day or so before the event you should check with the caterers that everything is in order and confirm the number of people attending. (Caterers refer to the number required as 'covers' – 12 covers would mean 12 people.) Quite often the numbers will change from the ones originally given to the caterer. If the caterers are external they may need a preparation room in which to change, prepare the foods and to place the dirty crockery when clearing the tables. The room should be of an adequate size, have easy access to washing facilities and be secure for personal belongings and property belonging to the caterers. You should check the requirements of the caterers when placing the booking.

After the caterers have laid out the food you should check that it is attractively displayed. To ensure that the food is fresh and unspoilt, it should remain covered until it is required.

The day before the event you should check that the room is prepared. If necessary, lay out anything that is needed for the meeting, and ensure that any equipment is in place and that there are sufficient chairs. Prepare an attendance list for your reception and if spaces have been reserved for visitors, remind the car park attendant. Other security measures to take will include preparing visitors' badges and clearance for the caterers (if they are external to the organisation).

■ DIY 12.3.4

Prepare a checklist, from all the information given, so that you do not miss anything out when assisting in arrangements for the provision of catering services at events in your organisation. This list can be used when discussing the requirements of future events with your colleagues and superiors.

Completing Element 12.3

To complete this element on assisting in the arrangements for the provision of catering services at events you will need to put all the DIY tasks in your folder and carry out a final assessment. Competence must be proven in dealing with events held internal and external to the organisation and catering used should include internal and external services. Keep a log of the events you assist with, as well as a list of the duties you actually carry out. Copies of letters, memos and forms completed will support your claim to competence.

Claiming credit

Once you have completed your final assessment, you will need to write in your record book or folder how, when, where and what you have done to prove that you are competent.

The following is an example of how one trainee completed this claim:

During my programme at College (September–June), I have assisted the division manager in making arrangements for refreshments and lunches to be available for meetings. The people attending the meetings have been internal staff and external visitors to the college. I made sure that I checked everything with the manager before confirming the arrangements. I made sure that the forms and confirmations were completed in good time to make sure that the deadlines were met. The department has 3 grades of refreshment – the one used most of the time is grade 3 which is the cheapest one, although this is sufficient for working lunches. The caterers tend to supply a mix of vegetarian and non-vegetarian food but will increase the quantity of vegetarian foods if requested.

On some occasions a booking is made at a local restaurant. This is usually telephoned but confirmed in writing (if time allows). Special dietary arrangements are not necessary as the restaurants used have a wide selection of foods, including vegan.

UNIT 13

Produce and present business documents from provided material

■ Element 13.1
PRODUCE BUSINESS DOCUMENTS FROM PROVIDED MATERIAL USING A KEYBOARD

Performance criteria

- Instructions are understood
- Approximately 1200 words are produced in the workplace, from provided material, in two and a half hours, with no more than 3 uncorrected spacing or typographical errors
- Uncertainties in text are identified, checked and rectified
- Completed documentation meets the requirements of the workplace
- Layout, spelling, grammar and punctuation are consistent, correct and in accordance with house style
- Corrections, when appropriate, are unobtrusive
- Security and confidentiality of information are maintained
- Copies and originals are correctly collated and routed, as directed
- Where work is not achievable within specified deadlines reasons are promptly and accurately reported
- Work is achieved within agreed deadlines

To be able to complete this unit it will be necessary for you to produce a variety of documents using a typewriter or word processor. Most books refer to the keyboard as a 'qwerty' keyboard. This means the keyboard has the keys in a particular order, ie the top row from the left is in the order of q, w, e, r, t, y. No doubt you have received training on how to use the 'home keys' (the middle row of the keyboard) and all the other keys, using the correct fingers. It is important for you to be able to 'touch type' without looking at the keys as this will improve the speed at which you can produce documents.

All skills improve with practice, whether you are ice skating, skiing or keyboarding. Keyboarding in particular will improve if you continually use the correct finger for the correct key, not looking at your keyboard or hands while you type. Frequent practice, say 30 minutes each day, is better than 3 hours on one day only once a week, as it is the continuous practice that improves the skill.

▶ *What printers are commonly used?*

If you have a word processor it will be connected to a printer. There are two different types of printer, one called impact (where contact is made with the paper) and the other non-impact (where contact is not made with the paper). Examples of impact printers are dot matrix and daisywheel. A dot matrix printer creates the letters and other characters by printing dots in the shapes of the character. The more dots the better the printing quality, as there is less space between the dots. The printer head is rectangular in shape and is made up of pin heads, the pins are pushed forward and form the shape of the character. Dot matrix printers can print up to 200 characters per second and can also produce diagrams and graphics.

A daisywheel printer is the same as the daisywheel on a typewriter, where the spokes of the printing wheel have characters on the end and it turns to allow the correct character to touch the paper. A daisywheel can print at up to 70 characters per second but cannot produce diagrams and graphics.

Dot matrix and daisywheel printers are fairly inexpensive to buy but are quite noisy. To reduce the noise, some companies cover the printer with an acoustic hood or screen as in Fig. 13.1, or when possible the printer may be located in a separate room.

Examples of non-impact printers are ink jet or laser printers. An ink jet printer squirts tiny jets of ink on to the paper to form the characters, and the quality is usually very good. An ink jet printer can produce up to 5 pages a minute and can also print pictures and graphics. A laser printer uses laser beams to transfer the characters on to a drum, which

351

Fig 13.1 A printer with an acoustic hood

turns and transfers the characters on to the paper. Lasers can produce a page of A4 typing in about 6 seconds. They can also produce excellent graphics.

Ink jet and laser printers are quiet to run but are more expensive to buy than impact printers. Laser printers can also be quite expensive to maintain as they require toner and parts to be changed when high numbers of copies are made. Colour printers are also available.

▶ *What health and safety precautions should you take?*

Switch off all machinery at the end of the day (the only exception may be the answer machine, which will take telephone calls in your absence, and the fax machine, which may send and receive messages during the night). Make sure that any connecting wires are not trailing across the floor, they should be taped under the desk or placed close against the walls. Do not overload sockets – multi-extension leads should be used when several items need to be plugged in at the same time; alternatively extra sockets should be installed.

Check the leads regularly for fraying or broken connections. New regulations under the Health and Safety at Work Act (HASAWA) (*see* page 37) and the Electricity at Work Act state that all electrical equipment must be regularly checked to confirm it is safe to use. Consult your tutor or health and safety representative if you are not sure about the state of any of the equipment you use.

▶ *Posture*

To make certain you do not suffer from strain and injury, you should sit in the most comfortable position for typing (*see* Fig. 13.2). Strain can occur to the neck, back, arms and legs, and on occasion can lead to serious complaints. It should allow you to sit with your feet flat on the floor (use a footrest if necessary), and have an adjustable back-rest to support your lower back. Desks for typing are generally lower than normal desks, to allow the keyboard to sit at the correct height.

Your head should be upright, otherwise you will find your neck will ache from constantly looking down at the desk. The document you are copying should be placed on a document holder, either to the right or left of your keyboard, whichever you find more comfortable.

▶ *Carrying out instructions*

Usually you will be given written documents or corrected typed documents to copy from, but occasionally someone may add a verbal instruction when they are handing you the work. Make sure that you write down the instructions, either on your notepad or on the document itself. You should not forget to follow the instruction when you do the work. An example may be 'Oh, could you do that in double line spacing for me – thanks' or 'Would you do 3 copies when you type this please.'

Verbal instructions are just as important as written instructions, but are easier to forget or overlook if you are disorganised and do not write them down.

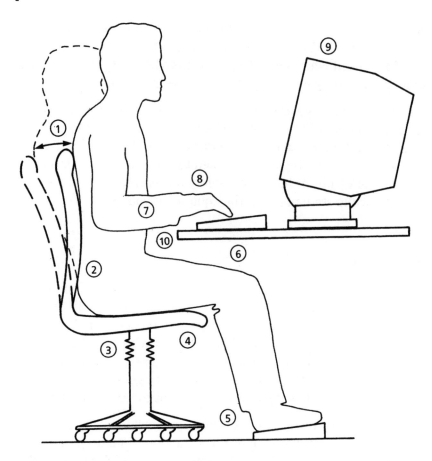

Seating and posture for typical office tasks

1   Seat back adjustability
2   Good lumbar support
3   Seat height adjustability
4   No excess pressure on underside of thighs and backs of knees
5   Foot support if needed
6   Space for postural change; no obstacles under desk
7   Forearms approximately horizontal
8   Minimal extension, flexion or deviation of wrists
9   Screen height and angle should allow comfortable head positions
10   Space in front of keyboard to support hands/wrists during pauses in keying

Fig 13.2 Good posture (Crown copyright)

354

Letters are normally typed on A4 headed paper, although some companies do use A5 letterhead. Memos on the other hand are commonly available in A4 and A5. A4 portrait paper is 210 mm × 297 mm, has 100 spaces across the top and 70 lines down (assuming you are using elite type which is 12 characters to 25 mm). A5 landscape paper is half this size, and has 100 spaces across the top and 35 lines down. The paper can be used in either the portrait position, with the short side put into the machine first, or landscape position, with the long side put in first (*see* Fig. 13.3).

The most commonly used envelopes are the C5 (229 mm × 162 mm), which takes A5 paper unfolded or A4 paper folded once; C6 (162 mm × 114 mm), which takes A5 paper folded once, or A4 paper folded in half twice; and DL (220 mm × 110 mm), which takes A4 paper folded into 3 and A5 paper folded once. (*See* page 239.)

The quality of stationery used will depend upon its purpose. Paper and envelopes used for business correspondence will be of good quality as the company will want to convey a good impression to its customers and clients. The quality of paper can be measured by its weight, or gsm (grams per square metre). Bond, copier and letterheaded paper is fairly thick and therefore heavier (usually by about 25 gsm) than paper such as bank, which would be cheaper and used for carbon copies.

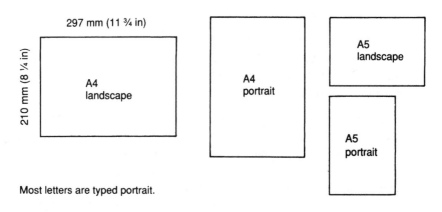

Most letters are typed portrait.

Fig 13.3 Paper sizes

▶ *What are correction signs?*

People working in offices have not always received the correct training regarding layout of letters, memos and other documents. They will rely upon you to turn their efforts into attractively displayed text. When they make corrections to documents they do not always use the approved correction signs. You will get to know each individual's signs, but if you are unsure at first, always ask. The accepted standard signs should be included as part of your training and you should always use them yourself when correcting work.

■ DIY 13.1.1

1 Type a copy of the list shown below. Next to each instruction insert the signs you would use to indicate the changes you wish to have made to a document.

Instruction	Signs
(1) New paragraph	1
(2) Change to capital letter	2
(3) Change to small letter	3
(4) Insert a space	4
(5) Insert a comma	5
(6) Insert a full stop	6
(7) Run-on one paragraph into another	7
(8) Close up a space	8
(9) Delete	9
(10) Transpose letters, words or paragraphs	10
(11) Leave a correction as it was	11

2 Copy type the following paragraph (complete with mistakes) and then insert, with a red pen, the corrections that have to be made to it. Remember to use the correct sign for each correction. When you have done this, retype the paragraph correctly.

asking questions to clarify the meaning of instructions is very important, In order to confirm under standing. youmust ensure that you are fully aware of what is expected From you. to do this you should ask quesitons and clarify the meaning if you do not not understnad what is expected. The person requesting you to carry out a task will be happie to answer questions, rather than receive a document that is totaly incorrect@ It may be the case that you are given written text to trans cribe into typewritten format. if this happens. it is a good idea to read thru the text first to make sure you understand it. If you do not, then you can ask questions before the person returns to their own work. It is also inportant that you clarify the persons instructions before they leave to make sure that you are clear as to whether you require copies of the document routing to other members ofstaff. and if they require a particular layout for the document. Remember that these insttuctions maybe verbal and should be writtend down so that you do not forget,

▶ *What are abbreviations?*

As well as using correction signs you will probably find that people also use a variety of abbreviations. These could include:

ack	acknowledge
ackd	acknowledged
amt	amount
amts	amounts
chq	cheque
co	company
del	deliver(y)
dept	department
ff	faithfully
fr	from
hv	have
mth	month
recd	received
rect	receipt
ref	reference
sec	secretary
sins	sincerely
sh	shall
shd	should
tel	telephone
th	that
tog	together
wd	would
wk	week
wh	which
wl	will
yr	your or year (the content of the sentence should tell you which)

Can you make sense of this instruction?

> Pls wd it be poss for me to hv nxt Fri off. I wd lk to del an amt of chqs to a co wh I nd a rect for. The sec tells me I mst del in person if I want to rec a rect. Wd you mind if we get tog nxt wk to discs or sh I tel?

The above paragraph is obviously exaggerated, but people will use abbreviations when drafting out letters, memos and reports for typing. You should always type the word in full: **never** use the abbreviation unless told to do so. If you are unsure of a word look it up in a dictionary, and if you cannot find it, ask for assistance.

▶ *What types of layouts are used?*

As well as making sure the content is correct, part of your job will be to make sure the correct layout is used. Most companies use a 'house style' – a particular style the company (the house) has approved and wishes all staff to use. An approved house style is used so that customers receive the same style of documentation, regardless of which department sends it. Some companies are extremely fussy about the house style, even stating what size print and style to use.

The most commonly used layout is the fully blocked style used without punctuation (except in the paragraphs of the letter). In this style everything starts at the left-hand side (*see* Fig. 13.4). This is the quickest style to type, as you do not need to work out spacing or spend time inserting unnecessary punctuation marks.

The date should always be written in the same way whether it is typed at the top of the letter or in one of the paragraphs, eg 25 May 1994 (without punctuation).

The layout for blocked memos would be as shown in Fig. 13.5.

The other style frequently used is semi-blocked. In this style the date is placed on the right-hand side and the signature block is centred. The rest of the letter remains at the left-hand side (*see* Fig. 13.7).

For memos typed in a semi-blocked layout the word 'Memorandum' would be moved to the centre and the date and reference across towards the right-hand side (*see* Fig. 13.6).

If an enclosure is mentioned in the letter or memorandum the letters 'Enc' or 'Encs' (if more than one) should be placed at the bottom of the page. It is normal practice not to sign memoranda, although some supervisors may prefer to put their initial at the bottom of the page to confirm the contents.

```
Reference

Date

Name
Address
Town
County
Postcode

Dear xxxxxxxx

HEADING  (if there is one)

Paragraphxxxxxxxxxxxxxxxxxxxxxxxxxxxxxxxxxxxxxxxxxxxxx
xxxxxxxxxxxxxxxxxxxxxxxxxxxxxxxxxxxxxxxxxxxxxxxxxxxxxx
xxxxxxxxxxxxxxxxxxxxxxxxxxxxxxxxxxxxxxxxxxxxxxxxxxxxxx
xxxxxxxxxxxxxxx

Paragraphxxxxxxxxxxxxxxxxxxxxxxxxxxxxxxxxxxxxxxxxxxxxx
xxxxxxxxxxxxxxxxxxxxxxxxxxxxxxxxxxxxxxxxxxxxxxxxxxxxxx
xxxxxxxxxxxxxxxxxxxxxxxxxxxxxxxxxxxxxxxxxxxxxxxxxxxxxx
xxxxxxxxxxxxxxx

Yours xxxxxxxx



Name
Department or position
```

Fig 13.4 Letter in fully blocked style

```
MEMORANDUM

To

From

Date

Ref

HEADING  (if there is one)

Paragraphxxxxxxxxxxxxxxxxxxxxxxxxxxxxxxxxxxxxxxxxxxxx
xxxxxxxxxxxxxxxxxxxxxxxxxxxxxxxxxxxxxxxxxxxxxxxxxxxxxxx
xxxxxxxxxxxxxxxxxxxxxxxxxxxxxxxxxxx

Paragraphxxxxxxxxxxxxxxxxxxxxxxxxxxxxxxxxxxxxxxxxxxxx
xxxxxxxxxxxxxxxxxxxxxxxxxxxxxxxxxxxxxxxxxxxxxxxxxxxxxxxx
xxxxxxxxxxxxx
```

Fig 13.5 Memo in fully blocked style

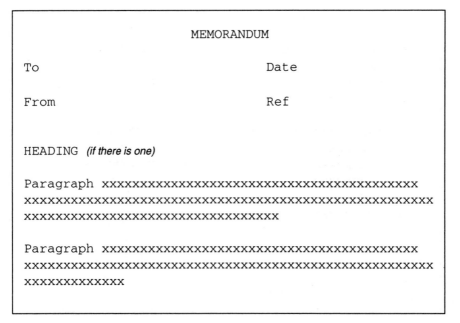

```
                    MEMORANDUM

To                           Date

From                         Ref


HEADING  (if there is one)

Paragraph xxxxxxxxxxxxxxxxxxxxxxxxxxxxxxxxxxxxxxxxxxxx
xxxxxxxxxxxxxxxxxxxxxxxxxxxxxxxxxxxxxxxxxxxxxxxxxxxxxxxx
xxxxxxxxxxxxxxxxxxxxxxxxxxxxxxxxxxx

Paragraph xxxxxxxxxxxxxxxxxxxxxxxxxxxxxxxxxxxxxxxxxxxx
xxxxxxxxxxxxxxxxxxxxxxxxxxxxxxxxxxxxxxxxxxxxxxxxxxxxxxxx
xxxxxxxxxxxxx
```

Fig 13.6 Memo in semi-blocked style

If you are asked to send copies of a document to other people you can indicate this at the bottom of the page. After the last line on the page or document leave a space and then type in 'Copy to:' and add the name(s) of the people copies are to go to. When the copies are prepared either tick or highlight a different name on each copy. This process is called 'routing', and when the original and the copies are ready to be dispatched you will be able to see easily who should receive each document (*see* page 125).

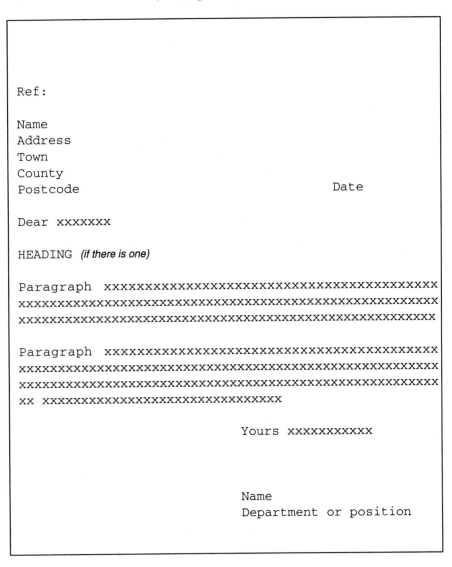

```
Ref:

Name
Address
Town
County
Postcode                              Date

Dear xxxxxxx

HEADING  (if there is one)

Paragraph  xxxxxxxxxxxxxxxxxxxxxxxxxxxxxxxxxxxxxxxxxxxx
xxxxxxxxxxxxxxxxxxxxxxxxxxxxxxxxxxxxxxxxxxxxxxxxxxxxxxxxx
xxxxxxxxxxxxxxxxxxxxxxxxxxxxxxxxxxxxxxxxxxxxxxxxxxxxxxxxx

Paragraph  xxxxxxxxxxxxxxxxxxxxxxxxxxxxxxxxxxxxxxxxxxxx
xxxxxxxxxxxxxxxxxxxxxxxxxxxxxxxxxxxxxxxxxxxxxxxxxxxxxxxxx
xxxxxxxxxxxxxxxxxxxxxxxxxxxxxxxxxxxxxxxxxxxxxxxxxxxxxxxxx
xx xxxxxxxxxxxxxxxxxxxxxxxxxxxxxx

                            Yours xxxxxxxxxxx




                            Name
                            Department or position
```

Fig 13.7 Letter in semi-blocked style

When starting a new job, it is your responsibility to find out the style required for documents; do not rely upon your existing knowledge, training and experience received at college or at previous companies. Some companies will produce a manual or guide for staff to ensure they follow the agreed layout for all documentation. If not, ask for examples for you to copy.

▶ Guidelines for typing envelopes

The guidelines for typing envelopes are given by the Post Office and suit the machinery installed to sort letters.

1 Type the address along the longer side of the envelope.
2 The first line of the address should start at about a third of the way across the envelope and half-way down.
3 Each line of the address should have a separate line.
4 The post town should be in CAPITALS.
5 The postcode should be the last line, in capitals, on its own and with one space between the two parts, eg GN3 2NN.

If there are any special instructions such as URGENT, CONFIDENTIAL, For the attention of ..., they should be typed two lines before the name and address (*see* Fig. 13.8).

```
            CONFIDENTIAL

            Dr D R Scott
            87 Wellington Drive
            NEWCASTLE
            NC32 6BB
```

Fig 13.8 Envelope layout

■ DIY 13.1.2

Type the following letter, using fully blocked layout, dated for today. Also prepare an envelope and mark it confidential. Leave a space of 5 cm at the top of the letter to allow for the letterhead. Choose suitable margins and size of paper. All abbreviations must be typed out in full. Address the letter to: Ms E Maidment, 58 Slovian Way, Birmingham, West Midlands, BM49 6PQ.

Dear ...
I ack rect of your recent app for the position of sales clerk. I wd be plsd if u cd tel me nxt wk to arrange an interview. My sec will take up refs prior to the interview wh I wd ask you to attend at the cos offices in Brighton. The Sales Dept has a large no of leads this mth and we are looking to recruit someone as qckly as poss. I lk forward to hearing fr u in the near future and hv enc a booklet on the co for yr info.
Yrs sncly
G Parkins
Personnel Director

▶ *Layout and presentation*

It may be left to you to decide how to lay out your documents and your job will be to ensure that you select the most suitable method for the document concerned. As said before, layout is important because it reflects an image of the business. The most important rule is to be consistent. If you decide to leave 2 lines between each paragraph in a report, you should not suddenly start leaving 3. Always look at previously typed documents to see how other staff have laid out the document, or ask for guidance from your supervisor.

▶ *What happens if you make mistakes?*

Everyone makes mistakes; the skill is in knowing when you make a mistake and correcting it – so that no one else knows! There is nothing worse than completing a letter or memorandum and passing it to your boss to be signed, only to find it comes back with a big circle round a silly typing mistake. If you are using a typewriter the whole document may have to be retyped.

It is most important to read everything you type before you hand it to the person for signature. You may believe that you 'know' when you make a typing error, but there could still be some that have gone unnoticed. Proofreading is a skill that has to be learned, in the same way as typing: the more you proofread the quicker you will become at identifying errors.

▶ *What is proofreading?*

This is when you read the document (proof) to ensure it is correct in content and layout. Most people find proofreading boring, and it probably is, but it is an essential part of document production. It is useful to get someone else to read an important document for you, as they will be unfamiliar with the content, will concentrate more and it is likely they will find errors that you may have overlooked. However, someone else can proofread for you only if the material is not confidential.

If you are unsure of how a word is spelt, look it up in a dictionary and keep a list of commonly misspelt words to refer to. If you have a word processor, it may have a spellcheck: make sure you use it. However, you will still need to proofread as the spellcheck will not find grammatical errors or words that are incorrect, eg 'it' instead of 'is', incorrect punctuation (eg a full stop instead of a comma), or words, sentences or paragraphs that have been missed out completely.

▶ *What is the best method for correcting errors?*

It depends on the type of error and the type of equipment you are using. Obviously, you cannot use correction fluid on a screen! A corrected error should be unobtrusive, which means you should not be able to notice it.

If you are using a typewriter you can use correction paper. This method is unobtrusive, as long as you have the character lined up correctly; otherwise the chalk covering misses and leaves some of the black character uncovered. This method should not be used for major errors such as changing two sentences round, or taking out a whole sentence. The other commonly used method is correcting fluid. Paint the error with the fluid, wait until it is dry, and then type the correct characters over the top. If you try to type in your corrections before the fluid has dried it will make a mess on the paper and can clog up the letters in your machine.

Many electric and electronic typewriters have correction facilities. The correction tapes will either be similar to correction paper or coated on one side with a sticky substance. The type of correction tape used will depend on the type of ribbon. Nylon ribbons use correction paper, and carbon ribbons use sticky correction tape which lifts the carbon image from the paper. If you look at the correction tape when you replace it you will see the carbon characters stuck to it. The disadvantage with this method of correction is that it leaves an indentation in the paper, and the better quality the paper the more obvious the indentation. This is not a problem if another character is to be typed on top but if it is between 2 words or at the end of a sentence the indentation may be noticeable.

Some electronic machines have an LCD (liquid crystal display) which displays each line of type. This facility can be set to allow you to correct words or sentences before you actually print them on to the paper.

When major errors occur in typewritten documents it may be possible to retype the one page necessary or to 'stick and paste'. This means that the correct paragraphs are cut out and glued round the newly typed paragraphs. The whole document is then photocopied. This method cannot be used for letters and it may be unsuitable for some occasions, for instance when your boss wants the original to be sent.

If you do use a word processor make sure that you proofread on screen properly – otherwise sheets of paper and time are wasted unnecessarily in printing work that is full of errors. The main advantage of proofreading on the screen is that errors are corrected before the document is printed – in this way the errors are totally unobtrusive.

If you are working as a general assistant, it may be that you send documents to the typing pool or clerk typist for typing. When they are returned to you for signature you must check thoroughly before signing and sending out. You should check spelling (look up any words you are not sure of), grammar, punctuation and content. Ensure that you use the approved correction signs whenever possible as this will make the typist's job easier and you will reduce the possibility of misunderstanding.

■ DIY 13.1.3

Type a copy of the following list. Below each word write down its meaning. Do not use a dictionary to help you. You will notice that although the words sound similar, they have very different meanings.

1	Accept	2	Except
3	Check	4	Cheque
5	Advise	6	Advice
7	Compliment	8	Complement
9	Ensure	10	Insure
11	Quiet	12	Quite
13	Stationary	14	Stationery
15	Principle	16	Principal
17	Insurance	18	Assurance
19	Affect	20	Effect

Now check your answers with a good dictionary and correct any mistakes you have made.

▶ *When should apostrophes be used?*

Apostrophes can easily be misused. The rules state that they should be used to form possessive nouns, that is, to show something belongs to someone or something, eg:

> Carly's pencil
> Natalie's lunch box
> Leila's coat

If the noun ends in 's' the apostrophe is placed after the 's'. Another 's' is added, eg:

> Kris's bike

If the noun is a plural (more than one), the apostrophe would still be after the 's', eg:

> the doctors' parking

366

This would mean more than one doctor; if it was the doctor's parking, it would mean only one doctor. Some nouns are changed slightly when becoming plural. 'Child' and 'woman' become 'children' and 'women'; in these cases the 's' is added and the apostrophe would appear before it, eg:

the children's socks
the women's handbags

An apostrophe is also used when a letter or letters are omitted from a word, for example don't, you're, aren't, can't, haven't, we've and I've. It's is used to mean 'it is' – the apostrophe takes the place of the letter 'i'.

■ DIY 13.1.4

Copy out the following sentences and put the apostrophes in the correct place.

1 The boys cat lay on its tail.
2 The dogs are in the kitchen eating the cats dinner.
3 Susans looking for her son.
4 Weve got to run or well be late for Sams speech.
5 I dont think youve got it.
6 Its too early now, well go later.
7 The trainees folders havnt been seen yet.
8 Peters trousers were covered in Pauls drink.
9 The 2 boys said theyd be 2 hours late.
10 The childrens party began at 2 but I dont know who went.

▶ Useful books

Apart from a dictionary, other useful reference books include a good thesaurus – this gives alternative words with the same meaning, and can help widen your written and verbal vocabulary; glossary – a specialised list of words and their meanings for your particular business; and a general office reference book such as *Chambers' Office Oracle*, *The Secretary's Handbook* or *The Secretary's Desk Book*.

▶ *Planning and organising your work*

It is important for you to get into the habit of sorting through your work first thing in the morning to put all your tasks into order of priority. As the day goes by other work will be given to you and you will be expected to fit this in if it takes higher priority than the work you already have. Keep an eye on your in-tray and rearrange tasks into order each time you are given more work to do.

You must schedule your work so that important tasks are not left to the last minute or forgotten completely. Your supervisor will not give you one piece of work at a time and wait until you have finished this before giving you more work to do. It is more likely that your supervisor will give you a number of tasks at once, indicating the ones that need to be given priority, and then keep topping you up with work as the day progresses.

Always sort your work into priority order, taking into account the time it will take to complete each task. If you have been given a report to type that will take all day, tell your supervisor so that arrangements may be made to share the report or pass other priority tasks to someone else. Never, under any circumstances, allow yourself to forget security and confidentiality even if you are under pressure to get a task finished.

▶ *What about security and confidentiality?*

If you are responsible for processing confidential documents make sure you keep them in a folder marked CONFIDENTIAL, and lock them away when not required. Text on a VDU can easily be read if the screen is left on and poor printouts thrown into the bin may be read at a later date. If you take carbon copies remember the carbon paper can be read after use giving full details of the document typed. Do not allow anyone to look over your shoulder when typing and put all documents out of the way if you have to leave the office for any reason. Remember to use passwords to protect documents held on disks.

■ DIY 13.1.5

Your boss, Mrs D Gerrard, is unhappy with the quality of work produced by your colleague and has asked you to retype the memos shown in Figs 13.9 and 13.10, inserting her name in the 'From:' section. Include today's date, amend all errors and insert the word 'Urgent' in the most appropriate place. Decide yourself upon the best print, style, layout and paper size to use.

MEMORANDUM

To: John Ball, Personnel Director

From:

Date:

Ref: Applications for Junior Clerk Typist post

To date i have received 5 aplications for the cletk
typist post advertised in last weeks evening Echo. I
have sugested a dealine date of tues. next, with
interview to be arranged for the following weds.
(date please).

Can I suggest that you drawer up a list of your
requirements to ade us in to select a shortlist and so
that we can base our interview questions around what
you want.

We need to discus salary as details will need to be
given to the aplkicants at inteview - it is it possible
to meet with your tomorrow and weather accom. can be
arranged for the interview pannel.

Fig 13.9

MEMORANDUM

To: Carol Barker, Head Receptionist

From:

Date:

Ref: <u>Annual Sales Awards Ceremony</u>

Regarding the above ceremony , would it be possible
for   you to   ask your stff to prepare sep. name
badges on the Kroy letering machine req'd for all
staff attending the eveing?

The ceremony will be held on the 14th of next month
and Mr Ball woud like all staff to were name badges
so that they can recognise colleagues who operate in
different regions. I will sent you a list of names once
we recieve all the tear-off portions detailing the how
many tickets are required and the names of members of
staff attending. Their should be about 200.

You may find yourself receiving telephone inquiries
regarding the ceremoney, and to help you answer these, I
have attached a draft copy of the memo and notice soon to
be sent out to all staff.

Yours faithfully

Fig 13.10

▶ *How do you route a document correctly?*

When a document has to be seen by a number of people or
departments or a copy is put on file, it is usual practice to route each
copy of the document. This is done by listing the names of people
and/or departments at the bottom of the document. The word 'File'
may also be included to show that one copy has to go on file. The usual
style to use is:

Copy to: Nigel Parker – Accounts
           Henry Spratt – Purchasing
           File

The original copy of the document is sent to the person named at the top of the document. The correct number of copies are then routed by ticking a different name on each copy. In the example above the first copy would have the name Nigel Parker ticked, the second copy, Henry Spratt and the last copy, File. In this way all copies are clearly marked and their destination known. The first 2 copies could be placed in the internal postal system for delivery and the last copy would go into the filing cabinet.

▶ *What is collating?*

This means putting the documents you have typed into the correct page order. If you prepare a multi-page document it is wise to number each page so that you do not become confused when the document has to be put together. If you are using a word processor you can instruct it to automatically insert a header or footer that includes the page number of each sheet in the document. It is important that all pages are collated in the correct order before they are stapled or fastened together, otherwise the text may not make sense.

When preparing a multi-page letter it is important to follow the correct house style. When typing letters it is normal practice to insert the page number, date and name of addressee at the top of each consecutive page. For example, a multi-page letter typed in block style is likely to have the following typed at the top of page 2:

2
20 February 1994
Mrs J D Carpenter

If the pages become separated, the information at the top of each page will identify where each page belongs. If typing a report, you may have to include the name of the report at the top or bottom of each page rather than a person's name. This would normally be set up as a header or footer.

If you have to prepare copies of the document, these must also be placed in the correct page order. If you are able to send documents to a reprographic service to be copied, make sure that you tell them to collate and fasten the documents for you as this will save you time and help to meet deadlines.

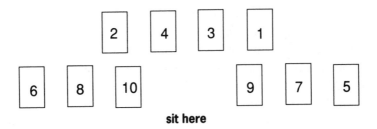

sit here

Fig 13.11

Collating by hand can take a long time, depending on how many pages and copies of the document you have to put together. If you are lucky, your company may have a photocopier that can be programmed to collate the pages as it is copying them, or you may have the use of a collating machine. Imagine if you have 25 copies of a 30-page report to collate by hand – it will take some time to put the pages in the correct order. You will need to have a work area where the 30 pages can be placed in separate heaps. Alternatively, you will have to sort the first 10 pages (or however many you can lay out) followed by the second set of 10 pages and then the third. These three heaps would then have to be collated into the final sets. You will need to lay out the documents in a logical sequence, either in page number order, or to speed up the process, an order where both hands can work at the same time. For example, a 10-page document could be laid out as in Fig. 13.11.

The left hand will take one copy of page 10 and place it in the space in front, and then the right hand will take one copy of page 9 and place it on top of page 10. Both hands can move at the same time and the document is collated back to front. Complete sets can be stacked away from the work area.

▶ *Preparing labels*

Self-adhesive labels can be purchased in rolls or in A4 sheets. Typing addresses on labels is quicker than typing on envelopes, and it is possible to use a label template on a word processor to print labels. Word processing software will allow you to set up a template that can be used to type address details on screen so that when they are printed out they are in the exact position on the roll or sheet of labels.

```
   Mr John Jameson
   14 Knights Road
   MANCHESTER
   MJ5 2LR
```

Fig 13.12 Label

Once you have set up a template that matches the exact size of labels used in your office or training centre, this should be saved so that it is ready for use again and again.

A4 sheets of labels can also be photocopied. First the addresses are typed on a plain piece of A4 paper which has a guide sheet behind to ensure the address is typed to the correct size. The typed copy is then placed on the photocopier and the sheet of labels passed through the machine. The addresses will be copied onto the labels ready for use. This is particularly worthwhile when sending documents regularly to the same addresses. The rules for typing addresses on envelopes also apply to labels (*see* page 240).

■ DIY 13.1.6

Your supervisor has asked you to complete the following work before lunch. It is important that it is finished on time but this only leaves you 2 hours and 30 minutes to carry out all the tasks. Your finished work must be 'mailable'. This means that it has been proofread and that you are satisfied with the end result. In order to pass this DIY you must complete all tasks within the time limit with no more than 3 uncorrected spacing or typographical errors. If there is any reason why you cannot achieve this deadline you must report the reason why, promptly and accurately to your supervisor. The tasks are on pages 375–85.

Before you start this DIY it is important that you read through each task first and clarify anything you are unsure of with your supervisor. The following instructions regarding each task should be discussed with your supervisor.

A Type or word process the advertisement. Use double-line spacing and display as attractively as possible. Choose a suitable size and quality of paper.

B Type or word process 10 labels using either a self-adhesive label roll or sheet. You must use the correct address layout and insert the word 'Confidential' in the correct position. If using a word processor, have you already prepared an address template?

C The letter of regret will eventually be sent to the 5 unsuccessful applicants. However, for the purpose of this task all you are requested to do is to prepare one draft letter, leaving a top margin of at least 10 cm.

D The letter of invitation will eventually be sent to the 5 applicants who are required for interview. However, for the purpose of this task all you are requested to do is to prepare one draft letter, leaving a top margin of at least 10 cm.

E This is the final article for the staff magazine and should be typed in single-line spacing. The article should fit on to one piece of A4 paper.

F Type or word process both lists on the same sheet of paper, in alphabetical order. Use the full amount of space on the sheet of A4, leaving enough clear space between each name and address to insert comments.

G Type or word process the report using double-line spacing. Produce one copy to be checked by your supervisor.

Prepare the relevant stationery before you begin and make sure you have a word processing label template or a photocopier label template available. You should also rearrange the tasks in priority order.

When your work is complete and fully proofread, hand it to your supervisor. You must finish all tasks within the 2 hours and 30 minutes time limit.

When your supervisor has checked your work, go back to tasks C, D and G and complete each task in full. This may require the use of a photocopier. Each task should have the correct number of copies produced, be collated in the correct order and routed in accordance with instructions. When you have done this pass your completed work to your supervisor so that it may be checked.

Please draft an advertisement for a~~s~~ secretary to the Personnel Director
It should be no more than 60 words long.

Previous office exp. necessary, shorthand/typing must be a minimum of 70/40. NVQ2 Administration essential, The job covers the whole range of secretarial skills and is very interesting. It would someone who is looking for a career in Personnel work. There is opportunity of progression for the right person. Age is not important. Salary starts at £9,500 pa with bonuses for additional, relevant qualifications. Hours 9–5. Holidays 4 weeks plus statutory bank holidays. Male or female candidates should apply to: Mr B Lewis, Personnel Officer, Coopers & Co, Lowther Rd, Fleetsbridge Poole.

(Ask for CV)

Please prepare address labels for
the following : (mark each "CONFIDENTIAL)

① Miss J Barlow
19 Landers Way
Poole BH15 9BJ

② Mrs F Jones
23 Urwin Cres
Bournemouth
BH3 9ZP

③ Mr P Cocker
76 Somerly Close
Poole BH14 8BB

④ Ms A Reblin
1 Union Street
Wareham
BH19 7PJ

⑤ Mr R Elcock
16 Saltash Sq
Poole BH16 2SP

⑥ Ms N Ahmed
89 Grenville Rd
Bournemouth
BH1 6PJ

⑦ Ms S Price
98 Shore Road
Southampton
SO9 6PQ

⑧ Mr P Francis
3 Wellington Rise
Ringwood
BH16 5TO

⑨ Ms J Anukot
76 Connaught Dr
Southampton
SO10 7PT

⑩ Mr P Davis
1 Lingwood Fields
Wareham
BH19 8PJ

Refer to your address labels list and send a letter of regret to Numbers 1, 2, 4, 5, 10. Copy the following for each, but remember to amend name, address and salutation.

Today's date

Dear . . .

(Type 1 draft. Leave top margin 10cm)

Thank you for your recent application in reply to our advertisement for a secretary to our ~~personnel~~ Director. [I regret to inform you that on this occasion your application has been unsuccessful.]

'However, I will keep your app. on file and will be pleased to ~~contact~~ write to you if a suitable position becomes available in the future.

I have taken this opportunity to enclose

a brochure on our company's goods
and hope that this will be of interest to you. We regularly up-date
our sales brochures and will be pleased
to forward them to you, if this is
acceptable.

May I take this opp. of thanking you
for showing interest in the company,
and wish you every success in finding a
suitable and enjoyable position of
work.

The company is developing new designs
and products that will be at the
forefront of the market. Our launch
date will be later this year and we
are expecting a resounding success.

Y.S.   Copy to: B Lewis
                                       File

Mr P Dennis   Personnel Director   ENCS

(D)

Refer to your address labels list and send a letter of invitation to numbers 3,6,7,8,9 Leave minimum top margin of 10 cm.

Today's date

Dear ...

Thank you for your recent application for the position of Secretary to our Personnel/Director.

I am pleased to inform you that you have been selected for interview on (it's ~~Thurs.~~ ~~Friday~~ next week, can you insert correct date) at 10.00 am. There are 5 candidates and it has been decided to show you all around the offices together. Coffee/tea will be served at 11.00 am and interviews* will commence after lunch*. Our Personnel ~~Director~~ Officer, Mr Lewis, will lead the interview panel. Each interview should last no more than 40 mins and a

*The Co. will provide lunch in the staff canteen

decision will be made on the day.

It will be necessary for you to bring the
following ~~along~~ documents with you. ~~on the day~~.

    1. Full CV
    2. certificates (copies not acceptable)
    3. NVQ evidence folder
    4. Record of achievement (if you have one)

Please contact me by no later than
Monday to confirm your appointment.
Once you have done so, references will
be contacted unless you inform us
otherwise in writing.

May I take this opp. of wishing you
every success in your interview. I look
forward to meeting you on ....(date).

Y.s.

Copy to: B Lewis
File

Liam, I have enclosed a sales brochure on the company that may be of help.

mr P Dennis
Personnel Dir

Encs

Please prepare article for staff magazine

DRAFT

Guidelines for composing a memo

The memo is a form of internal communication and can be hand
written or typed, usually on a pre-printed form. Memos can also
be transmitted electronically within an organisation using an
electronic mail system. *usually called Email* Telecom Gold operates a service that
allows its registered customers to access a central *electronic* mailbox where
messages can be left. The messages are collected by the
recipient who uses a special password to access his/her mailbox.
This system saves time and money and is becoming very popular.
However, it is wise to remember that even the most up-to-date
technological equipment cannot write the memo for you.
Therefore, it is important that all members of staff follow these
guidelines in order to make sure that their memos are composed
correctly.

1. There is no 'Dear' or 'Yours....'

8 2. *memos* They can be initialled, but not signed, by the sender.

3. Sentences should be short and concise.

4. A new paragraph should be used for separate info.

5. Use an appropriate style of language for the person *to whom* you are
writing to.

6. Try to keep the memo on one piece of paper.

7. If someone else has typed the memo for you, initial it to confirm it is correct.

2 8. Place only confidential or personal memos in an envelope.

Use a memo to:

1. Confirm facts discussed verbally

2. To request assistance

3. To provide info

4. To make a request

5. To seek clarification

6. Send instructions.

I hope that this article has helped to clarify the use of and composition of internal memos. It is important that in order to reflect a quality organisation we all start at the 'grass-roots' with our internal methods of communication.

ALYSON McKENZIE

COMMUNICATIONS OFFICER

Please prepare 2 lists giving details of the unsuccessful and successful applications for the /position of/ Personnel Director's secretary ~~advertisement~~. Display as follows.

SECRETARY — PERSONNEL DIRECTOR

Successful candidates   unsuccessful
called for interview   applicants
on . . . .

INSERT NAMES   INSERT NAMES
  & ADDRESSES   & ADDRESSES
HERE   HERE

alpha order please

Leave enough space between each name to insert details of confirmation for interview

DRAFT

Please type and make all necessary corrections. Prepare copies, collate & staple

Caps Sales Conference

Advertising, Sales and Marketing Managers with Managing Director.

Today's date

Report on Sales/Marketing ~~Program~~ *Project* 429

1. The *Sales* Manager thought that in light of the success of Project 326, it wd be ~~beneficial~~ *prudent* to run Project 429 in the same ~~way~~ *way.*

2. He urged further advertising to keep the company's name at the forefront of the market. An additional *budget* allowance of £15,000 was ~~endorsed.~~ *agreed*

✗ 3. The advertising Manager confirmed that without the additional allowance of £15,000 the team could not meet targets. It was felt tht the allowance *s*ould be well spent creating new and innovative ideas. *and would be earmarked for*

4. The Managing Director has agreed the additional allowance in theory but ~~but~~ added that there would have to be cuts elsewhere/ *in order* to raise the £15,000. She added that no further allowance would be made available, and asked the team for

5. their projected sales figs. [The following were put forward:

Single spacing between months and their figs. Indent and add @ signs. Months in full.

Jan	Feb	Mar	Apr
9,625	12,994	13,526	13,929

May	June	July	Aug
14,526	14,629	15,124	15,004

Sept	Oct	Nov	Dec
14,729	13,786	~~11,210,~~429 10,	9,949

5. The team advised that these figures were purely speculative *and were* based on the previous years *()* performance. They do however take in the anticipated sales resulting from Project 429.

The Managing Director said that she will consider the figs further and make a final decision next week. She then closed the meeting.

Copies to: Sales Man

Advertising Man

Marketing Man

File

Completing Element 13.1

To complete this element on producing business documents from provided material using a keyboard, you will need to put all the DIY tasks in your folder, and carry out a final assessment. This must prove that you are able to clarify and rectify uncertainties in text and use questions to ensure instructions are understood. Consistency in layout, spelling, grammar and punctuation must be in accordance with house style and security and confidentiality must be maintained. Corrections must be unobtrusive and copies and originals routed correctly. Approximately 1200 words must be produced in a working period of no longer than 2 hours and 30 minutes, with no more than 3 uncorrected spacing or typographical errors. When unable to meet specified deadlines you must show that you have reported this promptly and accurately to your supervisor.

The documents used to prove competence should include text, tabular material, listings and numeric material. You must prove that you are able to work from manuscript, amended typescript and unarranged material in draft. The documents you must be able to produce are letters, memos, short reports, labels, envelopes, notices for display, articles and lists.

Claiming credit

Once you have completed your final assessment, you will need to write in your record book or folder how, when, where and what you have done to prove that you are competent.

The following is an example of how one trainee completed this claim:

When I was working at Coopers & Co I produced a number of business documents including letters, memos, reports, articles and lists. I worked for 3 different people and therefore had to be able to understand their writing and layout preferences. If I was unsure of an instruction I asked the originator of the document to clarify the meaning. If I could not complete all of the tasks by the time requested I make sure that I told the person quickly and explained why I could not complete on time. I used consistent style, layout, grammar, spelling and punctuation. I chose the correct size and quality of paper for the task and made sure that I always produced tasks as attractively as possible. When I completed a 10–page report I photocopied it and collated it correctly. I used staplers to fasten the document and routed it correctly to all the named people on a provided list. I completed a timed task containing 1200 words in 2 hours and 30 minutes.

■ Element 13.2
PRESENT BUSINESS DOCUMENTS IN A VARIETY OF FORMATS USING A KEYBOARD

Performance criteria

- Instructions are understood
- Presentation, style and format are consistent, correct and in accordance with house style
- Completed presentation meets the requirements of the workplace
- Corrections, when appropriate, are unobtrusive
- Security and confidentiality of information are maintained
- Copies and originals are correctly collated and routed as directed
- Where work is not achievable within specified deadlines reasons are promptly and accurately reported
- Work is achieved within agreed deadlines

The performance criteria for Elements 13.2, 14.2 and 15.2 are exactly the same. Complete this Element to complete Unit 13, 14 or 15.

The equipment available for typing will vary from company to company but you may encounter manual typewriters, which have a distinct sloping keyboard and a carriage return lever. People who have been trained on manual typewriters find it quite easy to transfer to electric or electronic keyboards, but it is more difficult the other way round.

Electric typewriters are similar to manuals in that the keyboard slope is more or less the same. The difference is that less pressure is required to depress the keys. The carriage still moves from side to side but is controlled by a carriage return key instead of a lever. Automatic correction facilities may also be available in the form of correction tape. If a normal nylon ribbon is used a correction tape can be used to cover up the error; if a carbon ribbon is used a lift-off tape is required.

Electronic typewriters usually have a flatter keyboard than manual or electric machines; they also have a fixed carriage (*see* Fig. 13.13). A typing head moves along the carriage and a daisywheel, golf ball or ink jet will type the characters. Daisywheels and golf balls can be changed, which enables different typefaces and sizes to be used to enhance display. Electronic machines also have several features available which may include centring, justifying, memory, wider carriages, automatic

387

Fig 13.13 Electronic typewriter

correction, underscore, emboldening, carriage return and liquid crystal display. A typewriter with numerous, sometimes complicated, facilities may require operators to have specialist training – therefore it may be worth the company investing in word processors rather than complicated typewriters.

▶ *Why use a word processor?*

Word processors such as that shown in Fig. 13.14 have a wide range of facilities and guidance should be sought before purchasing. The software available on the market today has many advanced features which can be time saving, offer increased productivity and provide excellent quality display material. The majority offer mailmerge, spellcheck (specialised dictionaries may be available), various typefaces and sizes, automatic lines for tables and pictures, and moving and copying facilities.

Fig 13.14 A word processor

▶ *What is 'house style'?*

Written communication is one of the most important aspects of any business, as the appearance and quality of the documents represents the company image. Letters or other documents sent to customers with spelling, grammar or presentation errors will not project an efficient, businesslike image. The documents you produce should follow a 'house style'; this ensures that the documents received by the customer will reflect the same image regardless of the department that has sent them.

An organisation will decide upon the style in which letters, memos and other documents will be set out. Over the past few years more companies have moved from the indented, fully punctuated style to blocked, open punctuation, although combinations of both are sometimes used. The blocked, open punctuated style is quicker to type, easier to learn, and less presentation mistakes tend to be made (*see* Fig. 13.15). Some companies are particularly strict with their house style, even stating what size and style of type should be used. Whichever style is chosen by your organisation, it is important to make sure that all members of staff follow the rules so that all styles are consistent.

A major part of your job could be producing correspondence and other types of business documentation. Your typing skills should be quick but also 100 per cent accurate. This does not mean that you will never make an error, but that you should recognise and correct the error when proofreading the copy. When using a word processor it is likely that you will use a spellcheck to proofread your work for spelling mistakes. However, spellcheckers will only highlight a word that is not recognised by the computer's dictionary – any grammar or punctuation errors still need to be identified by you.

▶ What documents would you be expected to produce in an office?

You must be able to produce business correspondence, such as letters and memos, in the house style required by your organisation. You must be aware of the formats required for documents and enclosures and have the ability to use a variety of formats for the purpose of displays and graphics. You must also be able to use landscape and portrait display formats so that display material is produced as attractively and professionally as possible.

▶ What format should be used for letters?

Letters are received and dispatched on a daily basis from most companies, requesting information, supplying information or making arrangements. The aim is to get the information to the addressee, for it to be understood and acted upon. Most business letters are typed on letterheaded paper. This gives the basic facts about the company – the name, address, telephone number, fax and/or telex number, names of directors and company secretary, VAT registration number (if any) and possibly a logotype (commonly called a logo). A professionally designed letterhead makes the company immediately recognisable; some companies invest in a skilled designer to establish the logo which may also become a trade mark for the company. Letterheaded correspondence is normally produced on high quality paper; 80 gsm is usually used. The letters gsm stand for 'grams per square metre' which means that the higher the number the heavier and better quality the paper.

▶ *What format should be used for memos?*

These are used for internal communication only. Most companies have pre-printed forms in A4 and A5 size. They may have a company printed heading with either MEMO or MEMORANDUM, To and From, Date and Reference. A subject heading can be included if required. The content of a memo may be formal or informal. They do not have a complimentary close, but may be initialled by the sender to show approval or confirmation of the contents.

Special markings such as CONFIDENTIAL or PRIVATE are usually typed under the word Memorandum or centred at the top. If the memo is URGENT this would be typed in the top right-hand corner to ensure it was delivered quickly. Routed copies are indicated in the same way as letters, with 'Copy to' at the end of the memo, followed by the names/department of others that should receive a copy. Memo packs are available that have NCR paper ('No Carbon Required') this paper enables the original to be copied through onto the NCR paper without the use of carbon paper. Copies may be coloured to indicate circulation, for example original to addressee, pink copy to catering, blue to security, green file copy.

▶ *How do you indicate enclosures?*

If the letter or memo has enclosures mentioned, the letters Enc are typed at the bottom left-hand margin as a reminder to the sender to enclose them, and for the person receiving the letter to check that the enclosures are there. If there is more than one enclosure in a letter, 'Encs' may be followed by a number, for example 'Encs(3)'.

■ DIY 13.2.1

Collect examples of work that you have produced according to house style. You should include examples of letters and memos that have had enclosures included. Also include material that you have had to mark as confidential. Explain, in writing, how you would ensure that copies and originals are correctly collated and routed as directed.

24 October 19--

Carly-Jo Born
Top Go Salon
224 Lyndsey Road
Branksome
POOLE
BH30 6DB

Dear Carly-Jo

I have been requested by the French authorities
to send you copies of a work placement agreement,
and I am enclosing three copies, one copy to be
retained by you, one copy for the students and
one to be returned to me in the envelope provided.

The document is required in France by all
students carrying out work placement. Although
the document is not necessary under British law,
the French students are concerned that they will
not fulfil the requirements of their qualification
if this document is not part of their portfolio.

If you wish to delete any part of the document
please do so, or if there are any queries please
contact me.

Thank you for your co-operation.

Yours sincerely

Leila Blakemore
Co-ordinator

Encs

Fig 13.15 Blocked letter style

▶ *What format should be used for forms?*

Forms are usually typed in double line spacing to allow room to type or write on the lines. The lines are created by using the underscore or full stops and to ensure good presentation the right-hand margin is usually justified. When typing on forms the tails of descending letters such as p, q and j should be just above the line. When designing a form it is essential that adequate space is left for insertions to be made. How many forms have you used that do not allow enough space for you to insert your full address? Forms that are designed using a word processor can be made to look very professional by using the various display functions such as shadowing, tables, boxes, style, font and so on.

■ DIY 13.2.2

Design a form that can be used by staff to apply for annual leave. The form should cover a sheet of A4 paper and must be presented as attractively as possible. Design your own letterhead or use your own organisation's letter headed stationery on which to design the form.

▶ *What is the difference between landscape and portrait?*

A4 portrait paper is 210 mm × 297 mm, and has 100 spaces across the top and 70 lines down (assuming you are using elite type which gives 12 characters to the inch). A5 paper is exactly half this size, and A5 landscape has 100 spaces across the top and 35 lines down. The paper can be used either way: if the smaller side is put into the typewriter or printer first, this is portrait (as you would draw a person's face); if the longer side is put in first, this is landscape (as you would draw hills or a view) – *see* Fig. 13.3.

Portrait style is usual for business correspondence and is the style most commonly used in an office. Landscape style is used most often for display material that requires extra width. For example, an organisation chart is more likely to be produced on landscape paper as the chart grows in width each time a level is added. You may find that although you have produced correspondence, such as a business letter,

393

using portrait style, you may have to switch to landscape in order to display an accompanying enclosure.

▶ *What is a tabulated or table display format?*

The terms tabulation and table are used to describe information that has been laid out in rows and columns rather than in written text. Tabs and tables are used because they are easier to understand than written information. Look at the following examples – they both contain the same information, but which is the easier to understand?

A

FIRST NAME	SURNAME	PASSPORT?	LANGUAGES SPOKEN	AGE
Amanda	White	Y	German	19
Sally	Gower	N	French	20
David	Talbot	N	French	24
Mark	Harris	Y	Italian	23
Rachel	Markham	Y	Spanish	19
Jade	Hamell	Y	German	28
Perri	Franc	Y	French	24
Leila	Scott	N	Hindustani	19
Crystal	Maze	Y	French	30
John	Patel	N	Hindustani	23
Lynne	Christanou	Y	Greek	19
Shervin	Sepanje	N	Spanish	18

B The travel department has 12 new couriers. Amanda has a passport and speaks German; she is 19 years old. Sally does not have a passport but does speak French; she is 20 years old. David, Leila, John and Shervin do not have passports but Mark, Rachel, Jade, Perri, Crystal and Lynne do. David also speaks French as do Perri and Crystal. Jade is the only other courier that speaks German. Rachel and Shervin both speak Spanish and Leila and John speak Hindustani. Lynne is the only courier who speaks Greek. Rachel, Leila and Lynne are all 19; Shervin is the youngest and is only 18. The oldest member of the group is Crystal who is 30 years old.

It may be the case that you are given information written in the style used for example 'B'. If this is the case, use your common sense and ask if the person requesting the work would prefer if it was produced in a tabular or table format.

A tabular presentation is achieved by using the 'tab' key on your typewriter or computer keyboard. This key is used to align each column so that comparable information can read across or down. If you wish to prepare a lined tabulation using a typewriter, you will have to insert the horizontal lines as you go along. Some machines allow you to insert the vertical lines using a key on the keyboard, although in some cases you may have to insert vertical lines using a black pen and ruler.

Some word processing packages offer a tables option that will create on screen a table like the one in example 'A' above. Boxed in tables are particularly useful if information needs to broken down into separate parts. The boxes can be split or joined, shaded, enlarged and/or reduced to produce attractively displayed, and easy to understand material. *See* Fig. 13.16.

Ace Computer Supplies Catchpole Gardens London SE9				VAT. No. 423/75894/11
Invoice No: 55.2.78.94		Order No: C/7658/54		Date and Tax Point: 30.2.94
Qty	Description	Code	Price	Total
3	Comp. chairs	24-m-2309	57.69	173.04
6	Cartridges	34-n-3425	45.90	27.54
3 x 10	Diskettes	38-p-4879	8.90	26.70
3	PC stand	11-r-5888	27.50	82.50
2	Diskette Cases	56-o-3099	5.99	11.98
1	Continuous Paper	45-p-8759	9.99	FREE
TOTAL PRICE EXCLUDING VAT				569.65
VAT @ 17.5%			89.72	659.37
Goods delivered to: Bales Paint Supplies 144 Knight Lane Kinstone		Terms: 5% – 28 days 10% – 14 days E&OE		

Fig 13.16

■ DIY 13.2.3

Display the following material using a tabulated or table display. Use a heading of 'TRAINING OFFICE PAPER USAGE'.

1991 – 40 reams in each of the first 2 months of the year, 45 in March, 40 again in April and 37 in each of the last 2 months of the half year.

1992 – 52 reams used in each of the first 3 months, following 3 months dropped to 48, 45 and 40 respectively.

1993 – first 3 months of the half year 38, 36 and 34 reams respectively and the last 3 months levelled out at 33 reams each.

▶ *How can you display material effectively?*

Some documents may include items that need to be displayed, such as a letter or memo that requires a table in order to display information effectively. Documents may be required for display on a noticeboard, such as menus, advertisements, vacancies, programmes, etc. There are several ways of producing such material, but typing, word processing or using a desk-top publishing package will produce display material of a high quality.

Some spreadsheet programs will allow you to type the information in the form of a table, and by giving different commands the information can be printed in the form of a line graph, bar or pie chart (*see* Figs 13.17 to 13.19). Special flow chart programs can also be purchased, although it would not be worth buying these unless the package was going to be used frequently. Part of your job could be selecting the most effective method for displaying information.

Word processing packages allow you to change the size and style of the characters. The sizes are usually listed in point size (1 point = 0.0138"), the low numbers referring to the smaller sizes of print. The size of print commonly used on typewriters is 10, 12 or 15 pitch; for word processors it is between 11 pt and 13 pt. To display menus, programmes, tickets and posters you would need to select a size of print which would be effective for the purpose. On an A3 size poster 72 pt would be suitable for headings, and 36 pt for other information; programmes may require 24 pt for headings and 14 pt for information.

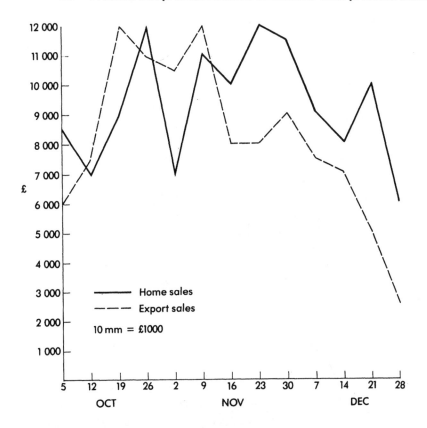

Fig 13.17 Line graph

Once you have selected an appropriate size of print for your
documents, the style can be selected to suit your needs. The fonts
most commonly used are Courier, Helvetica, Prestige and Roman.
Options may also be available for the styles to be in bold, normal, italic,
or bold and italic. You will need to experiment with the options
obtainable on the software available to you. If you are unfamiliar with
the options, it is useful to keep a printout of all available fonts and
styles as this saves time when selecting an attractive display for your
documents. (It is likely that your word processor manual will give
details of the fonts and styles available, although this may be governed
by the printer you are using.) It may also be possible to shadow or
outline your characters – this gives extra effect to displayed material.

NVQ Administration Level 2

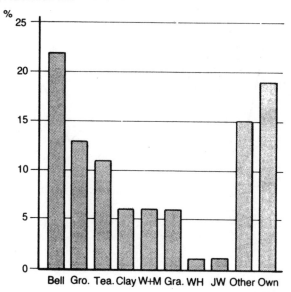

Fig 13.18 Bar chart

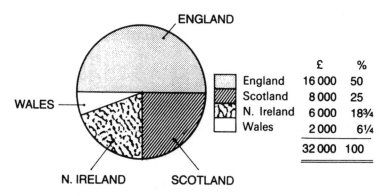

Fig 13.19 Pie chart

The following sizes are pica (10 cpi) converted to: small, large, very large and extra large:

NVQ LEVEL 2

NVQ LEVEL 2

NVQ LEVEL 2

NVQ LEVEL 2

398

The following styles are bold, underline, double underline, italic, outline, shadow, small capital, redline and strikeout:

BUSINESS ADMINISTRATION

BUSINESS ADMINISTRATION

BUSINESS ADMINISTRATION

BUSINESS ADMINISTRATION

BUSINESSS ADMINISTRATION

BUSINESS ADMINISTRATION

BUSINESS ADMINISTRATION

BUSINESS ADMINISTRATION

~~BUSINESS ADMINISTRATION~~

These examples have been created using a base font of Pica, which is 10 characters per inch (cpi). If you wanted to increase the size of the character all you would need to do is select a larger base font. Remember that the smaller the number the larger the font; this is because the number tells you the amount of characters that will fit into one inch.

The following base fonts are: elite, elite double-wide, pica, pica double-wide:

UNIT 13.2

UNIT 13.2

UNIT 13.2

UNIT 13.2

■ DIY 13.2.4

Use a spreadsheet to produce examples of a bar chart, line graph and pie chart. Select appropriate information yourself that will convert easily into each of the 3 formats required. Remember to label all parts and give your charts and graph a heading. Select a variety of styles, fonts and sizes to make your work as attractive as possible.

▶ *What other display facilities are there?*

Whichever type of document you are producing it is important to be accurate and consistent in layout and in your spelling, punctuation and grammar. It is not always possible to rely on your boss to use the correct spelling. Pay particular attention to words that you are not familiar with, or numerical information. These need to be checked carefully against the original data. The terminology used by a specialised organisation may be unfamiliar to you and this makes checking your documents more demanding. Keep a list of common specialist terms you use, or if you have a computerised spellcheck add them to the memory.

Mathematical signs and foreign text may also be typed and some machines have a secondary keyboard, that is the keys relate to special signs and characters which can be typed by keying in a special code. You will need to consult your typewriter manual or software manual to find out the facilities available, although you will find that some signs may need to be inserted by hand using a black pen. You may be able to find some of the following signs using your word processor or typewriter:

■ DIY 13.2.5

Take this opportunity to find out how to create signs and symbols like the ones above. If using a word processor or typewriter now is a good time to write down your own notes on what you have to do. Include with your notes examples of all the signs available on your typewriter or word processor.

Electronic machines will usually allow you to change the typeface, and embolden and outline characters to make your display material more attractive. Word processors have the best facilities which may include some graphics – it will depend on the package you are using, the speed at which your computer operates and the printer you have available. Alternatively you may be able to use a desk-top publishing package.

Many word processing packages also include graphics in the form of pictures which can be included in text. These are some of the easiest ones to use. If you become a specialist graphics operator then you will be able to create your own graphics to add to those already available. The following examples can be found on WordPerfect 5.1:

■ DIY 13.2.6

Display the following notices as attractively as possible. Use A4 landscape paper. Select or draw your own graphics to make the notices as attractive as possible.

1 Sports Club Members. Netball Team. Can you play? Would you like to learn? The Sports Club members would like to start a ladies' netball team. Training Monday 7–9 pm in the Sports Centre. League games 10–11 am at Green Lane Sports Ground. Please contact Sharon Mackett or Jayne Swaffield for more details on extension 1765.

2 Notice to all staff. Please note the new internal extension numbers. P J Adkins – 7689, A R Brown – 2869, T Lowe – 7869, T B Singh – 9860, L Betts – 9906, R Hawkins – 4811, N Petrovsky – 8868, A Groome – 7588, A R Brown – 2869, Y Yolland – 8113, T Murray – 2759, J P K Patel – 5583. Please display in alphabetical order.

▶ *What is a scanner?*

Scanners are useful for importing material onto a computer file, but again it will take specialist training for you to be able to master the techniques involved. Scanners can be used to copy to memory text and graphics from an original document so it can be used again and again from the hard disk, eg a company logo. The scanner is similar to a photocopier but it copies the document to disk instead of paper; this saves time as the document does not have to be keyed in and graphics are transferred automatically. However, it would be unusual for you to carry out this type of work often; if a company has a high demand for graphics they are likely to appoint a specialist graphics designer to deal with all the documents and requests.

Completing Element 13.2

To complete this element on presenting business documents in a variety of formats using a keyboard, you will need to put all the DIY tasks in your folder, and carry out a final assessment. This must prove that you are able to understand and carry out instructions, and that when deadlines are not achievable you are able to report this promptly and accurately. Your presentation style and format must be consistent and in accordance with house style. Corrections to your work must be unobtrusive and security and confidentiality must be maintained at all times. Copies and originals must be correctly collated and routed as directed. Competence must be proved dealing with documents and enclosures, displays and graphics using both portrait and landscape layout.

Claiming credit

Once you have completed you final assessment, you will need to write in your record book or folder how, when, where and what you have done to prove that you are competent.

The following is an example of how one trainee completed this claim:

While working at Coopers & Co I used WordPerfect 5.1 to produce tables and graphics. I produced multi-page documents, some with enclosures, that had to be collated, stapled and routed correctly. I produced a 20-page report for my supervisor that contained pie charts and tabulated material. The report was printed on portrait paper, but 2 pages which contained organisation charts had to be printed using landscape paper. When I was asked to use a new function on the computer I referred to the manual first; this happened when I was asked to use shaded boxes in a table. I always worked to deadlines, but if there had been a problem I would have reported this to my supervisor immediately. I made sure that my presentation style followed house style, which I was able to obtain from copies of other documents. I also used a package called Microsoft Works which allowed word processed, spreadsheet and database files to be integrated. I used this software to produce a sales brochure that had text and graphics contained in it (see evidence folder).

UNIT 14

Produce and present business documents from recorded material

- **Element 14.1**
  PRODUCE BUSINESS DOCUMENTS FROM RECORDED INSTRUCTIONS USING A KEYBOARD

  Performance criteria

  - Recorded instructions are correctly interpreted and followed
  - Approximately 600 words are produced in the workplace, from recorded instructions, in one and half hours, with no more than four uncorrected spacing or typographical errors
  - Uncertainties in text are identified, checked and rectified
  - Completed documentation meets the requirements of the workplace
  - Layout, spelling, grammar and punctuation are consistent, correct and in accordance with house style
  - Corrections, when appropriate, are unobtrusive
  - Security and confidentiality of information are maintained
  - Copies and originals are correctly collated and routed, as directed
  - Where work is not achievable within specified deadlines reasons are promptly and accurately reported
  - Work is achieved within agreed deadlines

Apart from giving you manuscript documents your manager may also use audio. Audio is quite often preferred to shorthand as the manager is able to record material away from the office, although the quality of such tapes can sometimes be poor, especially when dictation is carried out whilst travelling. You may find yourself trying to distinguish dictation from your manager's conversation with a taxi driver, or have the background noise of an airport, railway station or underground train.

404

The tapes given to trainees in a training centre are usually first class: the dictation is steady, no interruptions occur, some punctuation is usually given, and unusual words are spelt. In reality it would be most uncommon to receive such a tape when working. Most managers do not receive training in dictating material on to tapes, although most would benefit from it.

A common mistake made by managers is to give figures followed by the word 'pounds'. A manager who understands the way in which an audio typist works would know to say the word 'pounds' followed by the figures – in the same order that you would type the dictation. Another error may be the way in which your manager gives you instructions on the tape, quite often an afterthought – at the end of a letter you may hear 'Oh I forgot, I can't go on that date, delete the second paragraph and just leave the first and last' – not much help once you have typed the letter. However, the problems are not so severe if a word processor is used as documents can easily be altered before printing.

When working continually for the same person you will get to know their habits and the way in which they dictate; with experience you will be able to anticipate their requirements. It may be the case that you are responsible for transcribing audio material for a number of people, quite possibly from different departments. In this situation it is important the tapes are recorded with clear instructions. If you find one particular person's dictation always causes you problems, mention this to your supervisor.

▶ *What equipment do you need for audio?*

The manager will require a dictation machine and tapes. The most commonly used are small pocket machines like that in Fig. 14.1, which are easily carried and stored. The tapes for these machines can store 15 minutes of dictation on each side and are easily posted back to the office to be typed. Nevertheless, traditional machines are still in use and the standard C60, C90 and C120 cassettes operate on these. C60 is generally preferred as damage to a longer tape could result in a large amount of work being lost. The C60 tape is also the smallest and can be passed to the typist to start transcription while another tape can be used to carry on with dictation. Desk-top machines are available and

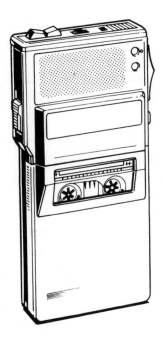

Fig 14.1 Dictating machine for audio transcription

may be preferred by managers who do not travel frequently. Some of the desk-top machines have special facilities such as telephone connection sockets used to record telephone conversations, for example containing measurements and numbers in a foreign language.

Transcription can be made by either playing the tape back and listening from the loudspeaker (although this would disturb colleagues) or through a set of headphones as in Fig. 14.2. The tape can be controlled by hand, using buttons on the machine, or by foot using a foot pedal. Foot pedals can have a play, reverse and a fast forward facility. When pressure is removed from the pedal the tape stops.

Most transcription machines have an index which can be used to mark the starting point of each separate document on the tape. This facility is not available on the hand-held dictation machines. A slip of paper is inserted into the indicator on the desk-top machine, and at the beginning of each document a mark is made on the paper, either by hand or by pressing a button on the machine. If the manager requires a particular document urgently, it would be a simple procedure to run the tape forward to the required point ready for transcription.

Fig 14.2 Audio transcription equipment

Alternatively, a tape counter may be used and the number recorded manually at the beginning of each piece of dictation to identify the position of each separate document.

Some of the more advanced machines have the same facility but the marks are made electronically and indexing would be automatically shown by bleeps or flashing lights.

■ DIY 14.1.1

Type or word process a brief report on how audio-typing is used in your office or training centre. Give examples of the kind of documents that are produced together with the name and type of equipment being used. Name each piece of equipment that you use in order to transcribe audio tapes and give details of how this equipment is set up.

▶ *How might larger companies use audio?*

Large companies may use a centralised dictation system which would allow access by all staff to audio facilities. Generally this system would be available through a centralised typing or secretarial service. A centralised system may also be connected to a networked computer system. This would enable documents to be sent via the electronic mail system for approval by the writer. There are 3 main methods.

1 Multi-bank. Several machines are located in the typing centre and

407

are connected to users via wires and the telephone system. Those wishing to use the system will dial the operator who will connect them to a free machine. Once the dictation is complete a supervisor will remove the tape and allocate the work to one of the audio typists.

2 **Tandem**. This is a similar system to the multi-bank, except that each audio typist has 2 machines on the desk, one for dictation and one for transcription. Connection to the system is still via the switchboard, but departments can be allocated particular audio typists. This system relieves the supervisor from allocating work and a typist can become familiar with a particular department's work or personal requirements and terminology.

3 **Continuous or loop technique**. Dictation is received on a continuous tape via the switchboard or a private line. Typists access the tape to transcribe. Urgent items can be indicated on some systems for priority treatment but normally transcription is carried out in the same order as the dictation was made. Some current systems include a visual display unit (VDU) which lists the documents waiting for transcription. It can also monitor the typists' productivity levels and will allow allocation of a department's work to a particular typist.

The cost of these systems can be enormous and careful research should be carried out before recommending a particular system for installation within a business. Central systems may also break down, which could result in business halting for a period of time. The effect of a central system on the audio typists should also be taken into consideration – would you like to sit in front of a typewriter or word processor all day doing nothing but transcribing audio tapes?

▶ *What about maintenance of equipment?*

All equipment, whether it is centralised or individual, should be regularly maintained. It is possible to keep the machine in good order by covering with a dust cover and using a cleaning tape – how often will depend on the machine usage. Connecting wires should not be allowed to trail around the desk and if a machine is not used on a regular basis it should be kept in a cupboard along with the attachments.

Earphones should be cleaned regularly and never lent out to other people. Using another person's earphones can result in ear infections. It is useful to use a mild disinfectant to clean ear pieces and when not in use your earphones should be kept in a container or plastic pocket where they cannot be damaged.

▶ *What types of headphones are there?*

Some people find that they can suffer from earache if constantly using headphones for transcription. There are several styles of headphone available on the market today, and one should be selected to suit your preferences. Most of the headphones supplied by the manufacturers have plastic tips which are placed just inside the ear and may have foam surrounds for increased comfort. The headphones used for personal stereos are suitable for audio typing and may be preferred.

If part of your job is to answer the telephone it can be inconvenient to be constantly taking off headphones to deal with telephone calls. A special adapter is available which is shaped to sit around the ear, the audio microphone is held in place on the ear, leaving one ear free for the telephone. However, the user can be easily distracted by surrounding noise and it is of course harder to listen with only one ear.

▶ *What skills are needed for audio?*

Good English is a must. A common error made by trainee audio typists is typing incorrect words, especially when they are pronounced the same but spelt differently – homonyms. These errors are not identified by a computerised spellcheck and the text must therefore be proof-read for sense as well as spelling, grammar and punctuation. Ensure that your office has a good dictionary and thesaurus, even if your computer has these facilities.

■ DIY 14.1.2

Type a copy of the following list. Below each word write down its meaning. Do not use a dictionary to help you. You will notice that although the words sound similar, they have very different meanings.

1	Accept	2	Except
3	Check	4	Cheque
5	Advise	6	Advice
7	Compliment	8	Complement
9	Ensure	10	Insure
11	Quiet	12	Quite
13	Stationary	14	Stationery
15	Principle	16	Principal
17	Insurance	18	Assurance
19	Affect	20	Effect

Now check your answers with a good dictionary and correct any mistakes you have made.

Interruptions can also create errors. In a busy office it is unlikely that you will be able to carry out any job for a long period without some kind of interruption. It could be the telephone, a visitor, a colleague's or manager's request, an emergency, change of priority, or it could be the end of the day. Your organisational skills are very important in this case to enable you to cope with routine transcription and deal with everyday interruptions at the same time.

After an interruption make sure you read through the last few sentences of text to familiarise yourself with the content: you will then be able to restart the tape and carry on where you left off. If using a word processor it is important to save text as you go along. If you are interrupted, save the work you have done and then deal with the interruption. Beware: work left on screen while you deal with another task can be read by anyone and may be deleted in error.

■ DIY 14.1.3

Your boss, Mrs D Gerrard, is unhappy with the quality of work produced by the new audio-typist and has asked you to photocopy and proofread the memos reproduced as Figs 14.3 and 14.4.

MEMORANDUM

To: Martin O'Connell

From: Iain Woods

Date:

Ref: <u>Applications for Publicity Manager</u>

We have recieved 8 aplications for the
post of publicity Manger in replie to our
our   advertisment in last weeks Evenning
Echo. i recomend a dealine date of fri.
next, with intervue to   be arranged for the
following wed. (date please).

Can I sugest that you let me had a copy of
the job discription which you are drawing uyp
to help us in to select a shortlist and so that
we can base our interview questions around this.

We need to discus salary as details will need to
be given to the apliciants at inteview - is it
possible to meet with your tomorrow and weather
accom. can be arranged for the interview pannel.

Fig 14.3

Your keyboarding skills are vital if you want to be competent at
transcribing audio dictation. You must be able to touch type to produce
an acceptable quantity of work in one day. Your presentation must be
good and your proofreading excellent. If you make an error it must be
corrected so it cannot be noticed. If you are working on a word
processor errors are easy to correct, but correcting errors on a
typewriter is time consuming and not always to the standard required.
It is important to remember that accurate typing will save time: you
will not be continually stopping to correct errors.

411

MEMORANDUM

To   Michelle Goujon

From   Olivia Skone

Date   5 May 199–

Ref   OS/MR

SALES CONFERENCE

The Salis Confence will take place in the last week of June. we has booked the Royal Hotel, as last year.

Could you plese insure that we have 20 setts of promotional literture on our latsest products for our sales representtives in advaance of this date?

Fig 14.4

■ DIY 14.1.4

Copy type the following list of commonly misspelled words. When you come across other words that cause you problems with spelling add these to your list. This list will build into your own personal reference – keep it close at hand when transcribing dictation.

accommodation	accessible	achieved
acknowledge	aggravate	all right
among	appearance	arrangement
beginning	believed	benefited
business	colleagues	coming
committee	completely	conscientious
correspondence	decision	definite
disappointed	especially	essential
excellent	expenses	extremely
February	friend	fulfilled
government	height	immediately
independent	instalment	knowledge

maintenance	minutes	necessary
noticeable	occasionally	occurrence
permanent	possesses	privilege
procedure	professional	quiet
recommend	referred	sentence
separate	similar	sincerely
successfully	surprise	transferred
twelfth	unnecessary	usually
view	Wednesday	withhold

▶ *What types of layouts are used?*

As well as making sure the content is correct, part of your job will be to make sure the correct layout is used. Most companies use a 'house style' – a particular style the company (the house) has approved and wishes all staff to use. An approved house style is used so that customers receive the same style of documentation, regardless of which department sends it. Some companies are extremely fussy about the house style, even stating what size print and style to use.

The most commonly used layout is the fully blocked style without punctuation (except in the paragraphs of the letter). In this style everything starts at the left-hand side (*see* Fig. 14.5). This is the quickest style to type, as you do not need to work out spacing or spend time inserting unnecessary punctuation marks.

The date should always be written in the same way whether it is typed at the top of the letter or in one of the paragraphs, eg 25 May 1994 (without punctuation).

The layout for blocked memos would be as shown in Fig. 14.6.

The other style frequently used is semi-blocked. In this style the date is placed on the right-hand side and the signature block is centred. The rest of the letter remains at the left-hand side (*see* Fig. 14.8).

For memos typed in a semi-blocked layout the word 'Memorandum' would be moved to the centre and the date and reference across towards the right-hand side (*see* Fig. 14.7).

If an enclosure is mentioned in the letter or memorandum the letters 'Enc' or 'Encs' (if more than one) should be placed at the bottom of the page. It is normal practice not to sign memoranda, although some supervisors may prefer to put their initial at the bottom of the page to confirm the contents.

```
Reference:

26 April 199-

Mrs R L George
14 Wood Road
BRACKNELL
Berks
BR4 6TU

Dear Mrs George

PICTURE FRAMING

Thank you for your request for a brochure
describing our product range.  We have pleasure
in enclosing our latest brochure, together with
our price list.

We look forward to hearing from you and to
receiving your order.

Yours sincerely


Olivia Skone
Marketing Executive

Enc
```

Fig 14.5 Letter in fully blocked style

MEMORANDUM

To   Michelle Goujon

From   Olivia Skone

Date   5 May 199-

Ref   OS/MR

SALES CONFERENCE

This will take place in the last week of June. We have booked the Royal Hotel, as last year.

Could you please ensure that we have 20 sets of promotional literature on our latest products for our sales representatives in advance of this date?

Fig 14.6 Memo in fully blocked style

MEMORANDUM

To	Michelle Goujon	**Date**	5 May 199-
From	Olivia Skone	**Ref**	OS/MR

SALES CONFERENCE

This will take place in the last week of June. We have booked the Royal Hotel, as last year.

Could you please ensure that we have 20 sets of promotional literature on our latest products for our sales representatives in advance of this date?

Fig 14.7 Memo in semi-blocked style

415

If you are asked to send copies of a document to other people you can indicate this at the bottom of the page. After the last line on the page or document leave a space and then type in 'Copy to:' and add the name(s) of the people copies are to go to. When the copies are prepared either tick or highlight a different name on each copy. This process is called 'routing', and when the original and the copies are

```
Ref: OS/MR

Mrs R L George
14 Wood Road
BRACKNELL
Berks
BR4 6TU                              26 April 199-

Dear Mrs George

PICTURE FRAMING

Thank you for your request for a brochure
describing our product range.  We have pleasure
in enclosing our latest brochure, together with
our price list.

We look forward to hearing from you and to
receiving your order.

                    Yours sincerely



                    Olivia Skone
                    Marketing Executive

Enc
```

Fig 14.8 Letter in semi-blocked style

ready to be dispatched you will be able to see easily who should receive each document (*see* page 422).

When starting a new job, it is your responsibility to find out the style required for documents; do not rely upon your existing knowledge, training and experience received at college or at previous companies. Some companies will produce a manual or guide for staff to ensure they follow the agreed layout for all documentation. If not, ask for examples for you to copy.

▶ *Guidelines for typing envelopes*

The guidelines for typing envelopes are given by the Post Office and suit the machinery installed to sort letters.

1 Type the address along the longer side of the envelope.
2 The first line of the address should start at about a third of the way across the envelope and half-way down.
3 Each line of the address should have a separate line.
4 The post town should be in CAPITALS.
5 The postcode should be the last line, in capitals, on its own and with one space between the two parts, eg GN3 2NN.

If there are any special instructions such as URGENT, CONFIDENTIAL, For the attention of ..., they should be typed two lines above the name and address (*see* Fig. 14.9).

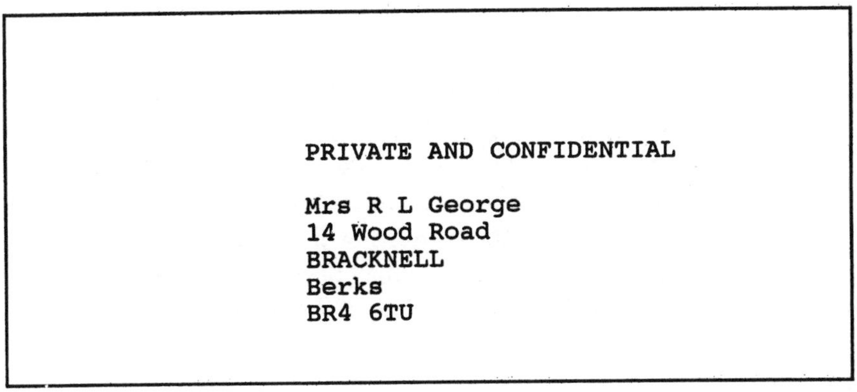

```
           PRIVATE AND CONFIDENTIAL

           Mrs R L George
           14 Wood Road
           BRACKNELL
           Berks
           BR4 6TU
```

Fig 14.9 Envelope layout

417

▶ *Layout and presentation*

It may be left to you to decide how to lay out your documents and your job will be to ensure that you select the most suitable method for the document concerned. As said before, layout is important because it reflects an image of the business. The most important rule is to be consistent. If you decide to leave 2 lines between each paragraph in a report, you should not suddenly start leaving 3. Always look at previously typed documents to see how other staff have laid out the document, or ask for guidance from your supervisor.

▶ *What happens if you make mistakes?*

Everyone makes mistakes; the skill is in knowing when you make a mistake and correcting it – so that no one else knows! There is nothing worse than completing a letter or memorandum and passing it to your boss to be signed, only to find that it comes back with a big circle round a silly typing mistake. If you are using a typewriter the whole document may have to be retyped.

It is most important to read everything you type before you hand it to the person for signature. You may believe that you 'know' when you make a typing error, but there could still be some that have gone unnoticed. Proofreading is a skill that has to be learned, in the same way as typing: the more you proofread the quicker you will become at identifying errors.

▶ *What is proofreading?*

This is when you read the document (proof) to ensure it is correct in content and layout. Most people find proofreading boring, and it probably is, but it is an essential part of document production. It is useful to get someone else to read an important document for you, as they will be unfamiliar with the content, will concentrate more and it is likely they will find errors that you may have overlooked. However, someone else can proofread for you only if the material is not confidential.

If you are unsure of how a word is spelt, look it up in a dictionary and keep a list of commonly misspelt words to refer to. If you have a word processor, it may have a spellcheck: make sure you use it. However, you will still need to proofread as the spellcheck will not find grammatical errors or words that are incorrect, eg 'it' instead of 'is', incorrect punctuation (eg a full stop instead of a comma), or words, sentences or paragraphs that have been missed out completely.

▶ *What is the best method for correcting errors?*

It depends on the type of error and the type of equipment you are using. Obviously, you cannot use correction fluid on a screen! A corrected error should be unobtrusive, which means you should not be able to notice it.

If you are using a typewriter you can use correction paper. This method is unobtrusive, as long as you have the character lined up correctly; otherwise the chalk covering misses and leaves some of the black character uncovered. This method should not be used for major errors such as changing two sentences round, or taking out a whole sentence. The other commonly used method is correcting fluid. Paint the error with the fluid, wait until it is dry, and then type the correct characters over the top. If you try to type in your corrections before the fluid has dried it will make a mess on the paper and can clog up the letters in your machine.

Many electric and electronic typewriters have correction facilities. The correction tapes will either be similar to correction paper or coated on one side with a sticky substance. The type of correction tape used will depend on the type of ribbon. Nylon ribbons use correction paper, and carbon ribbons use sticky correction tape which lifts the carbon image from the paper. If you look at the correction tape when you replace it you will see the carbon characters stuck to it. The disadvantage with this method of correction is that it leaves an indentation in the paper, and the better quality the paper the more obvious the indentation. This is not a problem if another character is to be typed on top but if it is between 2 words or at the end of a sentence the indentation may be noticeable.

Some electronic machines have an LCD (liquid crystal display) which displays each line of type. This facility can be set to allow you to correct words or sentences before you actually print them on to the paper.

When major errors occur in typewritten documents it may be possible to retype the one page necessary or to 'stick and paste'. This means that the correct paragraphs are cut out and glued round the newly typed paragraphs. The whole document is then photocopied. This method cannot be used for letters and it may be unsuitable for some occasions, for instance when your boss wants the original to be sent.

If you do use a word processor make sure that you proofread on screen properly – otherwise sheets of paper and time are wasted unnecessarily in printing work that is full of errors. The main advantage of proofreading on the screen is that errors are corrected before the document is printed – in this way the errors are totally unobtrusive.

If you are working as a general assistant, it may be that you send documents to the typing pool or clerk typist for typing. When they are returned to you for signature you must check thoroughly before signing and sending out. You should check spelling (look up any words you are not sure of), grammar, punctuation and content. Ensure that you use the approved correction signs whenever possible as this will make the typist's job easier and you will reduce the possibility of misunderstanding.

▶ *When should apostrophes be used?*

Apostrophes can easily be misused. The rules state that they should be used to form possessive nouns, that is, to show something belongs to someone or something, eg:

Carly's pencil
Natalie's lunch box
Leila's coat

If the noun ends in 's' the apostrophe is placed after the 's'. Another 's' is added, eg:

Kris's bike

If the noun is a plural (more than one), the apostrophe would still be after the 's', eg:

the doctors' parking

This would mean more than one doctor; if it was the doctor's parking, it would mean only one doctor. Some nouns are changed slightly when becoming plural. 'Child' and 'woman' become 'children' and 'women'; in these cases the 's' is added and the apostrophe would appear before it, eg:

the children's socks
the women's handbags

An apostrophe is also used when a letter or letters are omitted from a word, for example don't, you're, aren't, can't, haven't, we've and I've. It's is used to mean 'it is' – the apostrophe takes the place of the letter 'i'.

■ DIY 14.1.5

Copy out the following sentences and put the apostrophes in the correct place.

1 The boys cat lay on its tail.
2 The dogs are in the kitchen eating the cats dinner.
3 Susans looking for her son.
4 Weve got to run or well be late for Sams speech.
5 I dont think youve got it.
6 Its too early now, well go later.
7 The trainees folders havnt been seen yet.
8 Peters trousers were covered in Pauls drink.
9 The 2 boys said theyd be 2 hours late.
10 The childrens party began at 2 but I dont know who went.

▶ *Useful books*

Apart from a dictionary, other useful reference books include a good thesaurus – this gives alternative words with the same meaning, and can help widen your written and verbal vocabulary; glossary – a specialised list of words and their meanings for your particular business; and a general office reference book such as *Chambers' Office Oracle*, *The Secretary's Handbook* or *The Secretary's Desk Book*.

▶ *How do you route a document correctly?*

When a document has to be seen by a number of people or departments or a copy put on file, it is usual practice to route each copy of the document. This is done by listing the names of people and/or departments at the bottom of the document. The word 'File' may also be included to show that one copy has to go on file. The usual style to use is:

Copy to: Nigel Parker – Accounts
          Henry Spratt – Purchasing
          File

The original copy of the document is sent to the person named at the top of the document. The correct number of copies are then routed by ticking a different name on each copy. In the example above the first copy would have the name Nigel Parker ticked, the second copy Henry Spratt and the last copy File. In this way all copies are clearly marked and their destination known. The first 2 copies could be placed in the internal postal system for delivery and the last copy would go into the filing cabinet.

▶ *What is collating?*

This means putting the documents you have typed into the correct page order. If you prepare a multi-page document it is wise to number each page so that you do not become confused when the document has to be put together. If you are using a word processor you can instruct it to automatically insert a header or footer that includes the page number of each sheet in the document. It is important that all pages are collated in the correct order before they are stapled or fastened together, otherwise the text may not make sense.

When preparing a multi-page letter it is important to follow the correct house style. When typing letters it is normal practice to insert the page number, date and name of addressee at the top of each consecutive page. For example, a multi-page letter typed in block style is likely to have the following typed at the top of page 2:

2
20 February 1994
Mrs J D Carpenter

If the pages become separated, the information at the top of each page will identify where each page belongs. If typing a report, you may have to include the name of the report at the top or bottom of each page rather than a person's name. This would normally be set up as a header or footer.

If you have to prepare copies of the document, these must also be placed in the correct page order. If you are able to send documents to a reprographic service to be copied, make sure that you tell them to collate and fasten the documents for you as this will save you time and help to meet deadlines.

Collating by hand can take a long time, depending on how many pages and copies of the document you have to put together. If you are lucky, your company may have a photocopier that can be programmed to collate the pages as it is copying them, or you may have the use of a collating machine. Imagine if you have 25 copies of a 30-page report to collate by hand, it will take some time to put the pages in the correct order. You will need to have a work area where the 30 pages can be placed in separate heaps. Alternatively, you will have to sort the first 10 pages (or however many you can lay out) followed by the second set of 10 pages and then the third. These three heaps would then have to be collated into the final sets. You will need to lay out the documents in a logical sequence, either in page number order, or to speed up the process, an order where both hands can work at the same time. For example, a 10-page document could be laid out as in Fig. 14.10.

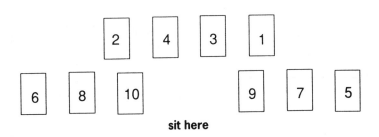

sit here

Fig 14.10

The left hand will take one copy of page 10 and place it in the space in front, and then the right hand will take one copy of page 9 and place it on top of page 10. Both hands can move at the same time and the document is collated back to front. Complete sets can be stacked away from the work area.

▶ *What type of stationery should you use?*

Letters are normally typed on A4 headed paper, although some companies do use A5 letterheads. Memos on the other hand are commonly available in A4 and A5. A4 portrait paper is 210 mm × 297 mm, has 100 spaces across the top and 70 lines down (assuming you are using elite type which is 12 characters to 25 mm). A5 landscape paper is half this size, and has 100 spaces across the top and 35 lines down. The paper can be used in either the portrait position, with the short side put in to the machine first, or landscape position, with the long side put in first (*see* Fig. 14.11).

The quality of stationery used will depend upon its purpose. Paper and envelopes used for business correspondence will be of good quality as the company will want to convey a good impression to its customers and clients. The quality of paper can be measured by its weight, or gsm (grams per square metre). Bond, copier and letterheaded paper is fairly thick and therefore heavier (usually by about 25 gsm) than paper such as bank, which would be cheaper and used for carbon copies.

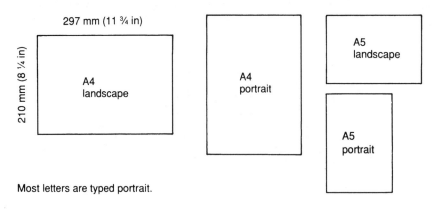

Most letters are typed portrait.

Fig 14.11 Paper sizes

424

▶ *Preparing labels*

Self-adhesive labels can be purchased in rolls or in A4 sheets. Typing addresses on labels is quicker than typing on envelopes, and it is possible to use a label template on a word processor to print labels. Word processing software will allow you to set up a template that can be used to type address details on screen so that when they are printed out, they are in the exact position on the roll or sheet of labels. Once you have set up a template that matches the exact size of labels used in your office or training centre, this should be saved so that it is ready for use again and again.

A4 sheets of labels can also be photocopied. First the addresses are typed on a plain piece of A4 paper which has a guide sheet behind to ensure the address is typed to the correct size. The typed copy is then placed on the photocopier and the sheet of labels passed through the machine. The addresses will be copied on to the labels ready for use. This is particularly worthwhile when sending documents regularly to the same addresses. The rules for typing addresses on envelopes also apply to labels (*see* page 417).

```
Mrs R Patel
19 Kings Gardens
EDINBURGH
E41 4IP
```

Fig 14.12 Label

▶ *What about security and confidentiality?*

If you are responsible for processing confidential documents make sure you keep them in a folder marked Confidential, and lock them away when not required. Text on a VDU can easily be read if the screen is left on, and poor printouts thrown into the bin can be read at a later date. If you take carbon copies remember the carbon paper can be read after use giving full details of the document typed. Do not allow anyone to look over your shoulder when typing and put all documents out of the way if you have to leave the office for any reason. Remember to use passwords to protect documents held on disks and keep your cassette tapes locked away so that they cannot be played by unauthorised personnel.

Completing Element 14.1

To complete this element on producing business documents from recorded instructions using a keyboard, you will need to put all the DIY tasks in your folder, and carry out a final assessment. This must prove that you are able to ask questions to clarify the meaning of recorded instructions and that you are able to confirm your understanding. You must be able to set up your audio equipment and transcribe recorded material using a typewriter or word processor. Correct grammar, spelling, punctuation and sense of recorded material must be evident and you must be able to select the appropriate layout, print and stationery for each task. A production rate of 600 words from recorded instructions must be achieved in 1 hour and 30 minutes, with no more than 4 uncorrected spacing or typographical errors; this must be carried out in workplace conditions ensuring security and confidentiality are maintained. You must prove that you are able to compose documents from recorded instructions and that you can copy, collate and route material to appropriate locations. If you are not able to meet deadlines you must provide valid reasons for non-achievement. Documents such as letters, memos, short reports, labels, envelopes, notices for display, articles and lists must be produced, and should include text, tabulation, listings and numeric information.

Claiming credit

Once you have completed you final assessment, you will need to write in your record book or folder how, when, where and what you have done to prove that you are competent.

The following is an example of how one trainee completed this claim:

While in the training centre I processed letters, memos, reports, notices, articles and lists using audio equipment (see evidence folder). I prepared envelopes or labels for letters. Included in the documents were text, tabulations, listings and numeric information. I carried out a timed assessment to prove that I am able to produce 600 words in 1 hour and 30 minutes with no more than 4 errors. I made sure my layout, spelling, grammar and punctuation were consistent and that I followed house style at all times. All corrections were unobtrusive and if I was unsure of anything I would ask my supervisor. Security

426

and confidentiality were always maintained; audio tapes were kept in a locked drawer and documents marked confidential were kept in a file. I produced a number of 2-page letters and a 10-page report. These were all collated and routed correctly. I always tried to work to agreed deadlines, but if unable to, I reported this to my supervisor and explained why immediately.

■ **Element 14.2**
PRESENT BUSINESS DOCUMENTS IN A VARIETY OF FORMATS USING A KEYBOARD

Performance criteria

- Instructions are understood
- Presentation, style and format are consistent, correct and in accordance with house style
- Completed presentation meets the requirements of the workplace
- Corrections, when appropriate, are unobtrusive
- Security and confidentiality of information are maintained
- Copies and originals are correctly collated and routed as directed
- Where work is not achievable within specified deadlines reasons are promptly and accurately reported
- Work is achieved within agreed deadlines

The performance criteria for Elements 13.2, 14.2 and 15.2 are exactly the same. Complete Element 13.2 (page 387) to complete Unit 13, 14 or 15.

UNIT 15

Produce and present business documents from dictated material

■ **Element 15.1**
PRODUCE BUSINESS DOCUMENTS FROM DICTATED INFORMATION USING A KEYBOARD

Performance criteria

- Information from notes dictated at a minimum of 70 wpm is transcribed accurately
- Instructions are understood
- Uncertainties in text are identified, checked and rectified
- Approximately 375–400 words are produced in the workplace, from dictated information, in one hour, with no more than 3 uncorrected spacing or typographical errors
- Completed documentation meets the requirements of the workplace
- Layout, spelling, grammar and punctuation are consistent, correct and in accordance with house style
- Corrections, when appropriate, are unobtrusive
- Security and confidentiality of information are maintained
- Copies and originals are correctly collated and routed, as directed
- Where work is not achievable within specified deadlines reasons are promptly and accurately reported
- Work is achieved within agreed deadlines

Shorthand is used to take down verbal information and transcribe it back later. It is usually transcribed using a typewriter or word processor and allows the boss to get on with work while the secretary prepares documents such as reports, letters, minutes and memoranda.

Shorthand is also used to note down instructions and messages – anything that needs to be written down quickly and accurately.

Most people speak at a speed of about 80–200 words per minute, but are able to write longhand at only 20–50 words per minute. Therefore, we must use some form of shorthand to record the words of even a slow speaker. Quick thinking and controlled penmanship are necessary if acceptable speeds are to be achieved. It is no use taking down dictation which cannot be accurately read back later.

Several forms of shorthand systems are available. It does not matter what system you use; what is important is that you are able to take down dictation and transcribe it accurately. You must also be familiar with house styles used by the organisation and transcribe documents using the correct layout and presentation. You will also have to judge the length of the document when typing it back to make sure you choose the correct size of paper. A sheet of A4 paper will hold approximately 200 typed words in double line spacing.

You must be good at spelling and grammar if you are to transcribe the dictation error free, with correct sentence construction and punctuation (your boss is unlikely while dictating to tell you where to put punctuation such as commas or full stops). Some shorthand systems are based on phonetics, ie the sound of the word, but when transcribed the word must be as it would be spelt and not spoken. Remember there are many words that sound the same but are spelt differently for different meanings – it is important that you have a good vocabulary and understand the meaning of words.

■ DIY 15.1.1

Your boss, Mrs D Gerrard, is unhappy with the quality of work produced by the new shorthand-typist and has asked you to photocopy and proofread the memos reproduced as Figs 15.1 and 15.2 on pages 430 and 431.

▶ *How could you improve your speed?*

All shorthand systems use short forms or common words. When a phrase is used often it can be written down as an abbreviation of the shorthand outline. Your shorthand book will give you details of all short

MEMORANDUM

To: Martin O'Connell

From: Iain Woods

Date:

Ref: Applications for Clerk Typist

So far i have received 9 aplications for the
cletk typist post advertised in last weeks
evening Echo. I recomend a dealine date of mon.
next, with interview to   be arranged for the
following tues. (date please).

Can I sugest that you drawer up a job discription
to help us in to select a shortlist and so that
we can base our interview questions around this.

We need to discus salary as details will need to
be given to the aplikants at inteview – it is it
possible to meet with your tomorrow and weather
accom. can be arranged for the interview pannel.

Fig 15.1

forms, and you are likely to design some of your own once you are
familiar with your boss's work. Phrases such as 'Thank you for your
letter of', 'Dear Sir/Madam', and complimentary closes such as 'Yours
sincerely' and 'Yours faithfully' will certainly be written as special
outlines.

You must practise every day to improve your speed. Always try to take
down a higher speed than normal to quicken your pace. Use shorthand
tapes or take dictation from the radio or television and always use a
proper shorthand notebook – it is designed for the purpose of taking
shorthand notes and will help you to improve your speed. You can use
a pen or pencil, depending on the system of shorthand being used,
although notes in pen are easier to read back for transcription
purposes. Special shorthand pens can be bought.

430

MEMORANDUM

To: Carol Baker

From: Iain Woods

Date:

Ref: <u>Annual Conference</u>

Regarding the above matter , would it be posible
for you to   ask your stff to prepare sep.
name badges req'd for all members attending the
conferance?

I will sent you a list of names once we recieve
all the booking slipss detailing the how many
delegates are coming and the names of
lecturers attending. Their should be about 150.

You may receiving telephone inquiries regarding
the conference, and to help you answer these, I
have attached a draft copy of the programme.

Yours faithfully

Fig 15.2

Always number and date the pages of your book and draw a wide
margin down one side to insert alterations. If your boss stops to think,
use the margin to write in any difficult or unusual words used that may
cause you problems later. Make sure your pencil is sharp and always
have another in reserve just in case the first pencil breaks in the
middle of dictation.

It is useful to put an elastic band round your book so it can be opened
easily at the relevant page. If your notebook is nearly finished, make
sure you have another readily to hand. As you transcribe each page,
draw a line through it to show the page is finished with; however, do
not destroy the shorthand as it may be needed later on to check a
query. Keep used notebooks for as long as it is company policy to do

so, and if you have confidential material in your notebook, make sure it is destroyed either in a shredder or incinerator.

■ DIY 15.1.2

Make a list of at least 10 short forms, and next to each short form write the correct shorthand outline. Practise these short forms daily by writing out each one at least 10 times. If you learn a new short form add this to your list.

If the dictation is too quick for you, say something. Do not sit quietly hoping to catch up later. It is likely that you will fall so far behind that the whole document will need to be dictated again – this will waste not only your time but also the valuable time of others. It is far better to ask the person to stop, and explain that the dictation is too fast – they will be happier going over a sentence or paragraph rather than repeating all the dictation.

▶ *What do you do if you cannot read an outline?*

The first thing to do is read through the whole passage and look for clues. The outline may be repeated somewhere else in your shorthand and may be clearer to understand. The outline can also be broken down into letters or sets of letters; try to put these together with different vowels filling the spaces. Look for alternatives; could the outline or stroke indicate another meaning or letter? Try to work through as many combinations as possible to give you clues as to the correct word.

If you are still unsure of an outline ask other shorthand users if they can decipher it. A different person may recognise the outline straight away. If all else fails, ask the person who gave the dictation for help. If this is not possible and you are familiar with the content of the text, you may be able to put a suitable word in yourself, but only do this if you know your boss will approve. Remember to take care, though, as you should never use a word that will change the meaning of the sentence.

When you first start a job it is a good idea to read back your shorthand notes to your boss – provided there is time available. This will help you to clarify difficult words and check on spelling. It may be the case that different terminology, such as medical or legal, is being used and you may need a little help in learning this.

■ DIY 15.1.3

Copy the following list of commonly misspelled words. Next to each word on your list fill in the correct outline. When you come across other words that cause you problems with spelling add these to your list. This list will build into your own personal reference – keep it close at hand when transcribing dictation.

accommodation	accessible	achieved
acknowledge	aggravate	all right
among	appearance	arrangement
beginning	believed	benefited
business	colleagues	coming
committee	completely	conscientious
correspondence	decision	definite
disappointed	especially	essential
excellent	expenses	extremely
February	friend	fulfilled
government	height	immediately
independent	instalment	knowledge
maintenance	minutes	necessary
noticeable	occasionally	occurrence
permanent	possesses	privilege
procedure	professional	quiet
recommend	referred	sentence
separate	similar	sincerely
successfully	surprise	transferred
twelfth	unnecessary	usually
view	Wednesday	withhold

You must have a dictionary if you want to transcribe shorthand competently. If you are ever unsure of a word – look it up. Do not rely upon others to spot and correct errors, it is your job to proofread and correct. Time will have already been spent dictating material; your boss will expect each piece of dictation to be typed and presented ready for signing or approval. If further time has to be spent reading through your work looking for errors, it is unlikely you will have the job for long!

You may be given additional instructions before, during and after dictation. Always make a note of these, do not try to remember later – it is more than likely you will forget. If your boss asks for copies of the finished transcription to be routed to other personnel, departments or file, indicate this at the bottom of the document. The usual style would be:

Copy to: Nigel Parker
             Henry Spratt
             File

The original copy would be sent to the person named at the top of the document. The copies would be routed by ticking or highlighting Nigel Parker on the first copy, Henry Spratt on the second and File on the third. In this way all copies are clearly marked and their destination known.

▶ What types of layouts are used?

As well as making sure the content is correct, part of your job will be to make sure the correct layout is used. Most companies use a 'house style' – a particular style the company (the house) has approved and wishes all staff to use. An approved house style is used so that customers receive the same style of documentation, regardless of which department sends it. Some companies are extremely fussy about the house style, even stating what size print and style to use.

The most commonly used layout is the fully blocked style used without punctuation (except in the paragraphs of the letter). In this style everything starts at the left-hand side (*see* Fig. 15.3). This is the quickest style to type, as you do not need to work out spacing or spend time inserting unnecessary punctuation marks.

The date should always be written in the same way whether it is typed at the top of the letter or in one of the paragraphs, eg 25 May 1994 (without punctuation).

The layout for blocked memos would be as shown in Fig. 15.4.

The other style frequently used is semi-blocked. In this style the date is placed on the right-hand side and the signature block is centred. The rest of the letter remains at the left-hand side (*see* Fig. 15.5).

```
Ref: LS/EF

5 October 199-

Dr D R Scott
87 Wellington Drive
NEWCASTLE
NC32 6BB

Dear Dr Scott

MEDICAL CONFERENCE, 14-15 OCTOBER

Thank you for your conference booking form and
fee.

I am pleased to confirm your request for a
single room with bath for the nights of 14 and
15 October.

We look forward to welcoming you to the
conference.

Yours sincerely



Lara Smith
Conference Secretary
```

Fig 15.3 Letter in fully blocked style

```
MEMORANDUM

To        Carol Baker

From      Lara Smith

Date      5 October 199-

Ref       LS/EF


MEDICAL CONFERENCE

Would you please arrange with the conference
centre for a slide projector and screen to be
available for Professor James's lecture on
15 October.

This will be required in addition to the OHP
and flipchart.
```

Fig 15.4 Memo in fully blocked style

For memos typed in a semi-blocked layout the word 'Memorandum' would be moved to the centre and the date and reference across towards the right-hand side (*see* Fig. 15.6).

If an enclosure is mentioned in the letter or memorandum the letters 'Enc' or 'Encs' (if more than one) should be placed at the bottom of the page. It is normal practice not to sign memoranda, although some supervisors may prefer to put their initial at the bottom of the page to confirm the contents.

If you are asked to send copies of a document to other people you can indicate this at the bottom of the page. After the last line on the page or document leave a space and then type in 'Copy to:' and add the name(s) of the people copies are to go to. When the copies are prepared either tick or highlight a different name on each copy. This process is called 'routing', and when the original and the copies are ready to be despatched you will be able to see easily who should

Ref: LS/EF

Dr D R Scott
87 Wellington Drive
NEWCASTLE
NC32 6BB   5 October 199-

Dear Dr Scott

MEDICAL CONFERENCE, 14-15 OCTOBER

Thank you for your conference booking form and
fee.

I am pleased to confirm your request for a
single room with bath for the nights of 14 and
15 October.

We look forward to welcoming you to the
conference.

                    Yours sincerely

                    Lara Smith
                    Conference Secretary

Fig 15.5 Letter in semi-blocked style

receive each document (see page 434).

When starting a new job, it is your responsibility to find out the style
required for documents; do not rely upon your existing knowledge,
training and experience received at college or at previous companies.
Some companies will produce a manual or guide for staff to ensure

```
                      MEMORANDUM

To        Carol Baker     Date  5 October 199-

From      Lara Smith      Ref   LS/EF


MEDICAL CONFERENCE

Would you please arrange with the conference
centre for a slide projector and screen to be
available for Professor James's lecture on
15 October.

This will be required in addition to the OHP
and flipchart.
```

Fig 15.6 Memo in semi-blocked style

they follow the agreed layout for all documentation. If not, ask for examples for you to copy.

▶ Guidelines for typing envelopes

The guidelines for typing envelopes are given by the Post Office and suit the machinery installed to sort letters.

1 Type the address along the longer side of the envelope.
2 The first line of the address should start at about a third of the way across the envelope and half-way down.
3 Each line of the address should have a separate line.
4 The post town should be in CAPITALS.
5 The postcode should be the last line, in capitals, on its own and with one space between the two parts, eg GN3 2NN.

If there are any special instructions such as URGENT, CONFIDENTIAL, For the attention of ..., they should be typed two lines before the name and address (see Fig. 15.7).

438

```
        PERSONAL

        Mr John Ball
        Martin Evans plc
        101 Princeton Lane
        HULL
        HR7 9NU
```

Fig 15.7 Envelope layout

▶ *Layout and presentation*

It may be left to you to decide how to lay out your documents and your job will be to ensure that you select the most suitable method for the document concerned. As said before, layout is important because it reflects an image of the business. The most important rule is to be consistent. If you decide to leave 2 lines between each paragraph in a report, you should not suddenly start leaving 3. Always look at previously typed documents to see how other staff have laid out the document, or ask for guidance from your supervisor.

▶ *What happens if you make mistakes?*

Everyone makes mistakes; the skill is in knowing when you make a mistake and correcting it – so that no one else knows! There is nothing worse than completing a letter or memorandum and passing it to your boss to be signed, only to find it comes back with a big circle round a silly typing mistake. If you are using a typewriter the whole document may have to be retyped.

It is most important to read everything you type before you hand it to the person for signature. You may believe that you 'know' when you make a typing error, but there could still be some that have gone unnoticed. Proofreading is a skill that has to be learned, in the same way as typing: the more you proofread the quicker you will become at identifying errors.

▶ *What is proofreading?*

This is when you read the document (proof) to ensure it is correct in content and layout. Most people find proofreading boring, and it probably is, but it is an essential part of document production. It is useful to get someone else to read an important document for you, as they will be unfamiliar with the content, will concentrate more and it is likely they will find errors that you may have overlooked. However, someone else can proofread for you only if the material is not confidential.

If you are unsure of how a word is spelt, look it up in a dictionary and keep a list of commonly misspelt words to refer to. If you have a word processor, it may have a spellcheck: make sure you use it. However, you will still need to proofread as the spellcheck will not find grammatical errors or words that are incorrect, eg 'it' instead of 'is', incorrect punctuation (eg a full stop instead of a comma), or words, sentences or paragraphs that have been missed out completely.

▶ *What is the best method for correcting errors?*

It depends on the type of error and the type of equipment you are using. Obviously, you cannot use correction fluid on a screen! A corrected error should be unobtrusive, which means you should not be able to notice it.

If you are using a typewriter you can use correction paper. This method is unobtrusive, as long as you have the character lined up correctly; otherwise the chalk covering misses and leaves some of the black character uncovered. This method should not be used for major errors such as changing two sentences round, or taking out a whole sentence. The other commonly used method is correcting fluid. Paint the error with the fluid, wait until it is dry, and then type the correct characters over the top. If you try to type in your corrections before the fluid has dried it will make a mess on the paper and can clog up the letters in your machine.

Many electric and electronic typewriters have correction facilities. The correction tapes will either be similar to correction paper or coated on one side with a sticky substance. The type of correction tape used will depend on the type of ribbon. Nylon ribbons use correction paper, and carbon ribbons use sticky correction tape which lifts the carbon image from the paper. If you look at the correction tape when you replace it you will see the carbon characters stuck to it. The disadvantage with this method of correction is that it leaves an indentation in the paper, and the better quality the paper the more obvious the indentation. This is not a problem if another character is to be typed on top but if it is between 2 words or at the end of a sentence the indentation may be noticeable.

Some electronic machines have an LCD (liquid crystal display) which displays each line of type. This facility can be set to allow you to correct words or sentences before you actually print them on to the paper.

When major errors occur in typewritten documents it may be possible to retype the one page necessary or to 'stick and paste'. This means that the correct paragraphs are cut out and glued round the newly typed paragraphs. The whole document is then photocopied. This method cannot be used for letters and it may be unsuitable for some occasions, for instance when your boss wants the original to be sent.

If you do use a word processor make sure that you proofread on screen properly – otherwise sheets of paper and time are wasted unnecessarily in printing work that is full of errors. The main advantage of proofreading on the screen is that errors are corrected before the document is printed – in this way the errors are totally unobtrusive.

If you are working as a general assistant, it may be that you send documents to the typing pool or clerk typist for typing. When they are returned to you for signature you must check thoroughly before signing and sending out. You should check spelling (look up any words you are not sure of), grammar, punctuation and content. Ensure that you use the approved correction signs whenever possible as this will make the typist's job easier and you will reduce the possibility of misunderstanding.

▶ *When should apostrophes be used?*

Apostrophes can easily be misused. The rules state that they should be used to form possessive nouns, that is, to show something belongs to someone or something, eg:

> Carly's pencil
> Natalie's lunch box
> Leila's coat

If the noun ends in 's' the apostrophe is placed after the 's'. Another 's' is added, eg:

> Kris's bike

If the noun is a plural (more than one), the apostrophe would still be after the 's', eg:

> the doctors' parking

This would mean more than one doctor; if it was the doctor's parking, it would mean only one doctor. Some nouns are changed slightly when becoming plural. 'Child' and 'woman' become 'children' and 'women'; in these cases the 's' is added and the apostrophe would appear before it, eg:

> the children's socks
> the women's handbags

An apostrophe is also used when a letter or letters are omitted from a word, for example don't, you're, aren't, can't, haven't, we've and I've. It's is used to mean 'it is' – the apostrophe takes the place of the letter 'i'.

■ DIY 15.1.4

Copy out the following sentences and put the apostrophes in the correct place.

1   The boys cat lay on its tail.
2   The dogs are in the kitchen eating the cats dinner.
3   Susans looking for her son.
4   Weve got to run or well be late for Sams speech.
5   I dont think youve got it.
6   Its too early now, well go later.
7   The trainees folders havnt been seen yet.
8   Peters trousers were covered in Pauls drink.
9   The 2 boys said theyd be 2 hours late.
10 The childrens party began at 2 but I dont know who went.

▶ *What is collating?*

This means putting the documents you have typed into the correct page order. If you prepare a multi-page document it is wise to number each page so that you do not become confused when the document has to be put together. If you are using a word processor you can instruct it to automatically insert a header or footer that includes the page number of each sheet in the document. It is important that all pages are collated in the correct order before they are stapled or fastened together, otherwise the text may not make sense.

When preparing a multi-page letter it is important to follow the correct house style. When typing letters it is normal practice to insert the page number, date and name of addressee at the top of each consecutive page. For example, a multi-page letter typed in block style is likely to have the following typed at the top of page 2:

2
20 February 1994
Mrs J D Carpenter

If the pages become separated, the information at the top of each page will identify where each page belongs. If typing a report, you may have to include the name of the report at the top or bottom of each page rather than a person's name. This would normally be set up as a header or footer.

If you have to prepare copies of the document, these must also be placed in the correct page order. If you are able to send documents to a reprographic service to be copied, make sure that you tell them to collate and fasten the documents for you as this will save you time and help to meet deadlines.

Collating by hand can take a long time, depending on how many pages and copies of the document you have to put together. If you are lucky, your company may have a photocopier that can be programmed to collate the pages as it is copying them, or you may have the use of a collating machine. Imagine if you have 25 copies of a 30-page report to collate by hand, it will take some time to put the pages in the correct order. You will need to have a work area where the 30 pages can be placed in separate heaps. Alternatively, you will have to sort the first 10 pages (or however many you can lay out) followed by the second set of 10 pages and then the third. These three heaps would then have

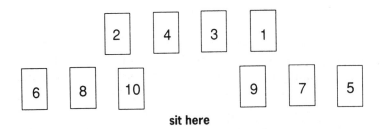

sit here

Fig 15.8

to be collated into the final sets. You will need to lay out the documents in a logical sequence, either in page number order, or to speed up the process, an order where both hands can work at the same time. For example, a 10-page document could be laid out as in Fig. 15.8.

The left hand will take one copy of page 10 and place it in the space in front, and then the right hand will take one copy of page 9 and place it on top of page 10. Both hands can move at the same time and the document is collated back to front. Complete sets can be stacked away from the work area.

▶ *What type of stationery should you use?*

Letters are normally typed on A4 headed paper, although some companies do use A5 letterheads. Memos on the other hand are commonly available in A4 and A5. A4 portrait paper is 210 mm × 297 mm, has 100 spaces across the top and 70 lines down (assuming you are using elite type which is 12 characters to 25 mm). A5 landscape paper is half this size, and has 100 spaces across the top and 35 lines down. The paper can be used in either the portrait position, with the short side put in to the machine first, or landscape position, with the long side put in first (*see* Fig. 15.9).

The quality of stationery used will depend upon its purpose. Paper and envelopes used for business correspondence will be of good quality as the company will want to convey a good impression to its customers and clients. The quality of paper can be measured by its weight, or gsm (grams per square metre). Bond, copier and letterheaded paper is

444

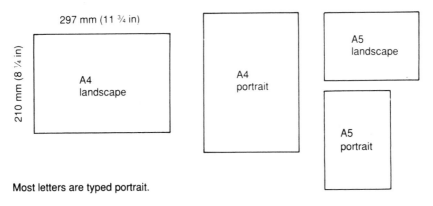

Most letters are typed portrait.

Fig 15.9 Paper sizes

fairly thick and therefore heavier (usually by about 25 gsm) than paper such as bank, which would be cheaper and used for carbon copies.

▶ *Planning and organising your work*

It is important for you to get into the habit of sorting through your work first thing in the morning to put all your tasks into order of priority. As the day goes by other work will be given to you and you will be expected to fit this in if it takes higher priority than the work you already have. Keep an eye on your in-tray and rearrange tasks into order each time you are given more work to do.

You must schedule your work so that important tasks are not left to the last minute or forgotten completely. Your supervisor will not give you one piece of work at a time and wait until you have finished this before giving you more work to do. It is more likely that your supervisor will give you a number of tasks at once, indicating the ones that need to be given priority, and then keep topping you up with work as the day progresses.

Always sort your work into priority order, taking into account the time it will take to complete each task. If you have been given a report to type that will take all day, tell your supervisor so that arrangements may be made to share the report or pass other priority tasks to someone else. Never, under any circumstances, allow yourself to forget security and confidentiality even if you are under pressure to get a task finished.

▶ *What about security and confidentiality?*

If you are responsible for processing confidential documents make sure you keep them in a folder marked CONFIDENTIAL, and lock them away when not required. Text on a VDU can easily be read if the screen is left on and poor printouts thrown into the bin may be read at a later date. If you take carbon copies remember the carbon paper can be read after use giving full details of the document typed. Do not allow anyone to look over your shoulder when typing and put all documents out of the way if you have to leave the office for any reason. Remember to use passwords to protect documents held on disks.

Ask your tutor or assessor to dictate the following passages to you. You will need to have a speed of at least 70 wpm and be able to complete transcription of 375–400 words in 1 hour. You should be able to transcribe 2 passages in 1 hour with no more than 3 uncorrected spacing or typing errors. You should not miss anything out or make number errors.

■ DIY 15.1.5

3 minutes at 70 wpm

Memo to all staff from the Communications Officer. The 8 guidelines must be typed as a list.
(*Dictation starts*)
The memo is a form of internal communication and can be hand-written or typed, usually on / a pre-printed form. Memos can also be transmitted electronically by an organisation using an electronic mail system.// The messages are collected by the recipient who uses a special password to access the mailbox. This /// system saves time and money and is becoming very popular.

However, even the most up-to-date equipment **(1)** cannot write the memo for you. Therefore, all members of staff must use these following guidelines to ensure / that their memos are composed correctly.

1. There is no 'Dear' or 'Yours'.
2. They can be // initialled, but not signed, by the sender.
3. Sentences should be short and concise.
4. A new /// paragraph should be used for separate information.

5. Use an appropriate style of language for the person you **(2)** are writing to.

6. Try to keep the memo on one piece of paper.

7. If someone / else has typed the memo for you, initial it to confirm it is correct.

8. Place only confidential // or personal memos in an envelope.

Use a memo to confirm facts discussed verbally, request information or /// to request assistance. They are also used to provide information, make a request, send instructions or seek clarification. **(3) (210 words)**

■ DIY 15.1.6

2.75 minutes at 70 wpm

Report on the increase in holiday travel to Australia.
(*Dictation starts*)
It would seem that Australia is now a very popular place for the British tourist to go / on holiday. The travel tour firms and the airlines report a large increase in the number of British // who went there last year. A record figure of more than five hundred thousand British tourists was /// reached and this year the amount is going to be much larger.

The reason is that while holiday **(1)** costs to most places are climbing up, air fares to Australia have come down. Also there has / been a drop in the value of Australian dollars and at present you can get a better exchange // rate because of this.

In previous years the majority of the holiday travel to Australia was to /// visit relatives and friends. Many of the people who managed to go to Australia had to save hard **(2)** to pay the fare. By the end of last year package tours to Australia had been offered / for no more than the cost of the same kind of tour to one of the top resorts // in America.

Take a look in your local travel agents and compare the costs of these holidays. **(2.75) (192 words)**

■ DIY 15.1.7

2.75 minutes at 70 wpm
TO: Ms K Davis, Deansway Conference Centre, Salterns Road, Salisbury
FROM: Pie Personnel Ltd, 88 Shaftesbury Square, Reading

One copy for file required.

A letter about the supply of staff for a conference centre.
(*Dictation starts*)
Dear Ms Davis, Thank you for your recent letter about part-time conference personnel.

I confirm that I / can provide the personnel you requested for your conference centre as I have a large number of // conference staff to call upon. I have passed on the details you sent to some of my relevant /// contacts, and have asked them to call at the centre for interview if they are interested in **(1)** any of your positions.

If you offer a place to any of them, please let me know / immediately. The rate is the same as in previous years, that is, £75 for each // person appointed. As you know, all staff are obliged by contract to inform me if a full-time /// job is offered to them. If this is the case, a further, additional fee of £75 **(2)** will be payable by you. A separate invoice will be sent to you for this. All payments will / of course be subject to 17.5 per cent VAT.

I hope that you will find // suitable conference personnel, but if you require further information, please do not hesitate to contact me.

Yours sincerely **(2.75)** **(193 words)**

■ DIY 15.1.8

2.75 minutes at 70 wpm
TO: M A Arnold, Head of Catering
FROM: P B Bishop, Staff Liaison Officer

One copy for file, and one to be sent to Claire Richards in Personnel.
A memorandum about the staff restaurant containing a list of 5 complaints received from staff.
(*Dictation starts*)
Several members of the staff have recently complained to me about the condition of the restaurant. I / am sure you will understand that it is very important indeed that this facility should be kept absolutely // clean at all times. I am told that at present this is far from being the case. ///

I list the following complaints that have been received by my office:

1 Staff who go into the **(1)** canteen at 12 o'clock for an early lunch often find that dirty breakfast plates are still on / the tables.

2 Bins have not been emptied.
3 The floor is littered with cigarette ends.
4 The // whole appearance of the room is unhealthy.
5 The food is often badly cooked and lukewarm.

In /// my opinion adequate staff are provided for the cleaning of the room, and there can be no excuse **(2)** for this dirty condition. The purpose of this restaurant is to provide good food at reasonable prices, and / I rely on the members of the catering staff to ensure that a good standard is achieved // at all times.

In view of these complaints, I must ask you to hold a meeting shortly. **(2.75)** **(192 words)**

■ DIY 15.1.9

2.75 minutes at 70 wpm

A letter to Mr J Hope, 89 Frederick Drive, Skelmersdale, Lancs.
FROM: GHP Estate Agency, 19 High Street, Edinburgh.
One copy for file.

A letter from an estate agent about houses in the Edinburgh area.
(Dictation starts)
Dear Mr Hope, We notice from your letter that you are interested in houses in the Edinburgh area. / We have a good selection of properties which we would be pleased to show you around. Enclosed are // photographs of 3 of them.

'Timberlands' cottage is set in a large garden on a very pretty /// estate, 2 miles out of town. It has 4 bedrooms and 2 reception rooms together with a **(1)** recently modernised kitchen. There are 2 en-suite bathrooms and an attractive ground floor toilet and shower room./

The smaller property is called 'Hillview' and has 2 bedrooms. The conservatory has an open view across // woodland to the hills. This is a very pleasant property which we are sure you would like /// to view.

The third property is a terraced house with a small garden to the rear. If you **(2)** want to live near to the town centre, this house is ideally situated. The 2 reception rooms / are large and the 2 bedrooms have recently been refurbished with modern decor and fittings.

These 3 properties cost // around £95,000 each. Appointments to view can be made on the above number.

Yours sincerely **(2.75)** **(193 words)**

■ DIY 15.1.10

This is a short report on converting imperial and metric measures. The basic conversions listed in the dictation must be typed as a tabulation. Take down the dictation word for word, but you can omit any words that you feel are unnecessary when presenting the information as a tabulation.

(*Dictation starts*)
Metric and imperial weights and measures may cause confusion in terms of length and weight. You will / find conversion tables in most good dictionaries that give quick equivalents to imperial and metric measurements. Some basic // conversions that you need to remember are as follows:

Conversions for length are: One inch is equal /// to 2.5 centimetres and one centimetre is equal to 0.4 inches. One foot is **(1)** equal to 0.3 metres and one metre is equal to 1.1 yards. One / yard is equal to 0.9 metres and one kilometre is equal to 0.6 miles. //

Conversions for weight are: One ounce is equal to 28 grams and one gram is equal /// to 0.03 ounces. One pound is equal to 0.4 kilograms and one kilogram **(2)** is equal to 2.2 pounds. One stone is equal to 6.3 kilograms.

Conversions / for capacity are: One pint is equal to 0.57 litres and one litre is equal // to 1.75 pints. One gallon equals 4.5 litres.

These conversions are approximate only. **(2.75) (193 words)**

Completing Element 15.1

To complete this element on producing business documents from dictated information using a keyboard, you will need to take dictation at a minimum speed of 70 wpm transcribed word for word, although word substitutions are allowed providing they do not change the meaning of the sentence. You must transcribe dictation of 375–400 words in a 1 hour working period with no more than 3 uncorrected spacing or typing errors. You are not allowed to miss anything out or make number errors.

You must prove competence by producing letters, memoranda and short reports which must contain text, tabulations, listings and numerical information. You must also include original shorthand notes. Your completed work must meet the requirements set and follow house style. If you are unsure of instructions you must clarify these with your supervisor by using questions to clarify dictated information. Where work cannot be completed within the required deadline, you must report this accurately and promptly. Collating, routing and your ability to decide upon layout, print and stationery to use will also be assessed.

If you use shorthand at work it is difficult for you to claim credit for this as your work is not timed. However, if you have a shorthand qualification you may be able to gain credit for this but will need to speak to your tutor or assessor.

Claiming credit

Once you have completed your final assessment, you will need to write in your record book or folder how, when, where and what you have done to prove that you are competent.

The following is an example of how one trainee completed their claim:

At college my assessor dictated reports, letters and memos at 70 wpm and I transcribed these word for word. If I was unsure of words I would read through my notes and look for clues. If I was really stuck I would ask my assessor for assistance. I transcribed 2 passages in 1 hour with no errors, I made no word substitutions. I used the layout requested by my assessor, but when told to do so I converted information into a tabulation or typed it as a list. All errors were corrected on screen before the document was printed out. I prepared extra copies if requested in correct page order and routed these as directed by ticking the relevant name. I only asked colleagues for help if the dictation was not confidential. Notebooks were kept in a safe place and would be destroyed if they contained confidential material. I was able to complete a number of assessments to the correct standard by the required deadline. However, if there had been a reason for me not completing on time I would have told my supervisor immediately.

■ Element 15.2
PRESENT BUSINESS DOCUMENTS IN A VARIETY OF FORMATS USING A KEYBOARD

Performance criteria

- Instructions are understood
- Presentation, style and format are consistent, correct and in accordance with house style
- Completed presentation meets the requirements of the workplace
- Corrections, when appropriate, are unobtrusive

- Security and confidentiality of information are maintained
- Copies and originals are correctly collated and routed as directed
- Where work is not achievable within specified deadlines reasons are promptly and accurately reported
- Work is achieved within agreed deadlines

The performance criteria for Elements 13.2, 14.2 and 15.2 are exactly the same. Complete Element 13.2 (page 387) to complete Unit 13, 14 or 15.

INDEX

The best route to NVQs in Administration

- Everything you need for assessing competence and APL at Levels 1, 2 and 3
- Everything students need to document competency and build portfolios at Levels 1, 2 and 3
- Fully in line with current NVQ standards awarded by LCCI, RSA and PEI
- **Unique updating service available** – to ensure the assessor and workbook material is always relevant, and to insure against NCVQ changes to NVQ standards
- All assessor and workbook material can be **photocopied**, under licence

For Assessors

NVQ LEVEL 1 AND 2 ADMINISTRATION
Effective Assessment Pack and User Guide
Barbara Clothier and Anne Fellowes, Lecturers and Course Development Managers for NVQ
A4 binder, ISBN: 0 273 60532 1
*Free update with the 1994 standards included
Updates also available priced separately:
ISBN 0 273 61084 8 (Level 1), ISBN 0 273 61085 6 (Level 2)

NVQ LEVEL 3 ADMINISTRATION
Effective Assessment Pack and User Guide
Barbara Clothier and Anne Fellowes
A4 binder, ISBN: 0 273 60526 7

For students and trainees

There are Workpacks giving tasks/assignment material for each NVQ Administration unit at Levels 1 to 3. These are available either as 34 separate Workpacks, or as complete sets at each Level, and are fully in line with the latest standards. Purchase of the Workpacks in complete sets, one for each level, gives an automatic right to photocopy the material. These packs are available as follows:

NVQ LEVEL 1 ADMINISTRATION
Complete set of Workpacks for all units
Margaret Dudley
A4 binder, ISBN: 0 273 60896 7

NVQ LEVEL 2 ADMINISTRATION
Complete set of Workpacks for all units
A4 binder, ISBN: 0 273 60897 5

NVQ LEVEL 3 ADMINISTRATION
Complete set of Workpacks for all units
A4 binder, ISBN: 0 273 60898 3

Underpinning knowledge texts for NVQ Administration

ADMINISTRATION NVQ LEVEL 1
Lynda Bourne and Pamela Scott
2nd Edition ISBN: 0 273 60618 2

ADMINISTRATION NVQ LEVEL 2
Lynda Bourne and Pamela Scott
2nd Edition, ISBN: 0 273 60619 0

ADMINISTRATION NVQ LEVEL 3
Lynda Bourne and Pamela Scott
ISBN: 0 273 03944 X

To place your orders, please write to Financial Times Professional,
12–14 Slaidburn Crescent, Southport, PR9 9YF
Or Tel: 01704 226881 or Fax: 01704 231970

For further information, please contact The Academic Marketing Department,
Financial Times Management, 128 Long Acre, London WC2E 9AN
Tel: 0171 447 2000   Fax: 0171 240 5771